250 ESSENTIAL CHINESE CHARACTERS

FOR EVERYDAY USE

Vol 1

by Philip Yungkin Lee
University of New South Wales, Australia

TUTTLE PUBLISHING
Tokyo • Rutland, Vermont • Singapore

Published by Tuttle Publishing, an imprint of Periplus Editions (HK) Ltd.,
with editorial offices at 364 Innovation Drive, North Clarendon, VT 05759
and 130 Joo Seng Road #06-01, Singapore 368357

LCC Card No. 2004297990
ISBN-10: 0-8048-3359-1
ISBN-13: 978-0-8048-3359-2

Distributed by:

North America, Latin America & Europe
Tuttle Publishing
364 Innovation Drive
North Clarendon, VT 05759-9436
Tel: (802) 773 8930; Fax: (802) 773 6993
Email: info@tuttlepublishing.com
Website: www.tuttlepublishing.com

Japan
Tuttle Publishing
Yaekari Bldg., 3F, 5-4-12 Osaki, Shinagawa-ku
Tokyo 141-0032
Tel: (03) 5437 0171; Fax: (03) 5437 0755
Email: tuttle-sales@gol.com

Asia Pacific
Berkeley Books Pte. Ltd.
130 Joo Seng Road, #06-01, Singapore 368357
Tel: (65) 6280 1330; Fax: (65) 6280 6290
Email: inquiries@periplus.com.sg
Website: www.periplus.com

Indonesia
PT Java Books Indonesia
Kawasan Industri Pulogadung
Jl. Rawa Gelam IV No. 9,
Jakarta 14240, Indonesia
Tel: (62-21) 4682 1088; Fax: (62-21) 461 0207
Email: cs@javabooks.co.id

10 09 08 07 06
10 9 8 7 6 5

Printed in Singapore

Contents

Introduction

One of the questions most frequently asked by beginning learners of Chinese is how many characters are needed to gain a basic knowledge of the written language. There is no simple answer to this question. Excluding specific characters which are often found in shop signs, street names, restaurant menus etc., the number of characters a beginning learner needs to know ranges from 250 to 500. The lower figure is needed for the construction of simple sentences and the higher figure to construct more complex sentences and utilize them to express oneself meaningfully in everyday contexts.

The first volume of *250 Essential Chinese Characters for Everyday Use* introduces the basic skills involved in writing Chinese characters. Each unit presents ten new characters which are shown in simplified form (*jiantizi*) along with Pinyin romanization and their English meaning. Just over a third of the selection also have traditional forms (*fantizi*) which are listed side by side after the respective simplified forms. Short notes relating to the origin of the character, how the simplified form is constructed, and in some cases a guide to pronunciation all aim to de-mystify each character and make the task of learning them less arduous.

As well as the basic meaning of each character, several examples are given of its use in combination with other characters to form compounds, and each of these compounds is contextualized in an example sentence to illustrate its use. In these example sentences the characters are lined up with their Pinyin romanization to allow you to identify the words and pronounce them if you wish. Please note that the English translation is given as a general guide to meaning only.

The book is arranged in 25 units of 10 characters, each of which is followed by a quiz in both characters and Pinyin romanization so that you can monitor you own progress.

At the end of each group of 5 units or 50 characters, there is a Character Building section in which characters are grouped together based on their meaningful parts known as the radicals, showing how character components are recycled to form other characters; a Review of characters and compounds arranged according to parts of speech to help you build up your skills in sentence formation; and a Word/Sentence Puzzle utilizing all the characters so far introduced which challenges you to pick out characters in meaningful combinations. Don't hesitate to use the Key whose purpose is to guide you in your efforts to solve the puzzle.

If you need a quick reference on the whereabouts in this book of a particular character and its example compounds and sentences, consult either the Alphabetical Index or the Radical Index, which is based on the number of strokes of the radicals.

Your job as a self-paced learner is to focus intently on the character at hand as you write it. Each character should be written stroke by stroke, following the correct stroke order. Note the stroke order and the number of strokes as you practice writing each character in the boxes provided. There is a short note to remind what you should bear in mind as you write each character.

Unlike the letters of the roman alphabet, Chinese characters are all squarish in shape, with their components conforming to a rule of symmetry and balance. They should not be written too rectangular or even roundish because that will destroy their visual integrity. In other words, you cannot practice writing the characters in just any shapes and sizes that you like, as you will need the visual images of your own handwriting to assist in recalling them. For this reason, this book provides you with a clear model for each character and a proper grid of squares in which to copy it over and over again until the habit is formed.

After you have practiced writing each character in its square grid, you will have learned to reproduce it yourself, corresponding very closely to the model character provided. To do this, you cannot rush each character since you must refer to the model character each time and follow the correct stroke order as you write it. When you do that, you will find that you get twice the result with half the effort.

Students' Guide

Chinese Characters

One of the great fascinations of learning Chinese lies in the Chinese writing system. Each character looks like a square-shaped box written in various strokes. Learners who are used to the alphabetical writing system find characters difficult to recognize, time consuming to write and near impossible to remember. In this book we teach 250 characters with a view to demonstrate how the large number of components you are learning both as visual and phonetical elements can be recycled and used in different combinations to form new characters. Through remembering the pronunication or meaning of these components, you will gain a basic knowledge on the compositions of Chinese characters — the radicals, the phonetic components and their configurations. This will establish a relationship between form, pronunciation and meaning in characters and will enable you to transfer what you already know when you learn new characters.

Structurally there are two types of characters: those that exist as an integral unit, and those that can be divided into radical and phonetic components. Integral characters are often radicals themselves. Thus some basic knowledge of a radical is desirable not just for learning a certain character but for using the radical index when looking up a character in a Chinese dictionary.

It is often said that radicals are categories of thought which the ancient Chinese used to describe the world around them. A combination of a radical and a sound element gives specific meaning under a certain category of meaning. As you come across radicals in this book you will learn to classify characters under these categories or radicals. *The Chinese-English Dictionary* (published in 1995 by the Foreign Language Teaching and Research Press in Beijing) uses 189 radicals to organize the characters contained in the dictionary. That dictionary is probably the most widely used Chinese-English Dictionary in the world and is deemed likely to be the dictionary most often consulted by users of this book. You will learn 90 radicals in this book. Of these about 50 are the most common radicals. We believe that the knowledge you gained from these radicals will enable you to guess the meaning of many common Chinese characters.

The Basic Strokes

Chinese characters are written in various strokes. Although we can identify over 30 different strokes, only 8 are basic ones and all the others are their variants. Certain arrangements of strokes form components or the building blocks for characters.

The strokes that make up a component of a character and by extension the whole character are given names. Below are the 8 basic strokes:

[—] The *héng* or 'horizontal' stroke is written from left to right.

[|] The *shù* or 'vertical' stroke is written from top to bottom.

[ )] The *piě* or 'downward-left' stroke is written from top-right to bottom-left.

[＼] The *nà* or 'downward-right' stroke is written from top-left to bottom-right.

[丶] The *diǎn* or 'dot' stroke is written from top to bottom-right, finishing firmly. It can also be finished to bottom-left, depending on how the dot is written.

[ㄱ] The *zhé* or 'turning' stroke can begin with a horizontal stroke with a downward turn, or it can be a vertical stroke with a horizontal turn to the right.

[亅] The *gōu* or 'hook' stroke is written by a quick flick of the pen or Chinese brush. There are five types of *gōu* 'hook' strokes. They are:

       [㇆] the *hénggōu* or 'horizontal hook',

       [亅] the *shùgōu* or 'vertical hook',

       [㇄] the *wān'gōu* or 'bending hook',

       [㇂] the *xiégōu* or 'slanting hook',

       [㇉] the *pínggōu* or 'level hook',

[㇀] The *tí* or 'upward stroke to the right' is written from bottom-left to top-right.

Stroke Order

It is important to remember that the components in a character are written according to some fixed rules or stroke order. The same stroke order should be used every time you write a character. If you write a character according to the prescribed order, you will find it easier to remember as repetition will develop muscular cues in your fingers which will assist in the recall of the character, much like remembering a figure in dancing. Thus, when writing a character, the following rules should be observed:

1. From top to bottom:

三		一	二	三	
学		丷	丷	学	学
是		日	旦	早	是

2. From left to right:

你		亻	亻	你	你
好		女	好	好	
她		女	如	她	她

3.   The horizontal before the vertical:

十		一	十		
七		一	七		
天		二	于	天	

4.   The horizontal before the down stroke to the left:

大		一	ナ	大	
有		一	ナ	冇	有
在		一	ナ	才	在

5.   The down stroke to the left before that to the right:

人		ノ	人		
八		ノ	八		
文		丶	亠	文	

6.   The enclosing strokes first, then the enclosed and finally the sealing stroke:

四		丨	冂	冂	四
国		冂	国	国	国
回		冂	回	回	回

7.   The middle stroke before those on both sides:

小		亅	小	小	
你		亻	竹	你	你
水		亅	刁	水	水

8. Inside stroke before side stroke:

Explanatory Notes for Character Entries

Below is an annotated character entry. It has been reduced to show the full range of information:

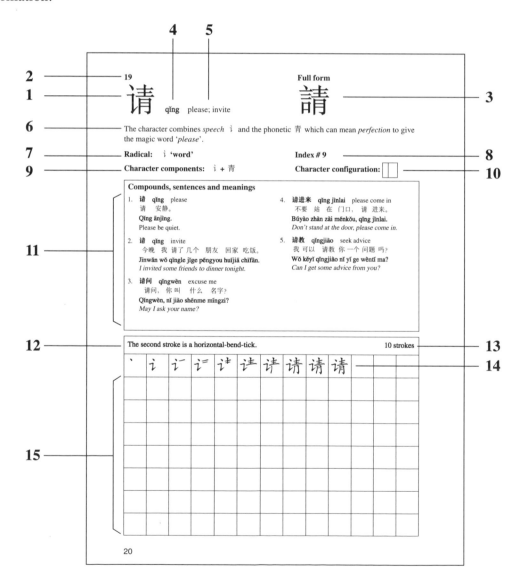

KEY:
1. the character
2. character serial number as sequenced in this book
3. full form of the character
4. pronunciation and tone
5. character definition
6. character explanation and points to note on the use of the character.
7. radical information
8. radical index number (based on *The Chinese-English Dictionary 1995*)
9. character components
10. character configuration
11. character combinations and example sentences with pronunciation and meaning
12. points to note when writing out the character.
13. total number of strokes of the character
14. stroke order
15. space to practice writing out the character

Simplified characters versus full characters

Out of the 250 characters studied in this book, 83 are simplified. This is under one-third which is generally the number of characters simplified for common usage. Where a simplified form exists, the full form is given as a reference. It is useful to know how the full form looks like as it is often used to illustrate how the character came to evolve to its present form.

Simplified characters have existed long before the Communist Chinese Government sanctioned their use with an official list in 1986. For example, the characters *cóng* 从 (from), *wàn* 万 (ten thousand) and *bǐ* 笔 (writing brush) existed side by side with their full forms 從, 萬 and 筆 in classical Chinese. The official sanction only means the abolition of the complex forms.

Several techniques were employed to create simplified characters. One was to replace the original component of a character with a component of fewer strokes but which had the same sound as the given character. For example, the simplified character for 'recognize' is *rèn* 认. The component 人 is pronounced as *rén* which is also the pronunciation for *rěn* 忍 in the full form (despite their different tones). Other examples are *shí* 识, *yàng* 样, *zhōng* 钟, *kuài* 块, *bāng* 帮, *yuán* 园, *yuǎn* 远 and *jí* 极 .

Another technique used was simply to take one section of a complex character and used it as the simplified one. Compare the full form for 'kin' 親 (*qīn*) and its simplified form 亲 which uses only the left component in simplification. Other examples in this collection are *ér* 兒 (son), *yī* 醫 (doctor), *xí* 習 (practice), *tiáo* 條 (classifier), *lǐ* 裡 (inside) and *qì* 氣 (gas, vapor) with their respective simplified forms 儿, 医, 习, 条, 里 and 气 .

Some characters are simplified on the basis of having adopted the cursive forms and in the process losing some of their strokes. For example, the radical 言 (speech) is simplified to 讠 by the adoption of its cursive form. Other radicals in this collection simplified on the same basis are 纟 (silk), 钅 (metal), 门 (door), 车 (vehicle) and 饣 (food). Note that simplification involving the radicals are responsible for many simplified forms being created as it is often the case that only the radicals are simplified. Examples are *shuō* 说, *huà* 话, *yǔ* 语, *shéi/shuí* 谁, *xiè* 谢, *qǐng* 请, *cí* 词, *dú* 读 for 讠 (word), *gěi* 给, *liàn* 练, *jīng* 经 for 纟 (silk), *qián* 钱, *tiě* 铁, *zhōng* 钟 for 钅 (metal), *wèn* 问, *jiān* 间 for 门 (door), *jiào* 较 for 车 (vehicle), and *fàn* 饭 for 饣 (food). Other cursive characters adopted as simplified forms are *ài* 爱, *dōng* 东, *jiàn* 见, *huì* 会, *xiě* 写, *shū* 书, *lái* 来, *jué/jiào* 觉, *lè/yuè* 乐, *cháng/zhǎng* 长 and *chē* 车.

Some cursive forms use an arbitrary form created for the sake of writing a character quickly. These are used to replace some complicated phonetic components. One common stereotype is *yòu* 又 made up of only two strokes. It is used in the characters *huān* 欢, *hàn* 汉, and *duì* 对 replacing 歡, 漢, and 對 respectively. Another such stereotype is *yún* 云 made up of only four strokes. It is used in the characters *yún* 云, *yùn* 运, and *dòng* 动 replacing 雲, 運, and 動 respectively.

The Pinyin System of Romanization

The system used in this book to write Chinese with Roman letters is the *Hanyu Pinyin* system which is standard in mainland China and is the system now used almost everywhere else in the world. The imitated pronunciation should be read as if it were English, bearing in mind the following main points:

Consonants
b, d, f, g, h, k, l, m, n, p, s, t, w, y as in English

c   like English **ts** in i**ts**
j   like English **j** in **j**eep
q   like English **ch** in **ch**eer, with a strong puff of air
r   like English **ur** in leis**ur**e, with the tongue rolled back
x   like English **see** (whole word)
z   like English **ds** in ki**ds**
ch like English **ch** in **ch**urch, with the tongue rolled back and a strong puff of air
sh like English **sh** in **sh**e, with the tongue rolled back
zh like English **j**, with the tongue rolled back

Vowels
a   like English **ar** in f**ar**
e   like English **ur** in f**ur**
i   like English **ee** in f**ee**
o   like English **or** in f**or**
u   like English **ue** in s**ue**
ü   like French **u**

Tones

A tone is a variation in pitch by which a syllable can be pronounced. In Chinese, a variation of pitch or tone changes the meaning of the word. There are four tones each marked by a diacritic. In addition there is a neutral tone which does not carry any tone marks. Below is a tone chart which describes tones using the 5-degree notation. It divides the range of pitches from lowest (1) to highest (5). Note that the neutral tone is not shown on the chart as it is affected by the tone that precedes it.

Tone chart

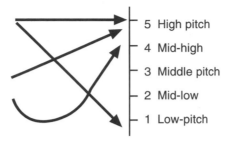

The first tone is a high-level tone represented by a level tone mark (–).

The second tone is a high-rising tone represented by a rising tone mark (ˊ).

The third tone is a low-dipping tone represented by a dish-like tone mark (ˇ).

The fourth tone is a high-falling tone represented by an falling tone mark (ˋ).

In addition to the above tones, there is a neutral tone which is pronounced light and soft in comparison to other tones. A neutral tone is not marked by any tone mark. A syllable is said to take on a neutral tone when it forms part of a word or is placed in various parts of a sentence.

How to use the Alphabetical Index

The words and phrases collected in the Chinese-English Glossary (approximately 1200 items) are arranged alphabetically according to the *Hanyu Pinyin* system of romanization. In this system each syllable (represented by a character) is a unit. The first character in a word or phrase is the head character. Each word or phrase is ordered in the first instance according to the phonetic value of this character. In a succession of entries having the same head character, alphabetical order is then determined by the phonetic value of the second character. This arrangement has the advantage of enhancing meaning by grouping together words which share a common character root, even though it is done at the expense of a straight alphabetical ordering.

The ordering of characters is affected by two other considerations. Firstly, in the case of characters represented by the same roman letters, alphabetization is determined by the tone of each character (represented in *Hanyu Pinyin* by diacritics), in the order first, second, third, fourth and neutral tone. Secondly, in the case of characters represented by the same Roman letters which also have the same tone, alphabetization follows the principle that simpler characters (those composed of fewer strokes) are listed before more complex characters (those composed of more strokes).

For example, the first 17 entries under Q have as their head character variations of the syllable 'qi' (pronounced like *chee* in English). These entries are *qī* — first tone (5 instances of a 2-stroke character, 1 of a 7-stroke character, 2 of a 12-stroke character); *qí* — second tone (1 instance); *qǐ* — third tone (4 instances of the same character); *qì* — fourth tone (1 instance of a 4-stroke character and 5 instances of a 7-stroke character). The neutral tone *qi*, written without any tone mark, is absent in this collection.

In the case of a character taking more than one tone, e.g. '*bu* 不' which can take on *bū*, *bù* or *bu*, the words or phrases sharing the head character are also arranged in the descending order of the tones.

How to use the Radical Index

The radical index is based on the 189 radicals used by *The Chinese-English Dictionary 1995*, published by the Foreign Language Teaching and Research Press in Beijing. When you look up a character, first determine which part of the character constitutes the radical and then count the remaining number of strokes to locate the character under that radical. Where a character is made up of two components which can function as radicals, it is sometimes classified under both radicals. For example, the character *měi* 美 'beautiful', is classified under both components which are treated as radicals: *yáng* 羊 'sheep' and *dà* 大 'big' in the same way as found in the *Chinese-English Dictionary 1995*.

1

一

yī / yí / yì   one

The character is pronounced in the 1st tone as *yī* when it is used in counting; in the 2nd tone as *yí* before a syllable in the 4th tone; and in 4th tone as *yì* before syllables in 1st, 2nd or 3rd tones.

Radical: 一 'horizontal stroke'   **Index # 2**

Character component: 一   **Character configuration:** ☐

Compounds, sentences and meanings

1. 一 **yī** one
一二三
yī èr sān
one two three

2. 一个 **yí ge** one (general objects, usually roundish)
请 给 我 一个 面包。
Qǐng gěi wǒ yí ge miànbāo.
Please give me a bread roll.

3. 一本(书) **yì běn (shū)** one (book)
我 买了 一本 书。
Wǒ mǎile yì běn shū.
I bought a book.

4. 一次 **yí cì** once
我 来过 北京 一次。
Wǒ láiguo Běijīng yí cì.
I've been to Beijing once.

5. 第一 **dìyī** first
这 是 第一次。
Zhè shì dìyī cì.
This is the first time.

Begin boldly and end firmly.   1 stroke

一

1

一 ➤

一——➤ èr two

The character, represented by two horizontal lines, indicates the number *two*.

Radical: 二 'two'

Character components: 一 + 一

Index # 10

Character configuration: ⊟

Compounds, sentences and meanings

1. 二 èr two
   一 加 一 等 于 二
   Yī jiā yī děngyú èr.
   One plus one equals two.

2. 二哥 èrgē second older brother
   我 二哥 是 中学 老师。
   Wǒ èrgē shì zhōngxué lǎoshī.
   My second oldest brother is a high school teacher.

3. 二月 Èryuè February
   北京 二月 还 很 冷。
   Běijīng Èryuè hái hěn lěng.
   Beijing is still quite cold in February.

4. 二等 èrděng second class
   我 买了 二等 舱 的 票。
   Wǒ mǎile èrděng cāng de piào.
   I've brought a second class cabin ticket.

5. 独一无二 dúyī-wú'èr unique
   她的 想法 独一无二。
   Tāde xiǎngfǎ dúyī-wú'èr.
   Her way of thinking is unique.

The bottom stroke is longer.   2 strokes

一	二										

三 sān three

The character, represented by three horizontal lines, indicates the number *three*.

Radical: 一 'horizontal stroke' **Index # 2**

Character components: 一 + 一 + 一 **Character configuration:**

Compounds, sentences and meanings

1. 三 **sān** three
    一不离二, 二不离三。
    Yī bù lí èr, èr bù lí sān.
    Things don't happen once; they come in twos and threes.

2. 三角形 **sānjiǎoxíng** triangle
    这 是 个 三角形。
    Zhè shì ge sānjiǎoxíng.
    This is a triangle.

3. 三个月 **sān ge yuè** three months
    我 来了 中国 三 个 月。
    Wǒ láile Zhōngguó sān ge yuè.
    I've been in China for three months.

4. 星期三 **Xīngqīsān** Wednesday
    今天 是 星期三。
    Jīntiān shì Xīngqīsān.
    Today is Wednesday.

5. 三心二意 **sānxīn-èryì** undecisive
    就 这样 吧, 别 再 三心二意 了。
    Jiù zhèyàng ba, bié zài sānxīn-èryì le.
    That settles it, don't be indecisive. (literally, three hearts, two minds)

The strokes are equally spaced, the middle stroke is the shortest. **3 strokes**

一 二 三

 **sì** four

The character originally depicted breath coming out of a mouth. It was suggested that the meaning of *four* came from breath spreading out in the *four* directions.

Radical: 囗 '4-sided frame'   **Index # 51**

Character components: 囗 + 儿   **Character configuration:**

Compounds, sentences and meanings

1. 四 **sì** four
   二二得四
   Èr èr dé sì.
   Two times two equals four.

2. 四方 **sìfāng** square
   我家有一个四方的盒子。
   Wǒ jiā yǒu yí ge sìfāng de hézi.
   I have a square box at home.

3. 四季 **sìjì** four seasons
   这里的气候四季如春。
   Zhèlǐ de qìhòu sìjì-rúchūn.
   The climate here is like spring in all seasons.

4. 四川 **Sìchuān** Sichuan (province; literally, four rivers, referring to the four tributaries of the Yangzi which flow through the province).
   四川菜 很 好吃。
   Sìchuāncài hěn hǎochī.
   Sichuan food is delicious.

5. 四通八达 **sìtōng-bādá** in all directions
   美国 的 公路 四通八达。
   Měiguó de gōnglù sìtōng-bādá.
   Highways of the United States go in all directions.

The inner strokes do not touch the frame.											5 strokes
丨	冂	冈	四	四							

 wǔ five

The character originally depicted the shape of a hand. The meaning of *five* comes from the *five* fingers.

Radical: 一 'horizontal stroke'　　　　**Index # 2**
or 二 'two'　　　　　　　　　　**Index # 10**
Character component: 五　　　　　　　**Character configuration:**

Compounds, sentences and meanings

1. 五　wǔ　five
五路　公共　汽车。
Wǔlù gōnggòng qìchē
No. 5 bus

2. 五月　Wǔyuè　May
五月　一号　是　劳动节。
Wǔyuè-yīhào shì Láodòngjié.
The first of May is Labor Day.

3. 五个月　wǔ ge yuè　five months
他的　汽车　买了　五个月。
Tāde qìchē mǎile wǔ ge yuè.
He bought his car five months ago.

4. 五体投地　wǔ tǐ tóu dī　prostrate oneself before someone (literally, the five extremities of the body).
他　为人　正直，　让　我　佩服得　五体
投　地。
Tā wéirén zhèngzhí, ràng wǒ pèifúde wǔ tǐ tóu dī.
I admire his uprightness greatly.

5. 五颜六色　wǔyán-liùsè　multi-colored
五颜六色　的　云霞　真　美丽。
Wǔyán-liùsè de yúnxiá zhēn měilī.
The multi-colored clouds are really pretty.

There is equal spacing between the 3 horizontal strokes.
The bottom stroke is longer than the ones above.

4 strokes

一	丁	开	五								

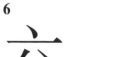 liù six

The character is romanized as *liù* with the tone mark placed on the main vowel *u*. This is because the pronunciation of *i* is unaffected by the tone change.

Radical: 亠 'the top of 六'   Index # 6

Character components: 亠 + 八   **Character configuration:**

Compounds, sentences and meanings

1. 六 liù six
   二三得六。
   Èr sān dé liù
   Two times three equals six.

2. 六月 Liùyuè June
   六月 十二号 是 我的 生日。
   Liùyuè-shí'èrhào shì wǒde shēngrì.
   The 12th of June is my birthday.

3. 星期六 Xīngqīliù Saturday
   星期六 我 不 上班。
   Xīngqīliù wǒ bú shàngbān.
   I don't go to work on Saturday.

4. 六一 Liùyī June 1st
   六一 是 国际 儿童节。
   Liùyī shì Guójì értóngjié.
   June 1st is International Children's Day.

5. 三头六臂 sāntóu-liùbì super-human
   (literally, three heads and six arms)
   你 别怕, 他 没有 三头六臂。
   Nǐ bié pà, tā méiyǒu sāntóu-liùbì.
   Don't be scared, he's not super-human.

End the last stroke firmly.   4 strokes

丶	亠	六	六								

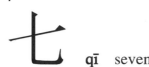 **qī** seven

The character represented a bent finger under a fist, an ancient way of signalling *seven*.

Radical: 一 'horizontal stroke'   **Index # 2**

Character components: 一 + 乚   **Character configuration:** ☐

Compounds, sentences and meanings

1. 七 **qī** seven
   七七四十九。
   Qī qī sìshíjiǔ.
   Seven times seven equals forty-nine.

2. 七天 **qī tiān** seven days
   一个 星期 有 七 天。
   Yí ge xīngqī yǒu qī tiān.
   There are seven days a week.

3. 七月 **Qīyuè** July
   北京 七月 很 热。
   Běijīng Qīyuè hěn rè.
   Beijing is very hot in July.

4. 七七八八 **qīqībābā** miscellaneous
   这里七七八八的 事情 很多。
   Zhèlǐ qīqībābā de shìqing hěnduō.
   There are plenty of odd jobs to do here.

5. 七上八落 **qīshàng-bāluò** be agitated
   (literally, like 15 buckets, 7 going up and 8 going down)
   我的 心头 如同 十五 个 吊桶
   Wǒde xīntóu rútóng shíwǔ ge diàotǒng,
   七上八落， 静不下来。
   qīshàng-bāluò, jìngbuxiàlai.
   My heart was racing erratically.

The second stroke ends with a hook.   2 strokes

一	七									

 **bā** eight

The character signifies something that can *easily be divided into two.*

Radical: 八 'eight'

Index # 17

Character component: 八

Character configuration:

Compounds, sentences and meanings

1. **八** **bā** eight
   我 家离 市区 八 公里。
   Wǒ jiā lí shìqū bā gōnglǐ.
   My house is 8 km from the city.

2. **八成** bāchéng 80 per cent
   事情 有了 八成 了。
   Shìqing yǒule bāchéng le.
   It's as good as settled.

3. **八折** **bāzhé** 20% discount
   八折 优惠 顾客。
   Bāzhé yōuhuì gùkè.
   80% discount.

4. **胡说八道** **húshuō-bādào** nonsense
   别 胡说八道。
   Bié húshuō-bādào.
   Don't talk nonsense.

5. **乱七八糟** **luànqībāzāo** in great disorder
   他的 屋子 乱七八糟 的。
   Tāde wūzi luànqībāzāo de.
   His room is in a mess.

Leave a gap at the top. 2 strokes

ノ	八										

 **jiǔ** nine

The character depicted a bent elbow, an ancient way of indicating the number *nine*.

Radical: 丿 'downward-left stroke'　　　　**Index # 4**

Character component: 九　　　　**Character configuration:** ☐

Compounds, sentences and meanings

1. **九** **jiǔ** nine
   三 三 得 九。
   Sān sān dé jiǔ.
   Three times three equals nine.

2. **九九表** **jiǔjiǔbiǎo** multiplication table
   你的 九九表 背熟 了吗?
   Nǐde jiǔjiǔbiǎo bèishú le ma?
   Did you learn the multiplication table?

3. **九级风** **jiǔjífēng** force 9 wind
   今天 吹 九级风。
   Jīntiān chuī jiǔjífēng.
   A strong gale is blowing today.

4. **九宫格儿** **jiǔgōnggér** 9-grid paper
   九宫格儿 是 用 来 写 汉字 的。
   Jiǔgōnggér shì yòng lái xiě Hànzì de.
   A 9-grid squared paper is used for writing characters.

5. **九一一** **Jiǔyīyī** September 11
   美国人 难忘 九一一。
   Měiguórén nǎnwàng Jiǔyīyī.
   Americans will never forget what happened on September 11.

The second stroke ends with a hook.　　　　2 strokes

丿	九									

10

十   **shí**   ten

The character signifies *all directions*.

Radical: 十 'ten'

Index # 11

Character component: 十

Character configuration: ☐

Compounds, sentences and meanings

1. 十   **shí**   ten
   我 妹妹 今年 十 岁。
   Wǒ mèimei jīnnián shí suì.
   My younger sister is ten years old.

2. 十分   **shífēn**   fully
   你 康复了，我 十分 高兴。
   Nǐ kāngfúle, wǒ shífēn gāoxìng.
   I'm very pleased that you've recovered.

3. 十足   **shízú**   100 per cent
   这 个 小伙子 干劲 十足。
   Zhè ge xiǎohuǒzi gànjìng shízú.
   This young man is full of energy.

4. 十字路口   **shízì lùkǒu**   intersection
   前面 有 个 十字 路口。
   Qiánmiàn yǒu ge shízì lùkǒu.
   There's an intersection further ahead.

5. 十全十美   **shíquán-shíměi**   be perfect in every way (literally, complete and beautiful)
   人生 很 难会 有 十全十美 的。
   Rénshēng hěn nán huì yǒu shíquán-shíměi de.
   It's very hard to find perfection in life.

The lower part of the vertical stroke is longer.   **2 strokes**

一	十								

Quiz 1 (1–10)

A. Join groups of 3 consecutive numbers in the 9-character grids below. They should be grouped together vertically, horizontally or diagonally.

一	九	七
二	三	六
三	四	五

七	二	三
五	六	四
七	六	五

八	七	六
四	九	五
八	九	十

B. Match characters with numbers by drawing lines.

(i)

十四	12
十二	15
十一	13
十五	11
十三	14

(ii)

五十九	65
三十七	48
二十六	59
四十八	37
六十五	26

C. Match the Chinese words with their English meaning.

(i)

dì 一	third
dì 三	first
dì 一 cì	third time
dì 三 cì	first time
dì 五 cì	fifth time

(ii)

二 yuè	four directions
六 ge yuè	fully
四 fāng	20% discount
八 zhé	six months
十 zú	February

D. Fill in the missing numbers with characters.

(i)

1. seventh   dì ___ 七 ___
2. four seasons   _____ jì
3. 70%   _____ chéng
4. 100%   _____ zú
5. second class   _____ děng

(ii)

6. Thursday   xīngqī _____
7. 10% discount   _____ zhé
8. multiplication table   _____ _____ biǎo
9. multi-colored   _____ yǎn _____ sè
10. undecisive   _____ xīn _____ yì

11

叫　jiào　be called

Full form

The full form combines *mouth* 口 and the phonetic 斗 which can mean *struggle*. It may be that it's a struggle to *yell out* someone's name to catch his or her attention. The simplified form uses a similar phonetic 丩 which joins the two dots to the horizontal stroke.

Radical: 口 'mouth'　　　　　　　　**Index # 50**

Character components: 口 + 丩　　　**Character configuration:**

Compounds, sentences and meanings

1. 叫　jiào　be called
   她 叫 什么 名字?
   Tā jiào shénme míngzi?
   What's her name?

2. 叫做　jiàozuò　be called
   这 种 汽油 叫做 含铅 汽油。
   Zhè zhǒng qìyóu jiàozuò hánqiān qìyóu.
   This type of petrol is called leaded petrol.

3. 叫门　jiàomén　call at the door
   有 人 在 叫门。
   Yǒu rén zài jiàomén.
   Someone is at the door.

4. 叫喊　jiàohǎn　shout
   请 别 在 这里 高声 叫喊。
   Qǐng bié zài zhèlǐ gāoshēng jiàohǎn.
   Please don't shout here.

5. 叫座　jiàozuò　draw a large audience
   这 个 电影 很 叫座。
   Zhè ge diànyǐng hěn jiàozuò.
   This movie is a box-office hit.

Write 口 half-way down the left strokes of 丩.　　　5 strokes

丨　丬　口　叱　叫

12

12

什 **shén** what?

甚

The simplified form must be used with the particle *me* 么 to give the meaning '*what?*'.

Radical: 亻 'upright person'

Index # 19

Character components: 亻 + 十

Character configuration: ▯

Compounds, sentences and meanings

1. **什么** shénme what
   你 叫 什么 名字?
   Nǐ jiào shénme míngzi?
   What's your given name?

2. **什么?** shénme Pardon me?
   什么? 请 再 说 一 遍。
   Shénme? Qǐng zài shuō yī biàn.
   Pardon? Please say that again.

3. **什么的** shénmede etc
   我 要 买鱼、肉、鸡蛋、什么的。
   Wǒ yào mǎi yú, ròu, jīdàn, shénmede.
   I have to buy fish, meat, eggs etc.

The left and right components do not join up. | 4 strokes

丿 亻 仁 什

me [particle]

麼

The character does not exist by itself but is used mostly after demonstrative pronouns and a few verbs.

Radical: 丿 'downward-left stroke'　　　　**Index # 4**
or　　厶 'private'　　　　　　　　　　**Index # 56**
Character components: 丿 + 厶　　　　**Character configuration:** ☐

Compounds, sentences and meanings

1. **这么　zhème**　so, such
   这么 做 就 行 了。
   Zhème zuò jiù xíng le.
   It should be fine if you do it this way.

2. **那么　nàme**　in that way
   别 走得 那么 快, 好不好?
   Bié zǒude nàme kuài, hǎobuhǎo?
   Don't walk so fast, okay?

3. **怎么　zěnme**　how
   这 个词儿英语 怎么 说?
   Zhè ge cír Yīngyǔ zěnme shuō?
   How do you say this word in English?

4. **多么　duōme**　to what extent
   多么 新鲜 的 水果 啊!
   Duōme xīnxiān de shuǐguǒ a!
   What fresh fruits!

5. **要么　yàome**　either or
   要么 他来, 要么 我 去, 我们 总 得
   Yàome tā lái, yàome wǒ qù, wǒmen zǒng děi
   见 个 面。
   jiàn ge miàn.
   Either he comes here or I go there; either way we've got to meet.

The first stroke only comes halfway down.　　　　3 strokes

丿	厶	么									

míng name

The character combines *mouth* 口 and *evening* 夕 which signifies that people at night identify themselves to others by calling out their *names*.

Radical: 口 'mouth'　　　　　　　　　**Index # 50**
or 　　　　夕 'sunset'　　　　　　　　　**Index # 56**
Character components: 夕 + 口　　　　**Character configuration:**

Compounds, sentences and meanings

1. 名　**míng**　name
   他 名 叫 王 刚。
   Tā míng jiào Wáng Gāng.
   His name is Wang Gang

2. 名字　**míngzì**　name
   我 有 中文 名字。
   Wǒ yǒu Zhōngwén míngzi.
   I have a Chinese name.

3. 名牌　**míngpái**　brand name
   北京 大学 是 名牌 大学。
   Běijīng Dàxué shì míngpái dàxué.
   Peking University is a prestigious university.

4. 名片　**míngpiàn**　business card
   这 是 我的 名片。
   Zhè shì wǒde míngpiàn.
   This is my business card.

5. 名胜　**míngshèng**　famous scenic spot
   南京 有 很多 名胜。
   Nánjīng yǒu hěnduō míngshèng.
   Nanjing has many famous scenic spots.

The third stroke does not cross through the second stroke. 　　　　**6 strokes**

ノ	ク	夕	夕	名	名						

字

zì character

The character combines *roof* or *house* 宀 with *child* 子 which by inference means a child is studying *characters* inside a house.

Radical: 宀 'roof'　　　　　　　　　**Index # 34**

Character components: 宀 + 子　　　**Character configuration:**

Compounds, sentences and meanings

1. **字** **zì** character, word
   你 这 个 字 写得 不对。
   Nǐ zhè ge zì xiěde búduì.
   You wrote this character incorrectly.

2. **字典** **zìdiǎn** dictionary
   你 有 汉英 字典 吗?
   Nǐ yǒu Hàn-yīng zìdiǎn ma?
   Do you have a Chinese–English dictionary?

3. **字母** **zìmǔ** alphabet
   汉语 拼音 用 的 是 拉丁 字母。
   Hànyǔ Pīnyīn yòng de shì Lādīng zìmǔ.
   Pinyin uses the Latin alphabet.

4. **字幕** **zìmù** subtitles, captions
   这 个 电影 有 中文 字幕。
   Zhè ge diànyǐng yǒu Zhōngwén zìmù.
   This movie has Chinese subtitles.

5. **汉字** **Hànzì** characters
   我 学了 十五 个 汉字。
   Wǒ xuéle shíwǔ ge Hànzì.
   I've learnt 15 Chinese characters.

The fifth stroke ends with a hook.　　　　　　　　　　　6 strokes

丶	丷	宀	宀	宁	字						

你 nǐ you

The right part of the character 尔 is the old form for *you*. The new form retains the same idea with the additional meaning of *person* 亻.

Radical: 亻 'upright person'   **Index # 19**

Character components: 亻 + 尔   **Character configuration:** ⊟

Compounds, sentences and meanings

1. **你** nǐ   you
   你 想 买 什么?
   Nǐ xiǎng mǎi shénme?
   What would you like to buy?

2. **你好** nǐ hǎo   hello
   你好! 认识 你, 我 很 高兴。
   Nǐ hǎo! Rènshi nǐ, wǒ hěn gāoxìng.
   Hi! I'm pleased to meet you.

3. **你们** nǐmen   you (plural)
   我 给 你们 介绍, 这是…, 这是…。
   Wǒ gěi nǐmen jièshào, zhè shì ..., zhè shì....
   Let me introduce, this is ..., this is ...

4. **你们好** nǐmen hǎo   hello everyone
   你们 好!
   Nǐmen hǎo!.
   Hi! Everyone!

5. **你们的** nǐmende   your, yours
   你们的 东西 放好 了吗?
   Nǐmende dōngxi fànghǎo le ma?
   Have you put away your things?

The fifth stroke is a vertical hook.   7 strokes

ノ	亻	亻	亻	你	你	你					

好

hǎo   good

The character signifies the old idea that being in possession of *woman* 女 and *child* 子 is *good*.

Radical: 女 'female'

Index # 65

Character components: 女 + 子

Character configuration:

Compounds, sentences and meanings

1. **好**   **hǎo**   good
   今天 天气 真 好。
   Jīntiān tiānqì zhēn hǎo.
   The weather is really lovely today.

2. **好办**   **hǎobàn**   easy to handle
   这 件 事 好办。
   Zhè jiàn shì hǎobàn.
   This matter can be settled.

3. **好吃**   **hǎochī**   delicious
   我 觉得 中餐 很 好吃。
   Wǒ juéde Zhōngcān hěn hǎochī.
   I think Chinese food is delicious.

4. **好处**   **hǎochù**   good points
   学 拼音 对 学 汉字 有 好处。
   Xué Pīnyīn duì xué Hànzì yǒu hǎochù.
   Learning pinyin helps you learn Chinese characters.

5. **好看**   **hǎokàn**   pretty
   你 说 这 条 裙子 好 不 好看?
   Nǐ shuō zhè tiáo qúnzi hǎo bu hǎokàn?
   Do you think this dress is pretty?

The first stroke travels down, turns and ends firmly.   6 strokes

し	乆	女	奵	奵	好						

wǒ I, me

The character combines *grain* 手 (written as 禾 in early sources) and *spear* 戈 to satisfy basic needs of food and security. From this the idea of *self* emerges.

Radical: 戈 'spear'

Index # 85

Character components: 手 + 戈

Character configuration:

Compounds, sentences and meanings

1. **我** **wǒ** I, me
   我 喜欢 学 汉字。
   Wǒ xǐhuan xué Hànzì.
   I like learning Chinese characters.

2. **我们** **wǒmen** we, us
   我们 互相 帮助, 好 不好?
   Wǒmen hùxiāng bāngzhù, hǎo buhǎo?
   Let's help each other, shall we?

3. **我们的** **wǒmende** our, ours
   我们的 将来 是 美好 的。
   Wǒmende jiānglái shì měihǎo de.
   Our future is bright.

4. **自我** **zìwǒ** self
   我 建议 大家 自我 介绍 一下儿。
   Wǒ jiànyì dàjiā zìwǒ jièshāo yīxiàr.
   I suggest that we introduce ourselves.

The fourth stroke comes up, the sixth stroke sweeps down.   7 strokes

丿	二	于	手	扰	我	我					

请 qǐng please; invite

Full form

請

The character combines *speech* 讠 and the phonetic 青 which can mean *perfection* to give the magic word '*please*'.

Radical: 讠 'word'

Index # 9

Character components: 讠 + 青

Character configuration:

Compounds, sentences and meanings

1. 请 qǐng please
   请 安静。
   Qǐng ānjìng.
   Please be quiet.

2. 请 qǐng invite
   今晚 我 请了几个 朋友 回家 吃饭。
   Jīnwǎn wǒ qǐngle jǐge péngyou huíjiā chīfàn.
   I invited some friends to dinner tonight.

3. 请问 qǐngwèn excuse me
   请问, 你 叫 什么 名字?
   Qǐngwèn, nǐ jiào shénme míngzi?
   May I ask your name?

4. 请进来 qǐng jìnlai please come in
   不要 站 在 门口, 请 进来。
   Búyào zhàn zài ménkǒu, qǐng jìnlai.
   Don't stand at the door, please come in.

5. 请教 qǐngjiào seek advice
   我 可以 请教 你 一个 问题 吗?
   Wǒ kěyǐ qǐngjiào nǐ yí ge wèntí ma?
   Can I get some advice from you?

The second stroke is a horizontal-bend-tick.   10 strokes

、	讠	丨	讠	讠	请	请	请	请	请			

20

问 **wèn** ask

Full form

問

The character signifies that one has to use the *mouth* 口 to ask a *question* and this usually takes place outside one's *door* 门 .

Radical: 门 'door'

Index # 37

Character components: 门 + 口

Character configuration: ⬜

Compounds, sentences and meanings

1. 问 **wèn** ask
   不 懂 就 问。
   Bù dǒng jiù wèn.
   Ask when you don't understand.

2. 问答 **wèndá** questions and answers
   我 现在 做 问答 练习。
   Wǒ xiànzài zuò wèndá liànxí.
   I'm doing questions and answers drills at present.

3. 问题 **wèntí** question
   没有 问题。
   Méiyǒu wèntí.
   There are no problems.

4. 问好 **wènhǎo** say hello to
   请 代 我 向 你父亲 问好。
   Qǐng dài wǒ xiàng nǐ fùqin wènhǎo.
   Please give my regards to your father.

5. 学问 **xuéwèn** learning
   他 是 一 位 学问 高深 的人。
   Tā shì yí wèi xuéwèn gāoshēn de rén.
   He is a very learned person.

The first stroke is a downward dot.   **6 strokes**

`　丶　讠　门　闩　问　问

21

Quiz 2 (11–20)

A. Look at the 9-character grid and CIRCLE words or phrases. They can be written horizontally from left to right or vertically. Look at the circled characters in the Key if unsure. COPY the word or phrase next to the grid and write the pinyin and meaning.

你	好	什
请	叫	么
问	名	字

	Word or phrase			Pinyin	Translation
(i)	你	好		Nǐ hǎo!	Hello!
(ii)					
(iii)					
(iv)					

B. Refer to the characters in the 9-character grid above and CONVERT the pinyin phrases into characters. You may like to check their English meaning in the Key. You might also need to refresh your memory on how to write the character wǒ 'I, me'.

(i)	Wǒ wèn nǐ.									
(ii)	Nǐ wèn wǒ shénme?									
(iii)	Wǒ jiào shénme míngzi?									

C. Match the Chinese words with their English meaning.

(i)

好 kàn   Come in
好 chī   characters
Hàn 字   dictionary
yǒu 名   delicious
字 diǎn   alphabet
请 jìnlai   business card
字 mǔ   pretty
名 piàn   famous

(ii)

xué 问   question
问 tí   etc.
叫 hǎn   say hello to
问 hǎo   what
请 jiào   shout
什么   seek advice
什么 de   how
zěn 么   learning

21

您

 nín   you (polite)

The character combines *you* 你 with *heart* 心 to express the *polite form* of *'you'*.

Radical: 心 'heart'   **Index # 76**

Character components: 你 + 心   **Character configuration:**

Compounds, sentences and meanings

1. 您   nín   you (polite)
    您 贵姓?
    Nín guìxìng?
    May I ask your name (surname)?

2. 您好   Nín hǎo!   How are you!
    老师，您好!
    Lǎoshī, nín hǎo!
    How are you, sir/ma'am (teacher)?

3. 您早   Nín zǎo!   Good morning!
    老师，您早!
    Lǎoshī, nín zǎo!
    Good morning, sir/ma'am (teacher)!

Note the position of the three dots in 心 .   11 strokes

ノ	イ	亻	价	伫	价	你	你	您	您	您		

23

guì expensive

When used as an honorific, the character means *your*. By itself, it means *expensive*. This comes from the time when shells were used as a form of money.

Radical: 贝 'seashell'

Index # 92

Character components: 中 + 一 + 贝

Character configuration:

Compounds, sentences and meanings

1. 贵 **guì** expensive
    这 本 书 很 好, 也 不 贵。
    Zhè běn shū hěn hǎo, yě bú guì.
    This book is good and is not expensive.

2. 贵姓 **guìxìng** your name (honorific)
    您 贵姓?
    Nín guìxìng?
    What's your surname, please?

3. 贵国 **guìguó** your country (honorific)
    贵国 是 哪国?
    Guìguó shì năguó?
    What nationality (polite form) are you?

The last stroke finishes firmly.   9 strokes

㇔	㇆	口	中	虫	串	贵	贵	贵				

姓

xìng surname

The character combines *woman* 女 and *birth* 生 to give the idea of *surname* inherited from the mother, which was the case in matriarchical societies.

Radical: 女 'female'   **Index # 65**

Character components: 女 + 生   **Character configuration:**

Compounds, sentences and meanings

1. **姓 xìng** to be surnamed
   我 姓 李, 名 叫 恩华。
   Wǒ xìng Lǐ, míng jiào Ēnhuá.
   My surname is Li, my given name is Enhua.

2. **姓名 xìngmíng** full name
   请 写下 你的 姓名。
   Qǐng xiěxià nǐde xìngmíng.
   Please write down your full name.

3. **姓氏 xìngshì** surname
   以 姓氏 笔划 为 序。
   Yǐ xìngshì bǐhuà wéi xù.
   Arranged by surname in the order of the number of strokes.

4. **老百姓 lǎobǎixìng** common people
   (literally, the 100 old names)
   中国 一般 老百姓 很 穷。
   Zhōngguó yībān lǎobǎixìng hěn qióng.
   In general, people in China are poor.

5. **同姓 tóngxìng** having the same surname
   以前 中国人 同姓 不 通婚。
   Yǐqián Zhōngguórén tóngxìng bù tōnghūn.
   In the past, people would not marry someone with the same surname.

The bottom horizontal stroke on the right hand side is longer.   8 strokes

ㄑ	女	女	女	女	妁	姓	姓				

 shì   be

Swearing under the *sun* 日 that something is true signifies the idea of certainty. Thus the character means *to be*.

Radical: 日 'sun'   **Index # 90**

Character components: 日 + 疋   **Character configuration:** ⊟

Compounds, sentences and meanings

1. 是 shì   to be
   她 是 日本人。
   Tā shì Rìběnrén.
   She is Japanese.

2. 是的 shìde   yes
   是的，日本人 也 用 汉字。
   Shìde, Rìběnrén yě yòng Hànzì.
   Yes, Japanese people also use Chinese characters.

3. 不是 búshì   not to be
   他 不是 日本人。
   Tā búshì Rìběnrén.
   He's not Japanese.

4. 是不是 shìbushì   to be or not to be
   他 是不是 日本人?
   Tā shìbushì Rìběnrén?
   Is he Japanese?

5. 还是 háishi   or
   她 是 日本人，还是 韩国人?
   Tā shì Rìběnrén, háishi Hánguórén?
   Is she Japanese or Korean?

Make sure that the last stroke is not too flat.									9 strokes
丶	冂	冃	日	旦	早	早	昰	是	

哪

nǎ which

The character combines *mouth* 口 with the phonetic 那 gives the character the sound element. By itself, it means *which*; with 儿, it means *where*.

Radical: 口 'mouth'　　　　　　　　　　**Index # 50**

Character components: 口 + 月 + 阝　　　　　**Character configuration:**

Compounds, sentences and meanings

1. **哪　nǎ** which one?
   你 喜欢 哪个 玩具?
   Nǐ xǐhuan nǎ ge wánjù?
   Which toy would you like?

2. **哪儿　nǎr** where?
   你 上 哪儿去?
   Nǐ shàng nǎr qù?
   Where are you going?

3. **哪里　nǎli** where?
   你 上 哪里去?
   Nǐ shàng nǎli qù?
   Where are you going?

4. **哪些　nǎxiē** which ones?
   你 去过 北京 哪些 地方?
   Nǐ qùguo Běijīng nǎxiē dìfang?
   Where have you been to in Beijing?

5. **哪国人　nǎguórén** which country?
   你 是 哪国人?
   Nǐ shì nǎguórén?
   What nationality are you?

The eighth stroke is written like the figure 3.　　　　　　　　**9 strokes**

丶	丬	卩	叮	叼	吗	明	哪	哪			

Full form

        guó   country

The simplified character signifies that when the best in the country as represented by *jade*
玉 is protected by a *wall* or *boundary* 囗, nationhood comes into being.

Radical: 囗 *'4-sided frame'*   **Index # 51**

Character components: 囗 + 玉   **Character configuration:** ▢

Compounds, sentences and meanings

1. 国 **guó** nation
   《一国 两制》 这个 政策 是

   <Yī guó liǎng zhì> zhè ge zhèngcè shì
   邓 小平 提出的。

   Dèng Xiǎopíng tíchū de.
   *It was Deng Xiaoping who proposed the policy
   of "One country, two systems."*

2. 国家 **guójiā** nation
   美国 是 民主 国家。

   Měiguó shì mínzhǔ guójiā.
   The United States is a democratic country.

3. 德国 **Déguó** Germany
   德国 在 欧洲。

   Déguó zài Ōuzhou.
   Germany is in Europe.

4. 国庆 **guóqìng** National Day
   十月 一号 是 中国   国庆节。

   Shíyuè-yīhào shì Zhōngguó Guóqìngjié.
   October 1st is Chinese National Day.

5. 国际 **guójì** international
   中国 的 国际 地位 提高 了。

   Zhōngguó de guójì dìwèi tígāo le.
   China's international status has improved.

The last stroke seals the enclosure.   8 strokes

丨	冂	冂	冃	用	国	国	国				

rén   person, people

The character is a pictograph of a *person* standing with his/her feet apart.

Radical: 人 'person'

Index # 18

Character component: 人

Character configuration: ☐

Compounds, sentences and meanings

1. **人** rén person, people
   房间 里 没有 人。
   Fángjiān li méiyǒu rén.
   There is no one in the room.

2. **人们** rénmen people
   人们 都 说 她 不错。
   Rénmen dōu shuō tā búcuò.
   People all speak well of her.

3. **中国人** Zhōngguórén Chinese (person)
   中国人 跟 日本人 不 一样
   Zhōngguórén gēn Rìběnrén bù yíyàng.
   Chinese people are different from Japanese.

4. **人口** rénkǒu population
   中国 的 人口 众多。
   Zhōngguó de rénkǒu zhòngduō.
   China has a large population.

5. **人山人海** rénshān-rénhǎi sea of people
   (literally, a mountain of people, a sea of people)
   广场 上 人山人海。
   Guǎngchǎng shang rénshān-rénhǎi.
   The square was crowded with many people.

Note the difference between 人 and 入. | 2 strokes

ノ	人								

zhōng   middle

The character signifies the idea of an arrow hitting the bull's eye right in the *center*.

Radical: 丨 'vertical stroke'   **Index # 3**

Character components: 口 + 丨   **Character configuration:** ☐

Compounds, sentences and meanings

1. 中 **zhōng** middle
   我 穿 中 号 的。
   Wǒ chuān zhōng hào de.
   I wear medium size.

2. 中级 **zhōngjí** intermediate level
   这 是 中级 课程。
   Zhè shì zhōngjí kèchéng.
   This is an intermediate course.

3. 中国 **Zhōngguó** China
   中国 是 世界 第三 大国。
   Zhōngguó shì shìjiè dìsān dàguó.
   China is the world's third largest country.

4. 中文 **Zhōngwén** Chinese language
   我 看不懂 中文 报。
   Wǒ kànbudǒng Zhōngwén bào.
   I can't read Chinese newspapers.

5. 中餐 **Zhōngcān** Chinese food
   我 爸爸 喜欢 吃 中餐。
   Wǒ bàba xǐhuan chī Zhōngcān.
   My father loves Chinese food.

The vertical stroke is in the middle of the rectangle.   4 strokes

丨	冖	口	中								

29

美 měi beautiful

The character combines *lamb* 羊 and *big* 大 to give the idea of *perfection* or *beauty*.

Radical: 羊 'sheep'   **Index # 133**
or   大 '**big**'   **Index # 43**
Character components: 羊 + 大   **Character configuration:**

Compounds, sentences and meanings

1. 美 **měi** good, satisfactory
   这里的 东西 物美 价廉。
   Zhèlǐ de dōngxi wùměi-jiālián.
   The things here are good and inexpensive.

2. 美丽 **měilì** beautiful
   这里的 风景 很 美丽。
   Zhèlǐ de fēngjǐng hěn měilì.
   The scenery here is beautiful.

3. 美好 **měihǎo** fine, happy
   我的 童年 是一个 美好 的 回忆。
   Wǒde tóngnián shì yí ge měihǎo de huíyì.
   I have good memories of my childhood.

4. 美化 **měihuà** beautify
   我们 应该 尽 可能 美化 环境。
   Wǒmen yīnggāi jìn kěnéng měihuà huánjìng.
   We should try our best to beautify the environment.

5. 美国 **Měiguó** USA
   美国 在 北 美洲。
   Měiguó zài Běi Měizhōu.
   The United States is in North America.

The last two strokes taper off   9 strokes

丶	丷	丷	兰	羊	羊	美	美	美			

吗 ma [particle]

Full form

嗎

The character combines *mouth* 口 which signifies *asking*, while the phonetic 马 gives the sound *ma*. Note that 吗 is always pronounced in the neutral tone.

Radical: 口 'mouth'

Index # 50

Character components: 口 + 马

Character configuration:

Compounds, sentences and meanings

1. **吗** **ma** question particle
   你 找 我 吗?
   Nǐ zhǎo wǒ ma?
   Are you looking for me?

2. **好吗** **hǎo ma** good?
   你 好 吗?
   Nǐ hǎo ma?
   How are you?

3. **忙吗** **máng ma** busy?
   你 忙 吗?
   Nǐ máng ma?
   Are you busy?

4. **干吗** **gàn ma** what are you doing?
   你 晚上 干 吗?
   Nǐ wǎnshang gàn ma?
   What will you be doing in the evening?

马 should be upright.

6 strokes

丶	冖	口	吗	吗	吗						

Quiz 3 (21–30)

A. Look at the 9-character grid and CIRCLE words or phrases. They can be written horizontally from left to right or vertically. Look at the circled characters in the Key if unsure. COPY the word or phrase next to the grid and write the pinyin and meaning.

您	哪	贵
中	国	姓
是	人	美

Word or phrase

(i)

贵	姓

(ii)

(iii)

Pinyin	Translation
Guìxìng	What's your name?

B. Refer to the characters in the 9-character grid above and CONVERT the pinyin sentences into characters. You might like to check their English meaning in the Key. Look up the characters you have learnt in previous sets.

(i)	Qǐngwèn, nín guìxìng?									
(ii)	Qǐngwèn, guìguó shì nǎguó?									
(iii)	Qǐngwèn, nǐ shì nǎguórén?									

C. Match the Chinese words with their English meaning.

(i)
哪 ge — which one
国 qìng — fine, happy
哪 xiē — beautiful
美 lì — country
美好 — which ones
国 jiā — National Day

(ii)
中 wén — population
是 de — Chinese food
hái 是 — name
人 kǒu — Chinese language
姓名 — or
中 cān — yes

33

 tā he

The character combines *person* 亻 and *also* 也 to suggest the idea of 'that male person also.' Thus it means *the third person*.

Radical: 亻 '**upright person**'   **Index # 19**

Character components: 亻 + 也   **Character configuration:** ▯

Compounds, sentences and meanings

1. **他** tā he
   他 是 我的 老朋友。
   Tā shì wǒde lǎopéngyou.
   He's an old friend of mine.

2. **他们** tāmen they
   他们 是 法国人, 不是 美国人。
   Tāmen shì Fǎguórén, búshì Měiguórén.
   They're French, not American.

3. **他人** tārén others
   别 吵, 这样 会 影响 他人。
   Bié chǎo, zhèyàng huì yǐngxiǎng tārén.
   Don't make so much noise as this will disturb people.

4. **他妈的** tāmāde damn it!
   他妈的,你 怎么 走路 看 也不看!
   Tāmāde, nǐ zěnme zǒulù kàn yě búkàn!
   Damn you, why don't you watch where you're going!

5. **其他** qítā other
   还有 什么 其他 事情 要 我们 做
   Háiyǒu shénme qítā shìqing yào wǒmen zuò
   吗?
   ma?
   Is there anything else you want us to do?

The third stroke ends with a hook.											5 strokes
ノ	亻	仂	他	他							

她 tā she

The character is a modern version of the pronoun 他 *he*, using the idea of *female* 女 and *also* 也 to suggest the idea of 'that female person also.' Thus it means *she*.

Radical: 女 'female'　　　　　　　**Index # 65**

Character components: 女 + 也　　　**Character configuration:**

Compounds, sentences and meanings

1. 她 **tā** she
   她 说 汉语 说得 很 好。
   Tā shuō Hànyǔ shuōde hěn hǎo.
   She speaks Chinese very well.

2. 她的 **tāde** her, hers
   她的 汉语 说得 很 地道。
   Tāde Hànyǔ shuōde hěn dìdao.
   Her spoken Mandarin is very idiomatic.

3. 她们 **tāmen** they, them (female)
   你认得 她们 是 谁 吗?
   Nǐ rènde tāmen shì shéi/shuí ma?
   Do you know who these girls/women are?

4. 她们的 **tāmende** their, theirs (female)
   她们的 衣服 都 很 时髦。
   Tāmende yīfu dōu hěn shímáo.
   The clothes they are wearing are very fashionable.

The fourth stroke ends with a hook.　　　　　　　　　6 strokes

乚	乙	女	如	如	她						

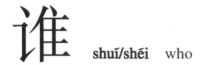 shuí/shéi who

Full form

The full character expresses the idea of asking for the identity of a *person,* or *who,* with the combination of the idea of *speech* 言 and the phonetic 隹，which contains *person.*

Radical: 讠 'word'

Index # 9

Character components: 讠 + 隹

Character configuration:

Compounds, sentences and meanings

1. **谁** shuí/shéi who
   有 谁 能 帮助 我 就 好了!
   Yǒu shuí/shéi néng bāngzhù wǒ jiù hǎo le!
   If only someone could help me!

2. **谁的** shuí/shéi'de whose
   这 是 谁的 中文 课本?
   Zhè shì shuí/shéi'de Zhōngwén kèběn?
   Whose Chinese textbook is this?

3. **谁知道** shuí/shéi zhīdao no one knows
   我 本 是 跟 她 开 玩笑, 谁 知道 她
   Wǒ běn shì gēn tā kāi wánxiào, shéi zhīdao tā
   生气 了。
   shēngqì le.
   I was only joking with her, I didn't expect her to get angry.

There is equal spacing between the horizontal lines.   10 strokes

丶	讠	讠	讠	讠	讠	讠	讠	谁	谁			

34

 的 **de** [particle]

Pronounced in the neutral tone. This particle, often indicating ownership, is the most frequently used character in Chinese.

Radical: 白 'white'　　　　　　　**Index # 125**

Character components: 白 + 勺　　**Character configuration:**

Compounds, sentences and meanings

1. 的　**de**　particle
她 有 一 双 大大的 眼睛。
Tā yǒu yī shuāng dàdà de yǎnjing.
She has big eyes (literally, a pair of big eyes).

2. 辣的　**là de**　chilli hot
我 爱 吃辣的。
Wǒ ài chī là de.
I love spicy food.

3. 昨天的　**zuótiān de**　yesterday's
这 是 昨天 的 报。
Zhè shì zuótiān de bào.
This is yesterday's newspaper.

4. 有的　**yǒude**　some
有的 是 新 的, 有的 是 旧 的。
Yǒude shì xīn de, yǒude shì jiù de.
Some are new, some are old.

Write the final stroke firmly.　　　　　　　　8 strokes

′ 亻 白 白 白 的 的 的

朋

péng friend

The character signifies two *friends* standing side by side.

Radical: 月 'flesh/moon'

Index # 103

Character components: 月 + 月

Character configuration:

Compounds, sentences and meanings

1. **朋** **péng** friend
   昨晚　亲朋　戚友聚在一起真
   Zuówǎn qīn-péng qī-yǒu jù zài yìqǐ zhēn
   高兴。
   gāoxìng.
   It was very happy to have relatives and friends gathered together last night.

2. **朋友** **péngyou** friend
   你有　中国　朋友吗?
   Nǐ yǒu Zhōngguó péngyou ma?
   Do you have any Chinese friends?

3. **男朋友** **nánpéngyou** boy friend
   她跟　男朋友　住在一起。
   Tā gēn nánpéngyou zhù zài yìqǐ.
   She lives with her boy friend.

4. **女朋友** **nǔpéngyou** girl friend
   你有　女朋友　了没有?
   Nǐ yǒu nǔpéngyou le méiyou?
   Do you have a steady girl friend?

5. **老朋友** **lǎopéngyou** old friend
   难得有机会跟　老朋友　聚在一起。
   Nándé yǒu jīhuì gēn lǎopéngyou jù zài yìqǐ.
   Old friends don't often get the chance to meet.

The right component is written slightly wider.   8 strokes

)	刀	月	月	朋	朋	朋	朋				

36

 友 yǒu friend

The character depicts two hands, a symbol of *friendship*.

Radical: 又 'again'   **Index # 24**

Character components: ナ + 又   **Character configuration:**

Compounds, sentences and meanings

1. **友** yǒu friend
他 是 我 十 多 年 的 好 友。
Tā shì wǒ shí duō nián de hǎo yǒu.
He has been my good friend for over ten years.

2. **友情** yǒuqíng friendship
他 很 重 友情。
Tā hěn zhòng yǒuqíng.
He values friendship greatly.

3. **友谊** yǒuyì friendship
友谊第一, 比赛第二。
Yǒuyì dìyī, bǐsài dì'èr.
Friendship first, competition second.

4. **友好** yǒuhǎo friendly
他 对 人 很 友好。
Tā duì rén hěn yǒuhǎo.
He's a friendly person.

5. **走亲访友** zǒu-qīn fǎng-yǒu visiting
relatives and friends
中国 普通 的 老百姓 走亲
Zhōngguó pǔtōng de lǎobǎixìng zǒu-qīn
访友 都 是 骑 自行车。
fǎng-yǒu dōu shì qí zìxíngchē.
Ordinary people in China use bicycles to visit their relatives and friends.

The long horizontal stroke covers 又.   4 strokes

一	ナ	方	友							

39

xué learn

The character combines a *child* 子 studying under a *roof* ⺌ to suggest *learning*.

Radical: 子 'child'

Index # 67

Character components: ⺌ + 子

Character configuration:

Compounds, sentences and meanings

1. 学 **xué** study, learn
   只要 努力,一定 能 学会。
   Zhǐyào nǔlì, yídìng néng xuéhuì.
   If you work hard, you will master it.

2. 学生 **xuésheng** student
   中国 学生 很 认真 学习。
   Zhōngguó xuésheng hěn rènzhēn xuéxí.
   Chinese students are very studious.

3. 学习 **xuéxí** learn
   应该 学习 别人 的 长处。
   Yīnggāi xuéxí biéren de chángchù.
   One should learn from others' strong points.

4. 学校 **xuéxiào** school
   这 个 学校 有 点儿 名气。
   Zhè ge xuéxiào yǒu diǎnr míngqì.
   This school has a good reputation.

5. 学费 **xuéfèi** tuition fees
   念 大学 一 年 的 学费 是 多少?
   Niàn dàxué yì nián de xuéfèi shì duōshao?
   How much are the annual university tuition fees?

The first two dots slant to the right.   8 strokes

丶	⺎	⺌	⺍	学	学	学	学				

bù / bú not

The character is usually pronounced in the 4th tone except when it is followed by another 4th tone syllable, which changes it into the 2nd tone.

Radical: 一 'horizontal stroke'　　　　　**Index # 2**

Character component: 不　　　　　　　**Character configuration:** ☐

Compounds, sentences and meanings

1. **不　bù**　not
   昨天 他 说　今天 不 来了。
   Zuótiān tā shuō jīntiān bù lái le.
   He said yesterday that he won't be coming today.

2. **不多不少　bùduō bùshǎo**　just right
   你 买 的 水果　不多 不少，　正　好。
   Nǐ mǎi de shuǐguǒ bùduō bùshǎo, zhèng hǎo.
   You bought just the right amount of fruit — not too much, not too little.

3. **不错　búcuò**　quite good
   这 个 字 写得 不错。
   Zhè ge zì xiěde búcuò.
   This character is quite well written.

4. **不好意思　bùhǎo yìsi**　embarrassed
   让 你 久 等 了，真 不 好意思。
   Ràng nǐ jiǔ děng le, zhēn bù hǎo yìsi.
   I'm sorry to have kept you waiting.

5. **不久　bùjiǔ**　not for a long time
   你 走了 不久,他 就 来 了。
   Nǐ zǒule bùjiǔ, tā jiù lái le.
   He came soon after you left.

The last stroke ends firmly.　　　　　　　　　　　　　**4 strokes**

一　丆　不　不

yīng hero

The character originally meant *flower*, it combines the grass radical ⺾ and the phonetic 央. It means *outstanding*.

Radical: ⺾ 'grass'

Index # 42

Character components: ⺾ + 央

Character configuration:

Compounds, sentences and meanings

1. **英 yīng** hero
   学校 开了 一个 群英会 庆祝
   Xuéxiào kāile yí ge qúnyīnghuì qìngzhù
   运动会 的结束。
   yùndònghuì de jiéshù.
   The school organized a celebration for the participants at the end of the sports carnival.

2. **英俊 yīngjùn** handsome
   这个 小伙子 长得 很 英俊。
   Zhè ge xiǎohuǒzi zhǎngde hěn yīngjùn.
   This young lad is quite handsome.

3. **英国 Yīngguó** England
   每年 去 英国 的 人 很多。
   Měinián qù Yīngguó de rén hěnduō.
   Many people travel to the UK every year.

4. **英语 Yīngyǔ** English language
   中国 有 很多 人 学 英语。
   Zhōngguó yǒu hěnduō rén xué Yīngyǔ.
   Many people in China study English.

5. **英里 yīnglǐ** mile
   美国 还 用 英里，不用 公里。
   Měiguó hái yòng yīnglǐ, búyòng gōnglǐ.
   The United States still uses miles, not kilometers.

The seventh stroke crosses the fifth stroke.   8 strokes

一	十	艹	艻	节	苙	莁	英				

wén script, language

The character represents a pattern used on ancient earthenware. It took on the meaning of character or *writing*.

Radical: 文 'script'

Index # 73

Character components: 亠 + 乂

Character configuration:

Compounds, sentences and meanings

1. 文　**wén**　language, script
   这 篇 文章 写得 文 不 对题。
   Zhè piān wénzhāng xiěde wén bú duì tí.
   This essay was irrelevant to the topic.

2. 英文　**Yīngwén**　English language
   你的 英文 说得 很 好。
   Nǐde Yīngwén shuōde hěn hǎo.
   You speak English very well.

3. 文字　**wénzì**　written language
   这 是 有 文字 可考 的 历史。
   Zhè shì yǒu wénzì kěkǎo de lìshǐ.
   This is a documented history.

4. 文化　**wénhuà**　civilization
   我 想 研究 中国 文化。
   Wǒ xiǎng yánjiū Zhōngguó wénhuà.
   I want to study Chinese civilization.

5. 文学　**wénxué**　literature
   我 想 研究 中国 文学。
   Wǒ xiǎng yánjiū Zhōngguó wénxué.
   I want to study Chinese literature.

The third stroke sweeps left.　　　　　　　　4 strokes

丶	一	亠	文								

Quiz 4 (31–40)

A. Look at the 9-character grid and CIRCLE words or phrases. They can be found horizontally from left to right or vertically. Look at the circled characters in the Key if unsure. COPY the word or phrase next to the grid and write the pinyin and meaning.

她	朋	友
学	英	文
不	谁	的

Word or phrase | Pinyin | Meaning

(i)

(ii)

(iii)

B. Refer to the characters in the 9-character grid above and CONVERT the pinyin sentences into characters. You might like to check their English meaning in the Key. Note that the pronouns for *he* or *she* have the same pronunciation *tā* but are written with different characters. Check the character for '*he.*'

(i)	Shuǐ/shéi'de péngyou?									
(ii)	Tā xué buxué Zhōngwén?									
(iii)	Bù, tā xué Yīngwén.									

C. Match the Chinese words with their English meaning.

(i)

中文 — the United Kingdom
文 huà — spicy (chilli hot)
là 的 — English language
yǒu 的 — Chinese language
zuótiān 的 — yesterday's
英 guó — civilization
英 lǐ — some
英文 — mile

(ii)

nǚ 朋友 — study
lǎo 朋友 — girl friend
友好 — school
学 sheng — a short time
学 xí — old friend/s
学 xiào — quite a few
不 jiǔ — friendly
不 shǎo — student

44

41   **huì** able to

Full form

The simplified form of the character combines *person* 人 with *speak* 云 to give the idea of people speaking in a *meeting*.

Radical: 人 'person'

Index # 18

Character components: 人 + 云

Character configuration:

Compounds, sentences and meanings

1. **会** **huì** be able to
   我 会 英语，不会 法语。
   Wǒ huì Yīngyǔ, búhuì Fǎyǔ.
   I speak English but I don't speak French.

2. **会** **huì** be likely to
   明天 会 下雨 吗?
   Míngtiān huì xiàyǔ ma?
   Will it rain tomorrow?

3. **一会儿** **yīhuìr** a moment
   请 你 等 一会儿。
   Qǐng nǐ děng yīhuìr.
   Please wait for a while.

4. **会话** **huìhuà** conversation
   学 语言 应该 多 听 会话。
   Xué yǔyán yīnggāi duō tīng huìhuà.
   You should listen to lots of conversation when learning a language.

5. **会议** **huìyì** meeting
   会议 进行 中，请 勿 打搅。
   Huìyì jìnxíng zhōng, qǐng wù dǎjiǎo.
   Meeting in progress, please do not disturb.

The last stroke ends firmly.　　　　　　　　　　　　　　　　　　**6 strokes**

ノ	人	厶	仐	会	会						

xiě write

The simplifed form combines *flat roof* 宀 with the character 与 and in the process loses the dot on the top. It means *to write*.

Radical: 宀 'flat roof'

Index # 8

Character components: 宀 + 与

Character configuration:

Compounds, sentences and meanings

1. **写** **xiě** write
   这 个 字 写得 很 好。
   Zhè ge zì xiěde hěn hǎo.
   This character is well-written.

2. **写作** **xiězuò** writing
   我 觉得 写作 最 难 学。
   Wǒ juéde xiězuò zuì nán xué.
   I think writing is the hardest thing to learn.

3. **大写** **dàxiě** upper case/capital letter
   名字 缩写 应该 用 大写。
   Míngzi suōxiě yīnggāi yòng dàxiě.
   Initials for names should be written in capital letters.

4. **小写** **xiǎoxiě** lower case
   一般 的 词 应该 用 小写。
   Yībān de cí yīnggāi yòng xiǎoxiě.
   Ordinary words should be written in lower case.

5. **书写** **shūxiě** hand-written
   书写 没有 打印 好看。
   Shūxiě méiyǒu dǎyìn hǎokàn.
   Handwriting doesn't look as good as printing.

The third stroke has two bends ending with a hook.　　　5 strokes

`	冖	写	写	写							

duō many, much

The character combines two evenings or moons to mean *many*.

Radical: 夕 'evening'   **Index # 56**

Character components: 夕 + 夕   **Character configuration:**

Compounds, sentences and meanings

1. **多** **duō** many
   里面 有 很多 人。
   Lǐmiàn yǒu hěnduō rén.
   There are many people inside.

2. **多少** **duōshao** how many
   你 认识 多少 汉字?
   Nǐ rènshi duōshao Hànzì?
   How many Chinese characters do you know?

3. **多半** **duōbàn** more often than not
   星期天 他 多半 上 这儿来。
   Xīngqītiān tā duōbàn shàng zhèr lái.
   He comes over on Sundays quite often.

4. **多数** **duōshù** majority
   我们 是 多数。
   Wǒmen shì duōshù.
   We are in the majority.

5. **多么** **duōme** how, what
   多么 新鲜 的 水果 啊!
   Duōme xīnxiān de shuǐguǒ a!
   How fresh the fruit is!

The top component rides on top of the lower one.   6 strokes

ノ	勹	夕	夘	多	多						

shǎo/shào   few, less; young

The character combines *small* 小 with an added 丿 stroke representing a sword, cutting a small object even smaller. It means *few*.

Radical: 小 'small'

Index # 49

Character components: 小 + 丿

Character configuration:

Compounds, sentences and meanings

1. **少**   shao   few
   上海　很少　下雪。
   Shànghǎi hěnshǎo xiàxuě.
   It seldom snows in Shanghai.

2. **不少**   bùshǎo   quite a lot
   这 次 旅行 花了 不少 钱。
   Zhè cì lǚxíng huāle bùshǎo qián.
   I spent quite a lot of money on this trip.

3. **少数**   shǎoshù   minority
   少数　服从　多数。
   Shǎoshù fúcóng duōshù.
   The minority is subordinate to the majority.

4. **多少**   duōshao   how many
   你 认识 多少 汉字?
   Nǐ rènshi duōshao Hànzì?
   How many Chinese characters do you know?

5. **少年**   shàonián   juvenile
   西方 国家 的 少年 犯罪 比较 多。
   Xīfāng guójiā de shàonián fànzuì bǐjiào duō.
   Juvenile delinquency is more common in Western countries.

The last stroke tapers off.   4 strokes

丨	小	小	少							

ge [classifier]

This character is pronounced in the neutral tone when used as *a general classifier* for most nouns. When used in the 4th tone, 个 means *individual*.

Radical: 人 'person'   **Index # 18**

Character components: 人 + 丨   **Character configuration:** ☐

Compounds, sentences and meanings

1. 个 **ge** classifier
   洗个澡，休息 休息。
   Xǐ ge zǎo, xiūxi xiūxi.
   Have a shower and then rest.

2. 两个 **liǎng ge** a couple of
   请 给 我 两 个。
   Qǐng gěi wǒ liǎng ge.
   Please give me two.

3. 个个 **gègè** each
   你的 孩子 个个 都 很 聪明。
   Nǐde háizi gègè dōu hěn cōngmíng.
   All your children are very bright.

4. 个人 **gèrén** individual
   我 个人 认为 这样 做 不对。
   Wǒ gèrén rènwéi zhèyàng zuò búduì.
   In my opinion this is not the way to do it.

5. 个别 **gèbié** individual (adjective)
   我 喜欢 个别 辅导。
   Wǒ xǐhuan gèbié fǔdǎo.
   I prefer individual tuition.

The second stroke joins the first stroke at the top.   3 strokes

ノ	人	个							

汉

Hàn ethnic Han Chinese

Full form

漢

The full form combines *water* 氵 with the phonetic 𦰩 to mean *the dominant ethnic group in China*. The phonetic is replaced by the stereotype 又 in simplification.

Radical: 氵 '3 drops of water'

Index # 32

Character components: 氵 + 又

Character configuration:

Compounds, sentences and meanings

1. **汉** **hàn** person
   不 到　长城　非 好汉。
   Bú dào Chángchéng fēi hǎohàn.
   You are not a true person if you haven't been to the Great Wall of China.

2. **汉语** **Hànyǔ** Chinese language
   你的 汉语　说得　很 不错。
   Nǐde Hànyǔ shuōde hěn búcuò.
   You speak Chinese very well.

3. **汉字** **Hànzì** Chinese characters
   我 觉得 汉字 很　有 意思。
   Wǒ juéde Hànzì hěn yǒu yìsi.
   I think Chinese characters are very interesting.

4. **汉族** **Hànzú** ethnic Han Chinese
   汉族 在 新疆　占 少数。
   Hànzú zài Xīnjiāng zhàn shǎoshù.
   Ethnic Hans are in the minority in Xīnjiāng.

5. **汉学** **Hànxué** Chinese studies
   她 研究 汉学。
   Tā yánjiū Hànxué.
   She is doing research in Chinese studies.

The third stroke simply lifts with no bend.

5 strokes

丶	冫	氵	氿	汉							

47

认 rèn recognize

Full form

認

The full form combines *speech* 言 and the phonetic 忍 to suggest the idea of *recognition*. The simplified form is 认 .

Radical: 讠 'word'　　　　　　　**Index # 9**

Character components: 讠 + 人　　　**Character configuration:** ⊟

Compounds, sentences and meanings

1. 认　rèn　recognize
你 变 多 了，都 认不出 你 了。
Nǐ biàn duō le, dōu rènbuchū nǐ le.
You've changed so much that I hardly recognized you.

2. 认识　rènshi　be acquainted with
认识 你，很 高兴。
Rènshi nǐ, hěn gāoxìng.
I'm pleased to meet you.

3. 认字　rènzì　read characters
我 现在 学 认字。
Wǒ xiànzài xué rènzì.
I'm learning to read characters.

4. 认得　rènde　know, recognize
你 还 认得 我 吗?
Nǐ hái rènde wǒ ma?
Do you still recognize me?

5. 认真　rènzhēn　conscientious
她 工作 很 认真。
Tā gōngzuò hěn rènzhēn.
She is conscientious in her work.

The last stroke joins the previous stroke mid-way down.　　　**4 strokes**

丶　讠　认　认

51

识 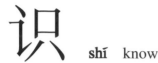 **shí** know

識

The full form combines *speech* 言 and the component 戠 to suggest the idea of *knowledge*. The simplified form is 识.

Radical: 讠 'word'

Index # 9

Character components: 讠 + 只

Character configuration: ▯

Compounds, sentences and meanings

1. 识 **shí** know
   这 个 农民 一字不识。
   Zhè ge nóngmín yízì-bùshí.
   This peasant is completely illiterate (literally, knows not one word).

2. 识别 **shíbié** distinguish
   他 不能 识别 真假 朋友。
   Tā bùnéng shíbié zhēnjiǎ péngyou.
   He cannot distinguish true friends from false ones.

3. 识货 **shíhuò** able to tell value in goods
   买 东西 要 识货。
   Mǎi dōngxi yào shíhuò.
   You need to know the value of things when shopping.

4. 识字 **shízì** become literate
   这 是 识字 课本。
   Zhè shì shízì kèběn.
   This is a reading primer.

5. 学识 **xuéshí** knowledge
   这 位 老先生 的 学识 很 广。
   Zhè wèi lǎoxiānsheng de xuéshí hěn guǎng.
   This old gentleman is very learned.

The last stroke finishes firmly.

7 strokes

`	讠	讥	识	识	识	识						

说　shuō　speak

Full form

説

The character combines *speech* 讠 and *exchange* 兑 to give the idea of oral communication between people. It means *to speak*.

Radical: 讠 'word'　　　　　　　　　　　**Index # 9**

Character components: 讠 + 兑　　　　　**Character configuration:**

Compounds, sentences and meanings

1. 说　shuō　speak
   请 听 我 说。
   Qǐng tīng wǒ shuō.
   Please listen to what I have to say.

2. 说话　shuōhuà　speak
   我 爸爸 不 太 爱 说话。
   Wǒ bàba bú tài ài shuōhuà.
   My father doesn't like to talk much.

3. 说谎　shuōhuǎng　tell a lie
   小孩子 不要 学 说谎。
   Xiǎoháizi búyào xué shuōhuǎng.
   Children should learn not to tell lies.

4. 说不定　shuōbudìng　maybe
   说不定 他 已经 走 了。
   Shuōbudìng tā yǐjīng zǒu le.
   Maybe he's already left.

5. 说服　shuōfú　convince
   她 说服了 我。
   Tā shuōfúle wǒ.
   She has convinced me.

The last stroke ends with a hook.　　　　　　　　　　　　　　　9 strokes

丶	讠	讠	讠	说	说	说	说	说				

Full form

语

语 yǔ language

語

The character combines *speech* 讠, *mouth* 口 and *five* 五 to mean *talking* or *language*.

Radical: 讠 'word'

Index # 9

Character components: 讠 + 五 + 口

Character configuration:

Compounds, sentences and meanings

1. **语 yǔ** language
   你的 法语 说得 很 好。
   Nǐde Fǎyǔ shuōde hěn hǎo.
   You speak French very well.

2. **外语 wàiyǔ** foreign language
   我 没 学过 外语。
   Wǒ méi xuéguo wàiyǔ.
   I have never studied a foreign language.

3. **语法 yǔfǎ** grammar
   中文 语法不太 难。
   Zhōngwén yǔfǎ bú tài nán.
   Chinese grammar is not too difficult.

4. **语言 yǔyán** language
   北京 语言 文化 大学。
   Běijīng Yǔyán Wénhuà Dàxué
   Beijing Language and Culture University

5. **语气 yǔqì** manner of speaking
   她用 婉转 的语气 说。
   Tā yòng wǎnzhuǎn de yǔqì shuō.
   She speaks in a tactful manner.

语 is easily confused with 话.

9 strokes

丶	讠	讠	订	语	语	语	语	语				

Quiz 5 (41–50)

A. Look at the 9-character grid and CIRCLE words or phrases. They can be written horizontally from left to right or vertically. Look at the circled characters in the Key if unsure. COPY the word or phrase next to the grid and write the pinyin and meaning.

Word or phrase	**Pinyin**	**Meaning**

多	少	说	(i)
写	会	汉	(ii)
认	识	语	(iii)

B. Refer to the characters in the 9-character grid above and CONVERT the pinyin sentences into characters and check their English meaning in the Key. Look up characters you have learnt in previous sets.

(i)	Nǐ huì shuō Hànyǔ ma?							
(ii)	Nǐ huì buhuì xiě Hànzì?							
(iii)	Nǐ huì xiě duōshao Hànzì?							
(iv)	Tā búhuì xiě Hànzì.							

C. Match the Chinese words with their English meaning.

(i)

多 shù	minority
少 shù	speak
说 huà	English language
说不 dìng	maybe
说 fú	majority
wài 语	convince
英语	grammar
语 fǎ	foreign language

(ii)

一会儿	become literate
会 huà	Chinese language
写 zuò	a moment
大写	writing
个人	conversation
认 de	capital letters
识字	individual
汉语	recognize

CHARACTER BUILDING 1 (1–50)

A. Memorize the following radicals and their English names. As a review exercise, write the pinyin and meaning of each example:

1. [一] 'horizontal stroke'

   一 (__yi__) ____one____ ; 三 (_____) _____ ;

   五 (_____) _____ ; 七 (_____) _____ ;

   不 (_____) _____ .

2. [丿] 'downward-left stroke'

   九 (_____) _____ ; 么 (_____) _____ ;

3. [讠] 'word'

   请 (_____) _____ ; 谁 (_____) _____ ;

   认 (_____) _____ ; 识 (_____) _____ ;

   语 (_____) _____ ; 说 (_____) _____ .

4. [人] 'person'

   人 (_____) _____ ; 个 (_____) _____ ;

   会 (_____) _____ .

5. [亻] 'upright person'

   你 (_____) _____ ; 他 (_____) _____ ;

   什 (_____) _____ .

6. [口] 'mouth'

   叫 (_____) _____ ; 哪 (_____) _____ ;

   名 (_____) _____ ; 吗 (_____) _____ .

7. [囗] '4-sided frame'

   四 (_____) _____ ; 国 (_____) _____ ;

8. [女] 'female'

   好 (_____) _____ ; 她 (_____) _____ ;

   姓 (_____) _____ .

B. Write the pinyin and meaning against the characters classified under the following radicals.

1. [丨] 'vertical stroke' 中 (_____) _____
2. [八] 'eight' 八 (_____) _____
3. [宀] 'flat roof' 写 (_____) _____
4. [二] 'two' 二 (_____) _____
5. [六] 'top of 六' 六 (_____) _____
6. [十] 'ten' 十 (_____) _____
7. [又] 'again' 友 (_____) _____
8. [氵] '3 drops of water' 汉 (_____) _____
9. [艹] 'grass' 英 (_____) _____
10. [小] 'small' 少 (_____) _____
11. [夕] 'sunset' 多 (_____) _____
12. [文] 'script' 文 (_____) _____
13. [心] 'heart' 您 (_____) _____
14. [戈] 'spear' 我 (_____) _____
15. [日] 'sun' 是 (_____) _____
16. [贝] 'sea shell' 贵 (_____) _____
17. [白] 'white' 白 (_____) _____
18. [羊] 'sheep' 美 (_____) _____

C. Write the pinyin and meaning against the characters which share the following components. (Note that these components are not necessarily used as radicals.)

1. [夕] 名 (_____) _____ ; 多 (_____) _____ .
2. [口] 名 (_____) _____ ; 问 (_____) _____ .
3. [中] 中 (_____) _____ ; 贵 (_____) _____ .
4. [子] 好 (_____) _____ ; 学 (_____) _____ .
                字 (_____) _____ ;
5. [又] 汉 (_____) _____ ; 友 (_____) _____ .
6. [也] 他 (_____) _____ ; 她 (_____) _____ .
7. [人] 人 (_____) _____ ; 认 (_____) _____ .
8. [小] 你 (_____) _____ ; 少 (_____) _____ .

REVIEW 1 (1–50)

The following are words and phrases classified under parts of speech. Write the pinyin and meaning for each word/phrase.

Pronouns 我 (___wǒ___) ___I, me___ ; 我的 (_____) _____ :

你 (_____) _____ ; 你的 (_____) _____ ;

他 (_____) _____ ; 他的 (_____) _____ ;

她 (_____) _____ ; 她的 (_____) _____ .

Interrogative 什么 (_____) _____ ; 哪 (_____) _____ ;

pronouns 谁 (_____) _____ ; 多少 (_____) _____ ;

Nouns 人 (_____) _____ ; 朋友 (_____) _____ ;

中文 (_____) _____ ; 英文 (_____) _____ ;

汉语 (_____) _____ ; 英语 (_____) _____ ;

汉字 (_____) _____ ; 中国 (_____) _____ ;

英国 (_____) _____ ; 美国 (_____) _____ .

Verbs 叫 (_____) _____ ; 姓 (_____) _____ ;

是 (_____) _____ ; 问 (_____) _____ ;

学 (_____) _____ ; 写 (_____) _____ ;

会 (_____) _____ ; 认识 (_____) _____ ;

Numbers 一 (_____) _____ ; 二 (_____) _____ ;

三 (_____) _____ ; 四 (_____) _____ ;

五 (_____) _____ ; 六 (_____) _____ ;

七 (_____) _____ ; 八 (_____) _____ ;

九 (_____) _____ ; 十 (_____) _____ ;

Classifiers 个 (_____) _____ .

Noun phrases 中文名字 (_____) _____ ;

英文名字 (_____) _____ ;

中国朋友 (_____) _____ ;

英国朋友 (_____) _____ ;

美国朋友 (_____) _____ ;

谁的朋友 (_____) _____ ;

哪国人 (_____) _____ .

WORD/SENTENCE PUZZLE 1

Find and CIRCLE words, phrases or sentences hidden in the puzzle. They can be found horizontally from left to right or vertically . The lines across and down are indicated by numbers. Write the meaning next to the pinyin. The first one is done for you.

ACROSS (left to right)

2. (i)   Zhōngguó péngyou   *Chinese friend/s* _____

   (ii) huì xiě   _____

3.   bù shuō   _____

4.   Nǐ rènshi duōshao Hànzì?   _____

8.   Guìguó shì nǎguó?   _____

DOWN

1.   Nǐ shì nǎguórén?   _____

2.   Yīngguó   _____

3 (i)   shízì   _____

   (ii) Nín guìxìng?   _____

5 (i)   bùshǎo   _____

   (ii) shìde   _____

6.   Nǐ huì shuō Hànyǔ ma?   _____

7.   Měiguórén   _____

	1	2	3	4	5	6	7
1	六	英	友	一	三	你	八
2	中	国	朋	友	叫	会	写
3	名	哪	写	您	不	说	十
4	你	认	识	多	少	汉	字
5	是	会	字	我	名	语	么
6	哪	七	五	英	多	吗	她
7	国	四	您	二	谁	他	美
8	人	的	贵	国	是	哪	国
9	问	请	姓	学	的	九	人

men [plural suffix]

Full form

The plural suffix is always pronounced in the neutral tone. It is mainly added to pronouns but occasionally used after nouns as a form of address for more than one person.

Radical: 亻 'upright person'　　　**Index # 19**

Character components: 亻 + 门

Character configuration:

Compounds, sentences and meanings

1. 你们　nǐmen　you (plural)
   请 你们 等 一下, 我 马上 回来。
   Qǐng nǐmen děng yíxià, wǒ mǎshàng huílai.
   Please wait a moment, I'll be right back.

2. 咱们　zánmen　we, us (referring to those spoken to)
   咱们 商量 一下。
   Zánmen shāngliang yíxià.
   Let's talk it over.

3. 女士们　nǔshìmen　ladies
   女士们 先生们, 你们 好!
   Nǔshìmen, xiānshengmen, nǐmen hǎo!
   Ladies and gentlemen! Greetings!

4. 男士们　nánshìmen　gentlemen
   通常 是 男士们 邀请 女士们
   Tōngcháng shì nánshìmen yāoqǐng nǔshìmen
   跳舞。
   tiàowǔ.
   Generally it is the men who ask the ladies for a dance.

5. 哥儿们　gērmen　buddies
   朋友 之间 分得 太 清 就 不够
   Péngyou zhījiān fēnde tài qīng jiù búgòu
   哥儿们 了。
   gērmen le.
   If friends become too calculating, then there's not much friendship between them.

The last stroke ends with a hook.								5 strokes
丿	亻	亻	们	们				

yǒu have

The character combines the pictograph 𠂇 , the figure of a *hand*, and *flesh* 月 to signify *flesh* in *hand*, thus giving the meaning of *to have* or *to exist*.

Radical: 月 'flesh/moon' **Index # 103**

Character components: 𠂇 + 月 **Character configuration:**

Compounds, sentences and meanings

1. 有 yǒu have, has
   我 有 一个 哥哥。
   Wǒ yǒu yí ge gēge.
   I have an older brother.

2. 有名 yǒumíng famous
   这个 演员 很有名。
   Zhè ge yǎnyuán hěn yǒumíng.
   This actor is very famous.

3. 有钱 yǒuqián rich
   很多 有钱 人 住 在 这里。
   Hěnduō yǒuqián rén zhù zài zhèlǐ.
   Many rich people live here.

4. 有意思 yǒu yìsi interesting
   今天 的 晚会 很 有意思。
   Jīntiān de wǎnhuì hěn yǒu yìsi.
   The performance tonight was enjoyable.

5. 有害 yǒuhài harmful
   吸烟 对 身体 有害。
   Xīyān duì shēntǐ yǒuhài.
   Smoking is harmful to one's health.

The stroke ends with a hook. 6 strokes

一	𠂇	才	右	冇	有						

méi   not have

The full form combines *water* 氵 with the phonetic 殳 to give the idea of *death by drowning*, or *not have*.

Radical: 氵 '3 drops of water'   **Index # 32**

Character components: 氵 + 殳   **Character configuration:**

Compounds, sentences and meanings

1. **没** méi   not have, did not
   昨天 银行 没 开门。
   Zuótiān yínháng méi kāimén.
   The bank was closed yesterday.

2. **没有** méiyǒu   not have
   里面 没有 人。
   Lǐmiàn méiyǒu rén.
   There's no one inside.

3. **没关系** méi guānxi   it doesn't matter
   他 来 不 来 都 没 关系。
   Tā lái bu lái dōu méi guānxi.
   It doesn't matter if he comes or not.

4. **没意思** méiyìsi   boring
   这 本 书 没意思。
   Zhè běn shū méiyìsi.
   This book is boring.

5. **没完没了** méiwán-méiliǎo   endless
   她 这么 没完没了 的 唠叨，烦死 人 了。
   Tā zhème méiwán-méiliǎo de láodao, fánsǐ rén le.
   Her endless chattering is really driving me up the wall.

The third stroke lifts with no bend.   7 strokes

丶	冫	氵	氵	氿	没	没						

54

和 hé and

The character combines *grain* 禾 and *mouth* 口 to suggest the idea of negotiating for *peace*.

Radical: 口 'mouth'   **Index # 50**
or 禾 'grain'   **Index # 124**
Character components: 禾 + 口   **Character configuration:**

Compounds, sentences and meanings

1. 和 hé and
他 和 我 一样 高。
Tā hé wǒ yíyàng gāo.
He's as tall as me.

2. 和好 héhǎo become reconciled
他们 吵过架, 现在 和好了。
Tāmen chǎoguojià, xiànzài héhǎo le.
They had a quarrel, but had made it up now.

3. 和平 hépíng peace
我们 应该 和平 解决 问题。
Wǒmen yīnggāi hépíng jiějué wèntí.
We should resolve problems peacefully.

4. 和睦 hémù harmonious
我们 一家 人 和睦 相处, 是 个
Wǒmen yì jiā rén hémù xiāngchù, shì ge
幸福 的 家庭。
xìngfú de jiātíng.
My family gets on well together, ours is a happy family.

5. 和气 héqì amiable
父亲 对 人 很 和气。
Fùqin duì rén hěn héqì.
My father is very friendly.

口 is slightly larger when written on the right.   8 strokes

ノ 二 千 禾 禾 禾 和 和

63

gē   older brother

The character signifies *older brother* carrying a sibling on his back.

Radical: 一 'horizontal stroke'   **Index # 2**
or   口 'mouth'   **Index # 50**
Character components: 可 + 可   **Character configuration:**

Compounds, sentences and meanings

1. 哥 **gē** older brother
   我 哥 去年 结婚 了。
   Wǒ gē qùnián jiēhūn le.
   My older brother married last year.

2. 哥哥 **gēge** older brother
   我 有 两 个 哥哥。
   Wǒ yǒu liǎng ge gēge.
   I have two older brothers.

3. 大哥 **dàgē** eldest brother
   今天 是 我 大哥的 生日。
   Jīntiān shì wǒ dàgē de shēngrì.
   Today is my oldest brother's birthday.

4. 二哥 **èrgē** second eldest brother
   二哥 出国 读书 了。
   Èrgē chūguó dúshū le.
   My second older brother has gone abroad to study.

5. 哥儿们 **gērmen** buddies
   朋友 之间 分得太 清 就 不够
   Péngyou zhījiān fēnde tài qīng jiù búgòu
   哥儿们 了。
   gērmen le.
   If friends become too calculating, then there's not much mateship between them.

The bottom vertical stroke ends with a hook.   10 strokes

一 丁 гТ 可 可 哥 哥 哥 哥

姐

jiě   older sister

The character combines *female* 女 and the phonetic 且 to give the idea of *older sister*.

Radical: 女 'female'   **Index # 65**

Character components: 女 + 且   **Character configuration:**

Compounds, sentences and meanings

1. **姐 jiě** older sister
我 姐 快 三十 岁了。
Wǒ jiě kuài sānshí suì le.
My older sister is nearly thirty.

2. **二姐 èrjiě** second oldest sister
我 二姐 大学 快 毕业了。
Wǒ èrjiě dàxué kuài bìyè le.
My second oldest sister will soon graduate from university.

3. **姐姐 jiějie** older sister
我 姐姐 比 我 大 十 岁。
Wǒ jiějie bǐ wǒ dà shí suì.
My older sister is 10 years older than me.

4. **姐夫 jiěfu** older sister's husband, brother-in-law
我 姐夫 很 照顾 我。
Wǒ jiěfu hěn zhàogu wǒ.
My brother-in-law looks after me very well.

5. **小姐 xiǎojie** Miss
王 小姐 今天 休假。
Wáng xiǎojie jīntiān xiūjià.
Miss Wang is off work today.

The last horizontal stroke is longer.   8 strokes

く	女	女	如	如	姐	姐	姐				

57

弟 **dì** younger brother

The character depicts stakes bound with twine. The inverted eight `ˇˇ` represents *low*, and from this came *younger brother*, who is low in position and short in height.

Radical: `ˇˇ` 'eight'   **Index # 17**

Character components: `ˇˇ` + 弔   **Character configuration:** ⊟

Compounds, sentences and meanings

1. 弟 **dì** younger brother
   三弟 今年 刚 进 中学。
   Sāndì jīnnián gāng jìn zhōngxué.
   My third youngest brother has just started secondary school.

2. 弟弟 **dìdi** younger brother
   你有 没有 弟弟?
   Nǐ yǒu méiyǒu dìdi?
   Do you have a younger brother?

3. 弟兄 **dìxiōng** brothers
   他就 弟兄 一个。
   Tā jiù dìxiōng yí ge.
   He's the only son of the family.

4. 弟媳 **dìxí** wife of younger brother, sister-in-law
   我 弟媳是 中国人。
   Wǒ dìxí shì Zhōngguórén.
   My younger brother's wife is Chinese.

5. 徒弟 **túdì** disciple, follower
   他们 是 师父徒弟 关系。
   Tāmen shì shīfu túdì guānxi.
   Theirs is a master – disciple relationship.

The fifth stroke ends with a hook.												7 strokes
`	`	丷	丷	弟	弟	弟						

58

妹

mèi   *younger sister*

The character combines *immature* 未 and *female* 女 to mean *younger sister*.

Radical: 女 'female'   **Index # 65**

Character components: 女 + 未   **Character configuration:** ⊟

Compounds, sentences and meanings

1. **妹   mèi**   younger sister
   我 妹 还 很 小。
   Wǒ mèi hái hěn xiǎo.
   My younger sister is still quite small.

2. **三妹   sānmèi**   third youngest sister
   我 三妹 在 中学 学习。
   Wǒ sānmèi zài zhōngxué xuéxí.
   My third youngest sister is in high school.

3. **小妹   xiǎomèi**   youngest sister
   我 小妹 在 小学 学习。
   Wǒ xiǎomèi zài xiǎoxué xuéxí.
   My youngest sister is in primary school.

4. **妹夫   mèifu**   younger sister's husband, brother-in-law
   我 妹夫 在 小学 教书。
   Wǒ mèifu zài xiǎoxué jiāoshū.
   My younger sister's husband teaches in a primary school.

5. **姐妹   jiěmèi**   sisters
   她 没有 姐妹，只 有 一 个 哥哥。
   Tā méiyǒu jiěmèi, zhǐ yǒu yí ge gēge.
   She has no sisters, only an older brother.

The horizontal stroke on the right-hand side is longer than the one above.   8 strokes

乚	乛	女	女	女	妹	妹	妹				

hái/huán   still, return

The full form combines *movement* 辶 with the phonetic *cycle* 睘. Thus, it means to *return*. Another meaning is *still*.

Radical: 辶 'movement'   **Index # 38**

Character components: 不 + 辶   **Character configuration:** ⊔

Compounds, sentences and meanings

1. 还 hái   still
    他 还 在 睡觉。
    Tā hái zài shuìjiào.
    He's still sleeping.

2. 还有 hái yǒu   still more
    我 有 一个 姐姐，还 有 一个 妹妹。
    Wǒ yǒu yǐ ge jiějie, hái yǒu yǐ ge mèimei.
    I have an older sister and a younger sister.

3. 还是 háishi   or
    他 是 日本人 还是 韩国人？
    Tā shì Rìběnrén háishi Hánguórén?
    Is he Japanese or Korean?

4. 还 huán   return
    下 个 月 我 就 还 你 钱。
    Xià ge yuè wǒ jiù huán nǐ qián.
    I'll repay the money next month.

5. 还价 huánjià   counter-offer, bid
    如果 你 不 想 买 就 别 还价。
    Rúguǒ nǐ bù xiǎng mǎi jiù bié huánjià.
    Don't bid if you don't intend to buy.

Write the middle component before 辶 .   7 strokes

一	丆	才	不	还	还	还							

liǎng   two

The character represents two people inside a room. It came to mean *a couple*.

Radical: 一 'horizontal stroke'   **Index # 2**

Character components: 一 + 冂 + 人 + 人   **Character configuration:**

Compounds, sentences and meanings

1. **两   liǎng**   two
   这 件 事 过 两 天 再 说。
   Zhè jiàn shì guò liǎng tiān zài shuō.
   Let's leave this matter for a couple of days.

2. **两个   liǎng ge**   two (of something)
   那 两 个 人 是 谁?
   Nà liǎng ge rén shì shéi?
   Who are those two people?

3. **两次   liǎng cì**   twice
   我 去过 两 次 中国。
   Wǒ qùguo liǎng cì Zhōngguó.
   I've been to China twice.

4. **两岁   liǎng suì**   two years (age)
   我 姐姐 比 我 大 两 岁。
   Wǒ jiějie bǐ wǒ dà liǎng suì.
   My older sister is 2 years older than me.

5. **两半儿   liǎngbànr**   two halves
   把 苹果 切成 两半儿。
   Bǎ píngguǒ qiēchéng liǎngbànr.
   Cut the apple into halves.

从 joins the horizontal stroke.   **7 strokes**

一	厂	冂	丙	两	两	两					

Quiz 6 (51–60)

A. Look at the 16-character grid and CIRCLE words or phrases. They can be written horizontally from left to right or vertically. Look at the circled characters in the Key if unsure. COPY the word or phrase next to the grid and write the pinyin and meaning.

					Word or phrase			Pinyin	Meaning
姐	个	妹	弟	(i)	美	国	人	Měiguórén	American/s
美	她	们	和	(ii)					
国	还	是	两	(iii)					
人	没	有	哥	(iv)					

B. Refer to the characters in the 16-character grid above and CONVERT the pinyin phrases into characters and then check their English meaning in the Key.

(i)	Wǒ yǒu liǎng ge mèimei.									
(ii)	Nǐ yǒu méiyǒu jiějie?									
(iii)	Tāmen shì Měiguórén. (all females)									
(iv)	Tā yǒu gēge hé dìdi.									

C. Match the Chinese words with their English meaning.

(i)

dà 姐	second younger sister
二妹	younger brother's wife
dà 哥	oldest sister
xiǎo 姐	sisters
姐妹	youngest sister
xiǎo 妹	Miss
弟 xí	disciple
tú 弟	oldest brother

(ii)

没 guānxi	twice
和 qì	it doesn't matter
还有	interesting
有 yìsi	famous
两 cì	peace
没 yìsi	boring
有名	still more
和 píng	amicable

70

xiōng older brother

The character combines *mouth* 口 and *son* 儿 to refer to the *first son*.

Radical: 口 'mouth'   **Index # 50**
or   儿 'son'   **Index # 21**
Character component: 口 + 儿   **Character configuration:**

Compounds, sentences and meanings

1. 兄 **xiōng** older brother
   你 听过 "长 兄 当 父"这 句 话
   Nǐ tīngguo "Zhǎng xiōng dāng fù" zhè jù huà
   吗?
   ma?
   Have you heard of the saying that the "oldest brother assumes the authority of the father?"

2. 兄弟 **xiōngdì** brothers
   你 有 几个 兄弟 姐妹?
   Nǐ yǒu jǐ ge xiōngdì jiěmèi?
   How many brothers and sisters do you have?

3. 老兄 **lǎoxiōng** brother (polite form of address between males)
   老兄, 火车站 在 哪儿?
   Lǎoxiōng, huǒchēzhàn zài nǎr?
   Excuse me, brother, where's the railway station?

4. 大兄弟 **dàxiōngdì** title for younger man (polite form)
   大兄弟, 这 件 事 就 托 你 了。
   Dàxiōngdì, zhè jiàn shì jiù tuō nǐ le.
   And so, brother, I'll leave the matter in your hands.

The last stroke finishes with a hook.   **5 strokes**

丶	冖	口	尸	兄							

 jiā family

The character combines *roof* 宀 with *pig* 豕, suggesting a place where pigs and humans are together. It means *home*.

Radical: 宀 'roof'   **Index # 34**

Character components: 宀 + 豕   **Character configuration:** ⬚

Compounds, sentences and meanings

1. 家 jiā family, home
   我 今天 晚上 不在 家。
   Wǒ jīntiān wǎnshang bú zài jiā.
   I won't be home tonight.

2. 家庭 jiātíng family
   我 有一个 幸福 的 家庭。
   Wǒ yǒu yí ge xìngfú de jiātíng.
   I have a happy family.

3. 家常菜 jiāchángcài home cooking
   我 喜欢 吃 家常菜。
   Wǒ xǐhuan chī jiāchángcài.
   I'm fond of home cooking.

4. 家务事 jiāwùshì housework
   家务事 总 做不完。
   Jiāwùshì zǒng zuòbuwán.
   Housework is never done.

5. 人家 rénjia other people
   人家 的 事情 我们 用不着 管。
   Rénjia de shìqing wǒmen yòngbuzháo guǎn.
   We needn't concern ourselves with others' affairs.

The sixth stroke ends with a hook.   10 strokes

丶	丷	宀	宀	宁	宁	宯	家	家	家		

63   **Full form**

   jǐ   how many?

The full character originally meant uncertainty. This meaning is lost when the character was simplified.

Radical: 几 'how many'   **Index # 22**

Character component: 几   **Character configuration:** ☐

Compounds, sentences and meanings

1. 几   jǐ   how many (for a small number)
   几点了?
   Jǐ diǎn le?
   What's the time?

2. 几个   jǐ ge   how many
   你 有 几个 中国 朋友?
   Nǐ yǒu jǐ ge Zhōngguó péngyou?
   How many Chinese friends do you have?

3. 几次   jǐ cì   how many times
   你 去过 中国 几次?
   Nǐ qùguo Zhōngguó jǐ cì?
   How many times have you been to China?

4. 几时   jǐshí   what time
   你们 几时 走?
   Nǐmen jǐshí zǒu?
   What time are you leaving?

5. 几分   jǐfēn   somewhat
   他 说 的 有 几分道理。
   Tā shuō de yǒu jǐfēn dàoli.
   There's something in what he said.

The character is closed at the top.   2 strokes

丿 几

73

口　　**kǒu**　　mouth

The character 口 represents the shape of a *mouth*.

Radical:　口 'mouth'　　　　　　**Index # 50**

Character component:　口　　　　**Character configuration:**

Compounds, sentences and meanings

1. 口　kǒu　classifier
   你家 有 几 口 人?
   Nǐ jiā yǒu jǐ kǒu rén?
   How many are there in your family?

2. 口福　kǒufú　gourmet's luck
   我 今天 口福 可 不浅。
   Wǒ jīntiān kǒufú kě bùqiǎn.
   I'm really in luck today where food is concerned.

3. 口味　kǒuwèi　taste of food
   今天 换换 口味, 吃 西餐 吧。
   Jīntiān huànhuan kǒuwèi, chī Xīcān ba.
   Let's have a change today and have Western food.

4. 口气　kǒuqì　tone of voice
   她 说话 有 埋怨 的 口气。
   Tā shuōhuà yǒu máiyuàn de kǒuqì.
   There was a note of complaint in what she said.

5. 口音　kǒuyīn　accent
   她 说 英语 带 美国 口音。
   Tā shuō Yīngyǔ dài Měiguó kǒuyīn.
   She speaks English with an American accent.

The last horizontal stroke travels from left to right.　　3 strokes

丨	冂	口									

bà father

The character combines *father* 父 with the phonetic 巴 to give the sound, and the meaning *father*.

Radical: 父 'father'　　　　　　　　**Index # 94**

Character components: 父 + 巴　　　　**Character configuration:**

Compounds, sentences and meanings

1. **爸** bà father
   我 爸 是 医生。
   Wǒ bà shì yīshēng.
   My father is a doctor.

2. **爸爸** bàba father
   我 爸爸 是 医生。
   Wǒ bàba shì yīshēng.
   My father is a doctor.

3. **后爸** hòubà stepfather
   后爸 也 叫 后爹。
   Hòubà yě jiào hòudiē.
   Another name for stepfather is hòudiē.

The last stroke ends with a hook.	8 strokes

ノ	八	少	父	爷	爷	爸	爸				

妈　　mā　mother

媽

The character combines *woman* 女 with the sound element 马 giving the character the meaning of *mother*.

Radical: 女 'female'

Index # 65

Character components: 女 + 马

Character configuration:

Compounds, sentences and meanings

1. 妈　mā　mother
   妈 最 疼 我。
   Mā zuì téng wǒ.
   Mum loves me most.

2. 妈妈　māma　mother
   妈妈　常常　给 我 补衣服。
   Māma chángcháng gěi wǒ bǔ yīfu.
   Mum often mends my clothes.

3. 后妈　hòumā　stepmother
   后妈 也 叫 后母。
   Hòumā yě jiào hòumǔ.
   Another name for stepmother is hòumǔ.

4. 姨妈　yímā　aunt (mother's married sister)
   姨妈 是 妈妈 已婚 的 姐姐 或 妹妹。
   Yímā shì māma yǐhūn de jiějie huò mèimei.
   Yímā refers to a married maternal aunt.

5. 姑妈　gūmā　aunt (father's married sister)
   姑妈 是 爸爸 已婚 的 姐姐 或 妹妹。
   Gūmā shì bàba yǐhūn de jiějie huò mèimei.
   Gūmā refers to a married paternal aunt.

The fifth stroke ends with a hook.						6 strokes
ㄥ	ㄥ	女	如	妈	妈	

67 **Full form**

 这 zhè this

 這

The full form combines *movement* 辶 with the phonetic 言 to suggest the idea of *this*. In simplification the phonetic 言 is changed to 文 for faster writing of the strokes.

Radical: 辶 'movement'   **Index # 38**

Character components: 文 + 辶   **Character configuration:** �

Compounds, sentences and meanings

1. 这 **zhè** this
   这 消息 我 知道 了。
   Zhè xiāoxi wǒ zhīdao le.
   I've already heard that news.

2. 这个 **zhè ge** this one
   我 就 买 这个。
   Wǒ jiù mǎi zhè ge.
   I'll buy this one.

3. 这儿 **zhèr** here
   这儿 不准 停车。
   Zhèr bùzhǔn tíngchē.
   Parking is prohibited here.

4. 这些 **zhèxiē** these
   这些 日子 我们 特别 忙。
   Zhèxiē rìzi wǒmen tèbié máng.
   We've been really busy lately.

5. 这样 **zhèyàng** this way
   我 觉得 这样 做 会 快 点儿。
   Wǒ juéde zhèyàng zuò huì kuàiyìdiǎnr.
   I think this way is faster.

The fourth stroke finishes firmly.   7 strokes

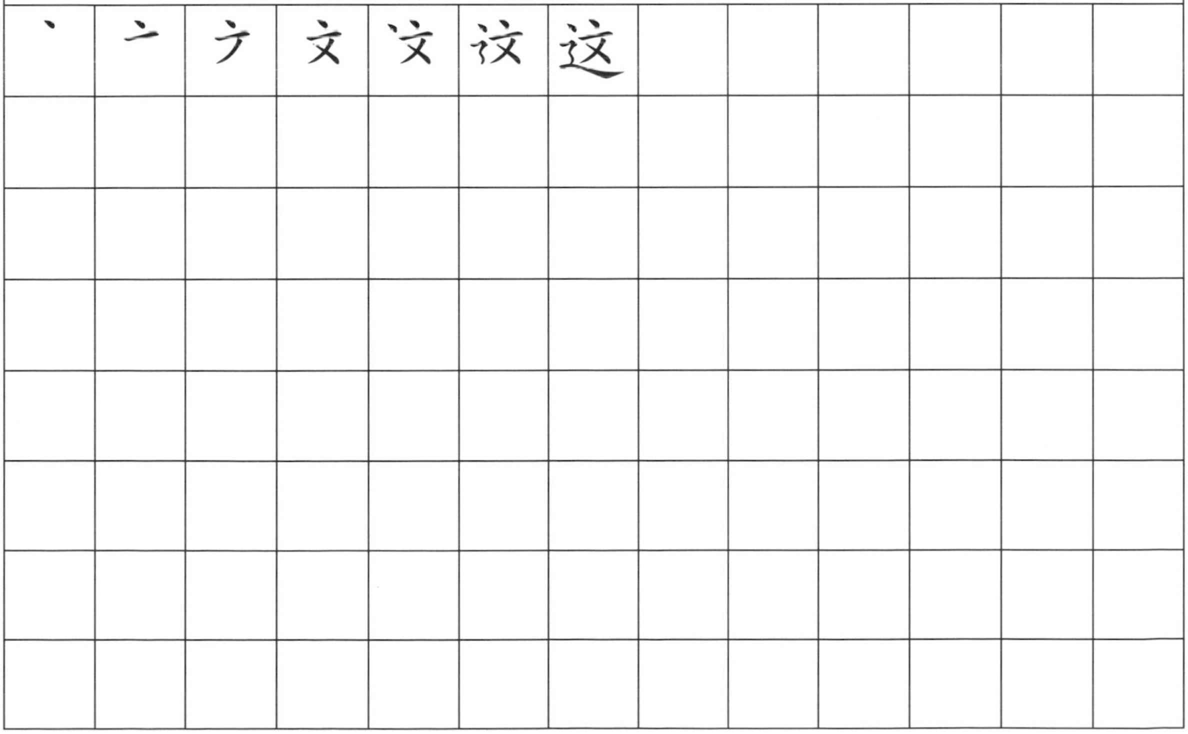

丶	二	亠	文	文	这	这					

77

 **yě** also

Not many characters contain this component 也. Certainly the pronoun 'he' has it and the pronoun 'she' also has it. It means *also*.

Radical: ㇆ **'horizontal-bend-hook'**   **Index # 5**

Character component: 也   **Character configuration:** ⬚

Compounds, sentences and meanings

1. 也 yě also
   我 妈妈 也 是 老师。
   Wǒ māma yě shì lǎoshī.
   My mother is also a teacher.

2. 也... 也 ... yě ... yě ...either ... or ...
   他 也 不 抽烟, 也 不 喝酒。
   Tā yě bù chōuyān, yě bù hējiǔ.
   He neither smokes nor drinks.

3. 也许 yěxǔ perhaps
   也许 我 不 该 告诉她。
   Yěxǔ wǒ bù gāi gàosu tā.
   Perhaps I shouldn't have told her.

4. ... 也罢 ... 也罢 ...yěbà ... yěbà whether ... or
   你 去也罢, 不去 也罢, 反正 是 一样。
   Nǐ qù yěba, bú qù yěbà, fǎnzhèng shì yíyàng.
   It makes no difference whether you go or not.

5. 也好 yěhǎo may as well
   你 说明 一下也 好。
   Nǐ shuōmíng yíxià yě hǎo.
   Maybe you'd better give an explanation.

The first stroke is a horizontal-bend-hook.   3 strokes

㇆	也	也									

老 lǎo old

The character is a pictograph depicting a long-haired hunchback holding a walking stick. It means *old*.

Radical: 老 'old'　　　　　　　　　　**Index # 136**

Character components: 土 + 丿 + 匕　　**Character configuration:**

Compounds, sentences and meanings

1. **老** lǎo old
   他 老 了, 走路 走 不 快 了。
   Tā lǎo le, zǒulù zǒu bú kuài le.
   He's getting old, he can no longer walk fast.

2. **老大** lǎodà oldest sibling
   我 家 三 兄弟, 我 是 老大。
   Wǒ jiā sān xiōngdì, wǒ shì lǎodà.
   Of the three brothers in my family, I'm the eldest.

3. **老婆** lǎopo wife
   他 说 他 老婆 不会 做饭。
   Tā shuō tā lǎopo búhuì zuòfàn.
   He says his wife can't cook.

4. **老外** lǎowài foreigner
   很多 老外 说 汉语 都 说得 很 好。
   Hěnduō lǎowài shuō Hànyǔ dōu shuōde hěn hǎo.
   Many foreigners can speak Mandarin very well.

5. **老实** lǎoshi frank, honest
   老实 说, 我 不 赞成 这 个 意见。
   Lǎoshi shuō, wǒ bù zànchéng zhè ge yìjiān.
   Frankly speaking, I don't like the idea at all.

The last stroke is a downward left stroke.　　　　　　　　**6 strokes**

一	十	土	耂	耂	老						

shī teacher

The full form combines *hill* 𠂤 with *going around* 帀 to give the idea of a leader who stands out from the rest of the crowd. It means *teacher*.

Radical: | 'vertical stroke'   Index # 3

or   巾 'napkin'   Index # 52

Character components: 丿 + 一 + 巾   **Character configuration:**

Compounds, sentences and meanings

1. **师** shī teacher
   我们 是 师生 关系。
   Wǒmen shī shīshēng guānxi.
   We have a teacher–student relationship.

2. **老师** lǎoshī teacher
   他 以前 是 老师, 现在 退休 了。
   Tā yǐqián shì lǎoshī, xiànzài tuìxiū le.
   He used to be a teacher, now he has retired.

3. **师父** shīfu master/teacher
   他 是 我的 师父, 我 是 他的 徒弟。
   Tā shì wǒde shīfu, wǒ shì tā de túdì.
   He's my master, I'm his disciple.

4. **师母** shīmǔ wife of master/teacher
   师母 很 好客, 经常 请 学生
   Shīmǔ hěn hàokè, jīngcháng qǐng xuésheng
   到 家里 吃饭。
   dào jiālǐ chīfàn.
   Our teacher's wife is very hospitable, she often invites students to dinner at her home.

5. **律师** lǜshī lawyer
   她 是 一个 很 有名 的 律师。
   Tā shì yí ge hěn yǒumíng de lǜshī.
   She's a very famous lawyer.

Note the difference between 师 and 帅.   6 strokes

丶	丿	广	广	师	师							

Quiz 7 (61–70)

A. Find and CIRCLE words, phrases or sentences hidden in the puzzle. They can be found horizontally or vertically from left to right. COPY the word or phrase next to the grid and write the pinyin and meaning.

						Word or phrase		Pinyin	Meaning
家	口	姐	人	(i)		老	师	lǎoshī	teacher
和	兄	妹	还	(ii)					
老	弟	爸	有	(iii)					
师	几	妈	哥	(iv)					

B. CONVERT the following pinyin sentences into characters. Some of the characters you need can be found in the 16-character grid above. Check the English meaning in the Key.

(i)	Wǒ jiā yǒu sì kǒu rén.								
(ii)	Bàba, māma, jiějie hé wǒ.								
(iii)	Wǒ māma shì lǎoshī.								
(iv)	Nǐ yǒu jǐ ge xiōngdì jiěmèi?								

C. Match the Chinese words with their English meaning.

(i)
家 tíng — wife
老大 — master
hòu 妈 — oldest sibling
师 fu — stepfather
兄弟 — family
gū 妈 — stepmother
老 po — father's married sister
hòu 爸 — brother

(ii)
这 xiē — honest
家 wùshì — perhaps
这 yàng — these
人口 — in this way
老 shi — housework
也 xǔ — population
这 èr — accent
口 yīn — here

81

 hěn very

The character combines *crossroad* 彳 with the figure of *a person looking back* 艮 to express the idea of *very*.

Radical: 彳 'double person'　　　　**Index # 54**

Character components: 彳 + 艮　　　　**Character configuration:** ⊞

Compounds, sentences and meanings

1. 很　hěn　very
   他 这 个 人 好得 很。
   Tā zhè ge rén hǎode hěn.
   He's a very good man.

2. 很好　hěn hǎo　very good/well
   这 个 汉字 你 写得 很 好。
   Zhè ge Hànzì nǐ xiěde hěn hǎo.
   You've written this Chinese character very nicely.

3. 很坏　hěn huài　very bad
   当心，这 个 人 很 坏。
   Dāngxīn, zhè ge rén hěn huài!
   Look out! This person is no good.

4. 很多　hěnduō　a lot of
   你 认识 很多 汉字。
   Nǐ rènshi hěnduō Hànzì.
   You recognize lots of characters.

5. 很近　hěn jìn　very near
   我 家 离 火车站 很 近。
   Wǒ jiā lí huǒchēzhàn hěn jìn.
   I live quite near the train station.

The last stroke tapers off.　　　　9 strokes

ノ	㇀	彳	彳	彳	彳	很	很	很				

zěn how?

The character combines *suddenly* 乍 and *heart* 心 to suggest the idea of an *instantaneous flash in the heart*. Thus it means *how* or *why*.

Radical: 心 'heart'   **Index # 76**

Character components: 乍 + 心   **Character configuration:**

Compounds, sentences and meanings

1. 怎 **zěn** why
   你 怎 不 早 说 呀?
   Nǐ zěn bù zǎo shuō ya?
   Why didn't you say so earlier?

2. 怎么 **zěnme** how
   这 个 词儿 英语 怎么 说?
   Zhè ge cír Yīngyǔ zěnme shuō?
   How do you say this word in English?

3. 怎样 **zěnyàng** how, what
   这 件 事 你 怎样 解释?
   Zhè jiàn shì nǐ zěnyàng jiěshì?
   How do you explain this matter?

4. 怎么样 **zěnmeyàng** what's it like?
   最近 怎么样, 忙 吗?
   Zuìjìn zěnmeyàng, máng ma?
   How have things been recently? Busy?

The top horizontal stroke is longer.   9 strokes

ノ	仁	仁	午	乍	乍	怎	怎	怎			

Full form

样

yàng appearance

様

The full form consists of 3 parts: *wood* 木, *sheep* 羊, and *permanent* 永. It was the name of a type of soft wood, resembling oak. Thus the idea of *like manner*.

Radical: 木 'tree'

Index # 81

Character components: 木 + 羊

Character configuration:

Compounds, sentences and meanings

1. 样 **yàng** appearance
   几 年 没 见面，他 还 是 那 个 样。
   Jǐ nián méi jiànmiàn, tā hái shì nà ge yàng.
   It's years since I last saw him, but he still looks the same.

2. 怎么样 **zěnmeyàng** what's it like?
   最近 怎么样，忙 吗?
   Zuìjìn zěnmeyàng, máng ma?
   How have things been recently? Busy?

3. 样子 **yàngzi** appearance
   这 件 大衣的 样子 很 好看。
   Zhè jiàn dàyī de yàngzi hěn hǎokàn.
   This coat is well cut.

4. 一样 **yíyàng** the same
   他们 兄弟 相貌 一样。
   Tāmen xiōngdì xiàngmào yíyàng.
   The brothers are alike in appearance.

5. 花样 **huāyàng** variety
   这 家 服装店 花样 很多。
   Zhè jiā fúzhuāngdiàn huāyàng hěnduō.
   There is a great variety of styles in this boutique shop.

The last stroke of 木 should be written firmly.

10 strokes

一	十	才	木	朮	栏	栏	栏	栏	样		

 **fù** father

The character was a pictograph of the right hand holding a cane. From this it came to mean the head of a family or *father*.

Radical: 父 'father'　　　　　　　**Index # 94**

Character component: 父

Character configuration:

Compounds, sentences and meanings

1. 父　**fù**　father
   以前 在 中国， 长兄 当 父。
   Yǐqián zài Zhōngguó, zhǎngxiōng dāng fù.
   Formerly in China, the oldest brother assumed the authority of the father.

2. 父亲　**fùqin**　father
   我 父亲 对 中国 很 有 兴趣。
   Wǒ fùqin duì Zhōngguó hěn yǒu xìngqù.
   My father is very interested in China.

3. 父母　**fùmǔ**
   下 个 月 我 父母 要 去旅行。
   Xià ge yuè wǒ fùmǔ yào qù lǚxíng.
   Next month my parents are going on a trip.

4. 祖父　**zǔfù**　paternal grandfather
   他的祖父 去世 了。
   Tāde zǔfù qùshì le.
   His paternal grandfather has passed away.

5. 继父　**jìfù**　stepfather
   他的继父 对 他 不错。
   Tāde jìfù duì tā búcuò.
   His stepfather is quite nice to him.

The last stroke tapers off.　　　　　4 strokes

丶　八　父　父

mǔ mother

The character was derived from a pictograph of a seated woman. The two dots represent the breasts. It means *mother*.

Radical: 母 'mother'

Index # 108

Character component: 母

Character configuration: ☐

Compounds, sentences and meanings

1. 母 **mǔ** female (animal)
   你 的 狗 是 公 的 还是 母 的?
   Nǐde gǒu shì gōng de háishi mǔ de?
   Is your dog male or female?

2. 母亲 **mǔqin** mother
   我 母亲 做 的 饭菜 最 好吃。
   Wǒ mǔqin zuò de fàncài zuì hǎochī.
   My mother cooks the best meals.

3. 父母 **fūmǔ** parents
   下 个 月 我 父母 要 去 旅行。
   Xià ge yuè wǒ fūmǔ yào qù lǚxíng.
   Next month my parents are going on a trip.

4. 母语 **mǔyǔ** mother tongue
   英语 是 我的 母语。
   Yīngyǔ shì wǒde mǔyǔ.
   English is my mother tongue.

5. 外祖母 **wàizǔmǔ** maternal grandmother
   他的 外祖母 每天 打 太极拳。
   Tāde wàizǔmǔ měitiān dǎ tàijíquán.
   His grandmother practices taichi every day.

The second stroke ends with a hook.   5 strokes

乙	母	母	母	母								

Full form

亲 qīn kin

親

The full form contains 3 parts: *stand* 立, *tree* 木, and *see* 見. It signifies a person standing on a tree eager to see his *loved one*.

Radical: 立 'erect'

Index # 111

Character components: 立 + 木

Character configuration:

Compounds, sentences and meanings

1. 亲 **qīn** close, intimate
   我 和 姐姐 最 亲。
   Wǒ hé jiějie zuì qīn.
   I'm very close to my older sister.

2. 亲人 **qīnrén** kin
   你 在 中国 有 没有 亲人?
   Nǐ zài Zhōngguó yǒu méiyǒu qīnrén?
   Do you have any relatives in China?

3. 父亲 **fùqīn** father
   我 父亲 对 中国 很 有 兴趣。
   Wǒ fùqīn duì Zhōngguó hěn yǒu xìngqù.
   My father is very interested in China.

4. 母亲 **mǔqīn** mother
   我 母亲 做 的 饭菜 最 好吃。
   Wǒ mǔqīn zuò de fàncài zuì hǎochī.
   My mother cooks the best meals.

5. 亲戚 **qīnqi** relatives
   我们 两 家 是 亲戚。
   Wǒmen liǎng jiā shì qīnqi.
   Our two families are related.

The middle horizontal stroke is the longest.   9 strokes

丶	亠	六	六	立	立	辛	辛	亲				

谢 **xiè** thank

Full form

謝

The full character combines *speech* 言 with *bowed body* 射. It suggests the idea that one should thank people with bowed body. It means *to thank*.

Radical: 讠 'word'

Index # 9

Character components: 讠 + 射

Character configuration:

Compounds, sentences and meanings

1. **谢** **xiè** thank
   不用 谢。
   Búyòng xiè.
   Don't mention it. [literally, no need to thank]

2. **谢谢** **xièxie** thank
   谢谢 你。
   Xièxie nǐ.
   Thank you.

3. **多谢** **duōxiè** many thanks
   多谢, 再见!
   Duōxiè, zàijiàn!
   Thanks a lot, good-bye!

4. **感谢** **gǎnxiè** thank
   非常 感谢。
   Fēicháng gǎnxiè.
   Many thanks.

5. **谢天谢地** **xiètiān-xièdì** thank heavens
   (literally, thank heaven and earth)
   谢天谢地, 没 发生 事故。
   Xiètiān-xièdì, méi fāshēng shìgù.
   Thank goodness, there was no accident.

The ninth stroke is downward-left.   12 strokes

丶	讠	讠	订	订	诀	诮	诮	谢	谢	谢	谢

身　　shēn　body

The character is a pictograph depicting a man with a pot belly walking on his short legs. It means *body*.

Radical: 身 'body'　　　　　　　**Index # 168**

Character component: 身

Character configuration: ☐

Compounds, sentences and meanings

1. 身　**shēn**　body, oneself
   身 在 福 中 不 知 福。
   Shēn zài fú zhōng bù zhī fú.
   When you're happy you don't know it.

2. 身体　**shēntǐ**　health
   跳舞 可以 锻炼 身体。
   Tiàowǔ kěyǐ duànliàn shēntǐ.
   Dancing can improve your physique.

3. 身上　**shēnshang**　(carry something) on one
   你 身上 有 零钱 吗?
   Nǐ shēnshang yǒu língqián ma?
   Have you got any change on you?

4. 身材　**shēncái**　body line
   王 菲 的 身材　苗条。
   Wáng Fēi de shēncái miáotiáo.
   Faye Wong has a slim figure.

5. 身高　**shēn'gāo**　stature
   王 菲 身 高 一点六五 米。
   Wáng Fēi shēn'gāo yīdiǎnliùwǔ mǐ.
   Faye Wong is 1.65 meters tall.

The third stroke ends with a hook.　　　　　　　　　**7 strokes**

´	亻	冂	甸	自	身	身					

tǐ body

Full form

體

The full form combines *bone* 骨 and the phonetic 豊 to suggest the idea of *body*. The simplified form uses *person* 亻 and *foundation* 本 to give the same meaning.

Radical: 亻 'upright person'　　　　**Index # 19**

Character components: 亻 + 本　　　　**Character configuration:**

Compounds, sentences and meanings

1. **体** tǐ style of writing
   你 写 的 是 什么 体?
   Nǐ xiě de shì shénme tǐ?
   What style of calligraphy are you writing?

2. **身体** shēntǐ health
   跳舞 可以 锻炼 身体。
   Tiàowǔ kěyǐ duànliàn shēntǐ.
   Dancing can improve your physique.

3. **体温** tǐwēn body temperature
   你的 体温 是 39 度，发烧 了。
   Nǐde tǐwēn shì sānshíjiǔ dù, fāshāo le.
   You have a fever, your temperature is 39 degrees.

4. **体力** tǐlì bodily strength
   运动 能 增强 体力。
   Yùndòng néng zēngqiáng tǐlì.
   Sports can build up your strength.

5. **体贴** tǐtiē considerate
   他 对妻子 很 体贴。
   Tā duì qīzi hěn tǐtiē.
   He's very considerate to his wife.

The bottom horizontal stroke is shorter.　　　　7 strokes

丿 亻 仁 什 什 休 体

都 **dōu/dū** all; city

The character combines *city* 阝 with *people* 者 to indicate a large *city* or *capital*. From the meaning of *general capital of all* 'dū' is evolved the idea of *all* with a different pronunciation: 'dōu'.

Radical: 阝 **'right ear-lobe'**   Index # 28

Character components: 者 + 阝   **Character configuration:**

Compounds, sentences and meanings

1. 都 **dōu** all
   大家 都 到 了 吗?
   Dàjiā dōu dào le ma?
   Is everybody here?

2. 都市 **dūshì** city
   上海 是 一个 大 都市。
   Shànghǎi shì yí ge dà dūshì.
   Shanghai is a big city.

3. 首都 **shǒudū** capital city
   北京 是 中国 的 首都。
   Běijīng shì Zhōngguó de shǒudū.
   Beijing is the capital of China.

The first stroke of 阝 looks like the figure 3.   10 strokes

一	十	土	少	才	者	者	者	都	都			

Quiz 8 (71–80)

A. Look at the 16-character grid and CIRCLE words or phrases. They can be written horizontally from left to right or vertically. Look at the circled characters in the Key if unsure. COPY the word or phrase next to the grid and write the pinyin and meaning.

						Word or phrase			**Pinyin**	**Meaning**
怎	很	都	谢	(i)		怎	样		zěnyàng	how
样	爸	身	这	(ii)						
父	母	体	家	(iii)						
语	亲	还	汉	(iv)						

B. CONVERT the following pinyin phrases into characters and check their English meaning in the Key. Some of the characters you need can be found in the 16-character grid above, the rest in the grid of the last character set.

(i)	Nǐ fùmǔ shēntǐ hǎo ma?									
(ii)	Tāmen dōu hěn hǎo, xièxie.									
(iii)	Nǐde Hànyǔ zěnmeyàng?									
(iv)	Hái hǎo, xièxie.									

C. Match the Chinese words with their English meaning.

(i)

怎么样	parents
父母	variety
母语	appearance
母的	what's it like?
一样	female (animal)
huā 样	relatives
亲 qi	mother tongue
样 zi	same

(ii)

都 shì	health
体 wēn	thank-you
体 lì	body temperature
身体	strength
身 cái	capital
身 gāo	city
谢谢	body height
shǒu 都	body shape

那 nà that

The character represented the state far in the west of Sichuan. Later it was borrowed to denote *thither*. It means *that*.

Radical: 阝 'right ear-lobe'   **Index # 28**

Character components: 刅 + 阝   **Character configuration:**

Compounds, sentences and meanings

1. **那 nà** that
   那 是 谁?
   Nà shì shéi/shuí?
   Who is that?

2. **那个 nà ge** that one
   那 个 孩子 很 可爱。
   Nà ge háizi hěn kě'ài.
   That child is cute.

3. **那么 nàme** in that way
   别 走得 那么 快, 好不好?
   Bié zǒude nàme kuài, hǎobuhǎo?
   Don't walk so fast, okay?

4. **那边 nàbian** over there
   请 把 东西 放 在 那边。
   Qǐng bǎ dōngxi fàng zài nàbian.
   Please put those things over there.

5. **从那儿起 cóng nàr qǐ** since then
   从 那儿起, 他 就 用心 念书 了。
   Cóng nàr qǐ, tā jiù yòngxīn niànshū le.
   He's been studying hard since then.

The fifth stroke looks like the number 3.   6 strokes

丁	了	彐	刅	那	那					

lǐ   inside

Full form

裡／裏

There are two full forms of this character: 裡 and 裏 . Both forms combine *clothing* 衣 with *inside* 里 to suggest *lining* or *inside*. The simplified form uses only the latter component.

Radical: 里 'inside'

Index # 163

Character component: 里

Character configuration: ☐

Compounds, sentences and meanings

1. 里 **lǐ** inside
   家里没 人。
   Jiāli méi rén.
   There is no one home.

2. 哪里 **nǎli** where?
   你 上 哪里 去?
   Nǐ shàng nǎli qù?
   Where are you going?

3. 这里 **zhèlǐ** here
   我们 这里 的 东西 很 便宜。
   Wǒmen zhèlǐ de dōngxi hěn piányi.
   Our merchandise is inexpensive.

4. 里边 **lǐbian** inside
   这 个 箱子 里边 有 什么?
   Zhè ge xiāngzi lǐbiān yǒu shénme?
   What's inside this box?

5. 里头 **lǐtou** inside
   这 个 箱子 里头 有 什么?
   Zhè ge xiāngzi lǐtou yǒu shénme?
   What's inside this box?

The bottom horizontal stroke is slightly longer.   7 strokes

丶	冂	日	日	旦	甲	里					

儿 ér son

兒

The full form comes with a head and two eyes 兒. In simplification, only the lower part of the body 儿 is retained.

Radical: 儿 'son'   **Index # 21**

Character component: 儿   **Character configuration:** ☐

Compounds, sentences and meanings

1. 儿 ér suffix (transcribed as r)
   你 去 哪儿?
   Nǐ qù nǎr?
   Where are you going?

2. 儿子 érzi son
   我的 大儿子 今年 二十六 岁了。
   Wǒde dà érzi jīnnián èrshíliù suì le.
   My eldest son is 26 this year.

3. 儿女 érnǚ sons and daughters
   我的儿女 都 长大 成人 了。
   Wǒde érnǚ dōu zhǎngdà chéngrén le.
   My children have all grown up.

4. 儿歌 érgē children's song
   今天 我 学了 一 首 儿歌。
   Jīntiān wǒ xuéle yì shǒu érgē.
   I learnt a nursery rhyme today.

5. 儿童 értóng children
   这 是 儿童 医院。
   Zhè shì értóng yīyuàn.
   This is a children's hospital.

Note the difference between 儿 and 儿.   2 strokes

ノ	儿								

zǐ child

The character represents a *baby* with a large head and both arms extended. It means a *child*.

Radical: 子 'child'   **Index # 67**

Character component: 子   **Character configuration:** ☐

Compounds, sentences and meanings

1. **子** **zǐ** noun suffix
   桌子 是 旧的,椅子是 新的。
   Zhuōzi shì jiùde, yǐzi shì xīnde.
   The desk is old but the chair is new.

2. **孩子** **háizi** child
   这 个 孩子 很 淘气。
   Zhè ge háizi hěn táoqì.
   This kid is very naughty.

3. **子女** **zǐnǚ** sons and daughters
   五十年代 的 人大 都 子女 成群。
   Wǔshíniándài de rén dà dōu zǐnǚ chéngqún.
   In the 50s, most people had lots of children.

4. **子孙** **zǐsūn** descendants
   中国人 叫 自己 炎黄 子孙。
   Zhōngguórén jiào zìjǐ Yánhuáng zǐsūn.
   The Chinese people call themselves descendants of the Yellow Emperor.

5. **妻子** **qīzi** wife
   我 来 介绍, 这 是 我 妻子。
   Wǒ lái jièshào, zhè shì wǒ qīzi.
   Let me introduce my wife.

The second stroke is a vertical hook.   3 strokes

㇇	了	子									

85

女 nǚ female

The character was derived from the figure of a woman in a graceful pose. Thus the character came to mean *woman*.

Radical: 女 'female' **Index # 65**

Character component: 女 **Character configuration:** ☐

Compounds, sentences and meanings

1. 女 nǚ female
   中国 的 女 运动员 都 很 出色。
   Zhōngguó de nǚ yùndòngyuán dōu hěn chūsè.
   The female Chinese athletes are outstanding.

2. 女儿 nǚ'ér daughter
   我 女儿 在 上海 教 英语。
   Wǒ nǚ'ér zài Shànghǎi jiāo Yīngyǔ.
   My daughter teaches English in Shanghai.

3. 女强人 nǚqiángrén a strong woman
   现在 女孩子 喜欢 当 女强人。
   Xiànzài nǚháizi xǐhuan dāng nǚqiángrén.
   These days girls want to be strong women.

4. 女生 nǚshēng female student
   学 语言 的 女生 比 男生 多。
   Xué yǔyán de nǚshēng bǐ nánshēng duō.
   Female language students outnumber male students.

5. 妇女 fùnǚ woman
   我 母亲 是 家庭 妇女。
   Wǒ mǔqin shì jiātíng fùnǚ.
   My mother is a housewife.

End the first stroke firmly. 3 strokes

㇛	女	女								

男 nán male

The character combines *field* 田 with *strength* 力 to express the idea that *men* do the strenuous work in the rice fields.

Radical:　田 'field'　　　　　**Index # 119**
or　　　　　力 'strength'　　　**Index # 31**
Character components: 田 + 力　　**Character configuration:**

Compounds, sentences and meanings

1. **男**　*nán*　man
   我们 家里男 女 平等。
   Wǒmen jiāli nán nǚ píngděng.
   In our household, we have equality of the sexes.

2. **男孩儿**　*nánháir*　boy
   男孩儿 比较 淘气。
   Nánháir bǐjiào táoqì.
   Boys are more mischievous.

3. **男朋友**　*nánpéngyou*　boy friend
   她 跟　男朋友　住 在 一起。
   Tā gēn nánpéngyou zhù zài yìqǐ.
   She lives with her boy friend.

4. **男高音**　*nán'gāoyīn*　tenor
   他的 声音 是 男 高音。
   Tāde shēngyīn shì nán'gāoyīn.
   He's a tenor.

5. **男厕所**　*náncèsuǒ*　men's toilet
   那边 有 男厕所。
   Nàbiān yǒu náncèsuǒ.
   There's a men's toilet over there.

Finish the top component first.　　　　　7 strokes

丿 冂 冂 田 田 畀 男

孩 hái child

The character combines *child* 子 with *cough* 亥 to suggest the presence of a *child* by the sound of coughing.

Radical: 子 'child'   **Index # 67**

Character components: 子 + 亥   **Character configuration:**

Compounds, sentences and meanings

1. **孩** **hái** child (usually used with suffix *zi* or *ér*)
   这 个 孩子 很 淘气。
   Zhè ge háizi hěn táoqì.
   This child is very naughty.

2. **男孩儿** **nánháir** boy
   男孩儿 比较 淘气。
   Nánháir bǐjiào táoqì.
   Boys are more mischievous.

3. **女孩子** **nǚháizi** girl
   这 个 女孩子 很 聪明。
   Zhè ge nǚháizi hěn cōngmíng.
   This girl is very clever.

4. **孩子气** **háiziqì** childish
   你 已经 十六 岁 了,别 那么 孩子气!
   Nǐ yǐjīng shíliù suì le, bié nàme háiziqì!
   You shouldn't be so childish, you're 16 now!

5. **孩子话** **háizihuà** childish talk
   你 已经 十六 岁 了,别 说 孩子话!
   Nǐ yǐjīng shíliù suì le, bié shuō háizihuà!
   You shouldn't talk like a child, you're 16 now!

The last stroke ends firmly.   9 strokes

㇇	了	子	孑	孑	孑	孩	孩	孩			

狗 gǒu dog

In this character, the animal radical 犭 combines with the phonetic 句 to give the idea of *dog*.

Radical: 犭 'animal'　　　　　　　**Index # 58**

Character components: 犭 + 句　　　**Character configuration:** ⊟

Compounds, sentences and meanings

1. **狗** **gǒu** dog
   我们 家 的 狗 是 公 的。
   Wǒmen jiā de gǒu shì gōng de.
   Our dog is a male.

2. **小狗** **xiǎogǒu** puppy
   这 只 小狗 真 可爱。
   Zhè zhī xiǎogǒu zhēn kě'ài.
   This puppy is really cute.

3. **母狗** **mǔgǒu** female dog, bitch
   这 只 母狗 已经 很 老 了。
   Zhè zhī mǔgǒu yǐjīng hěn lǎo le.
   This female dog is quite old.

4. **狗熊** **gǒuxióng** black bear
   狗熊 有 时候 吃 人。
   Gǒuxióng yǒu shíhou chī rén.
   Black bears sometimes eat people.

5. **狗屁** **gǒupì** rubbish (literally, dog's fart)
   这 篇 文章 写得 狗屁 不通。
   Zhè piān wénzhāng xiěde gǒupì bùtōng.
   The article is mere rubbish.

The second stroke finishes with a hook.								8 strokes
ノ	犭	犭	犭	狗	狗	狗	狗	

māo   cat

Full form

In the simplified form, the animal radical 犭 combines with the phonetic 苗 to give the idea of *cat*. The word *māo* sounds like a cat miawing. Note the full form uses a different radical which also means 'animal'.

Radical: 犭 'animal'

Character components: 犭 + 苗

Index # 58

Character configuration:

Compounds, sentences and meanings

1. 猫   **māo**   cat
   这 只 猫 是 公 的。
   Zhè zhī māo shì gōng de.
   This is a tomcat.

2. 母猫   **mǔmāo**   female cat
   这 母猫 很 老 了。
   Zhè mǔmāo hěn lǎo le.
   This female cat is quite old.

3. 小猫   **xiǎomāo**   kitten
   这些 小猫 太 可爱 了!
   Zhèxiē xiǎomāo tài kě'ài le!
   These kittens are so cute!

4. 大熊猫   **dàxióngmāo**   panda
   我 要 去 中国 看 大熊猫。
   Wǒ yào qù Zhōngguó kàn dàxióngmāo.
   I want to go to China to see the panda.

5. 猫头鹰   **māotóuyīng**   owl
   猫头鹰 吃 老鼠。
   Māotóuyīng chī lǎoshǔ.
   Owls eat rats.

The second stroke is a curving hook.   11 strokes

| ノ | 犭 | 犭 | 犭 | 犭 | 犭 | 犭 | 猫 | 猫 | 猫 | 猫 | | |

Full form

只 **zhī** [classifier]

The full form combines *bird* 隹 and *again* 又 to represent the *classifier* for animals. In simplification, the phonetic 只 is used. See also *zhǐ* in character #200.

Radical: 口 'mouth'	**Index # 50**
or 八 'eight'	**Index # 17**
Character components: 口 + 八	**Character configuration:**

Compounds, sentences and meanings

1. **只 zhī** classifier
   这 只 猫 是 公 的。
   Zhè zhī māo shì gōng de.
   This is a tomcat.

   两只老虎 **Liǎng zhī lǎohu** ("Two Tigers") is a well-known children's song.

两 只老虎, 两 只老虎;	一 只 没有 眼睛,
Liǎng zhī lǎohu, liǎng zhī lǎohu;	**Yī zhī méiyǒu yǎnjing,**
Two tigers, two tigers;	*One has no eyes,*
跑得 快, 跑得 快,	一 只 没有 尾巴;
Pǎode kuài, pǎode kuài;	**Yī zhī méiyǒu wěiba;**
They run fast, they run fast;	*One has no tail;*
	真 奇怪! 真 奇怪!
	Zhēn qíguài! Zhēn qíguài!
	It's really strange! It's really strange!

The last stroke finishes firmly.	5 strokes

丶	冂	口	尸	只							

Quiz 9 (81–90)

A. Look at the 16-character grid and CIRCLE words or phrases. They can be written horizontally from left to right or vertically. Look at the circled characters in the Key if unsure. COPY the word or phrase next to the grid and write the pinyin and meaning.

		Word or phrase		**Pinyin**	**Meaning**

Grid:

猫	女	哥	两
男	孩	那	有
母	里	儿	没
只	狗	子	家

(i) 男 孩 — nánhái — boy

(ii)

(iii)

(iv)

B. Refer to the characters in the 16-character grid above and CONVERT the pinyin phrases into characters and check their English meaning in the Key.

(i)	Nǐ gēge yǒu méiyǒu háizi?								
(ii)	Wǒ gēge yǒu liǎng ge nǚ'ér.								
(iii)	Nǐ jiā yǒu méiyǒu gǒu?								
(iv)	Méiyǒu, wǒ jiā yǒu yì zhī māo.								

C. Match the Chinese words with their English meaning.

(i)

儿子 — daughter
哪儿 — strong woman
女儿 — descendants
子 sūn — where
女 qiáng 人 — son
女 shēng — boy friend
男孩儿 — female student
男朋友 — boy

(ii)

母狗 — here
里 biān — female dog
孩子 qì — men's toilet
男 cèsuǒ — panda
xiǎo 猫 — over there
那 biān — childish
这里 — inside
dàxióng 猫 — kitten

 **dà** big

The character depicts a person standing with arms outstretched, giving the idea of *big*.

Radical: 大 'big' **Index # 43**

Character component: 大 **Character configuration:**

Compounds, sentences and meanings

1. **大** **dà** big
   把 收音机 开 大一点。
   Bǎ shōuyīnjī kāi dàyìdiǎn.
   Turn the volume of the radio up a bit.

2. **大声** **dàshēng** loudly
   请 别 大声 说话。
   Qǐng bié dàshēng shuōhuà.
   Please don't speak so loudly.

3. **大家** **dàjiā** everybody
   请 大家 坐好。
   Qǐng dàjiā zuòhǎo.
   Please be seated, everyone.

4. **大小** **dàxiǎo** size (literally, big small)
   这 双 鞋 大小 正 合适。
   Zhè shuāng xié dàxiǎo zhèng héshì.
   These shoes fit me perfectly.

5. **大概** **dàgài** in general
   我 只 知道 个 大概。
   Wǒ zhǐ zhīdao ge dàgài.
   I have only a general idea.

The last stroke tapers off.   3 strokes

一	大	大									

92

 **xiǎo** small

The character represents a large object being divided into two *small* objects. It means *small*.

Radical: 小 'small'   **Index # 49**

Character component: 小   **Character configuration:** ☐

Compounds, sentences and meanings

1. 小 **xiǎo** little
   我 比 你 小。
   Wǒ bǐ nǐ xiǎo.
   I'm younger than you.

2. 小时 **xiǎoshí** hour
   我 每天 工作 八 个 小时。
   Wǒ měitiān gōngzuò bā ge xiǎoshí.
   I work eight hours every day.

3. 小时候 **xiǎoshíhou** in one's childhood
   这 是 她 小时候 的 照片。
   Zhè shì tā xiǎoshíhou de zhàopiàn.
   These are her childhood photos.

4. 小吃 **xiǎochī** snacks
   北京 的 小吃 很 出名。
   Běijīng de xiǎochī hěn chūmíng.
   Beijing is famous for its snacks.

5. 小心 **xiǎoxīn** be careful (literally, little heart)
   过 马路 要 小心。
   Guò mǎlù yào xiǎoxīn.
   Be careful when crossing the road.

The middle stroke ends with a hook.   3 strokes

亅	小	小								

Full form

岁

   suì   age in years

歲

The simplified form combines *hill* 山 and *evening* 夕 to give the idea of *age in years.*

Radical: 山 'hill'   **Index # 53**

or   夕 'sunset'   **Index # 56**

Character components: 山 + 夕   **Character configuration:**

Compounds, sentences and meanings

1. **岁** **suì**   age in years
   李 老师 今年 五十七 岁。
   Lǐ lǎoshī jīnnián wǔshíqī suì.
   Teacher Li is 57 years old.

2. **岁数** **suìshù**   age (used in question)
   您 今年 多 大 岁数 了?
   Nín jīnnián duō dà suìshù le?
   How old are you? [question directed at older people as sign of respect]

3. **年岁** **niánsuì**   age
   他 是 上了 年岁 的 人。
   Tā shì shàngle niánsuì de rén.
   He is a person who is getting on in years.

4. **岁月** **suìyuè**   years
   岁月 不 居。
   Suìyuè bù jū.
   Time and tide wait for no one.

The dot is written last.   **6 strokes**

丿	凵	山	岁	岁	岁						

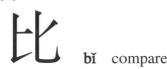

比 bǐ compare

The character represents the figure of two persons standing side by side when comparing heights. It means *compare*.

Radical: 比 'compare'　　　　　　**Index # 86**

Character components: 比 + 匕　　　　**Character configuration:**

Compounds, sentences and meanings

1. 比 **bǐ** compare to
   我 比 我 哥哥 小 两 岁。
   Wǒ bǐ wǒ gēge xiǎo liǎng suì.
   I'm 2 years younger than my brother.

2. 比较 **bǐjiào** comparatively
   最近 我 比较 忙。
   Zuìjìn wǒ bǐjiào máng.
   I've been busy of late.

3. 比赛 **bǐsài** competition
   今晚 有 一个 足球比赛, 你 看 吗?
   Jīnwǎn yǒu yí ge zúqiú bǐsài, nǐ kàn ma?
   Are you going to watch the soccer match tonight?

4. 比方 **bǐfāng** analogy
   可以 给 我 打 个 比方 吗?
   Kěyǐ gěi wǒ dǎ ge bǐfāng ma?
   Can you give me an example?

5. 比不上 **bǐbushàng** not as good as
   我的 汉语 比不上 他。
   Wǒde Hànyǔ bǐbushàng tā.
   My Chinese is not as good as his.

The first stroke is a vertical lift.　　　　　　　**4 strokes**

比	比	比	比								

做 zuò do

The character combines *person* 亻 with *cause* 故 which signifies that a person causes something to happen by *doing* or *making*.

Radical: 亻 'upright person'　　　　　**Index # 19**

Character components: 亻 + 古 + 攵　　　**Character configuration:**

Compounds, sentences and meanings

1. **做** zuò do, make
   这 是 你 自己 做 的 吗?
   Zhè shì nǐ zìjǐ zuò de ma?
   Did you do/make this yourself?

2. **做菜** zuòcài cook
   她 丈夫 很 会 做菜。
   Tā zhàngfu hěn huì zuòcài.
   Her husband is very good in cooking.

3. **做事** zuòshì work
   他 做事 做得 很 认真。
   Tā zuòshì zuòde hěn rènzhēn.
   He does his work conscientiously.

4. **做生意** zuò shēngyì do business
   我 爸爸 做 生意 的。
   Wǒ bàba zuò shēngyì de.
   My father is a businessman.

5. **做梦** zuòmèng dream
   昨晚 我 做了 一 个 可怕 的 梦。
   Zuówǎn wǒ zuòle yí ge kěpà de mèng.
   I had a terrible dream last night.

The last stroke tapers off.　　　　　　　　　　　　　**11 strokes**

| ノ | 亻 | 亻 | 什 | 什 | 估 | 估 | 佔 | 做 | 做 | 做 | | |

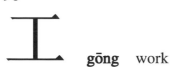

gōng work

The character depicts an ancient carpenter's square from which the meaning of *work* was derived.

Radical: 工 'work'   **Index # 39**

Character component: 工   **Character configuration:** ☐

Compounds, sentences and meanings

1. 工 **gōng** work
   假期的 时候, 他去 打工 挣
   Jiàqī de shíhou, tā qù dǎgōng zhèng
   零花钱。
   línghuāqián.
   During the holidays, he does menial work to earn some pocket money.

2. 工作 **gōngzuò** work
   你做 什么 工作?
   Nǐ zuò shénme gōngzuò?
   What work do you do?

3. 工资 **gōngzī** wage or salary
   一个 月的 工资 有 多少?
   Yǐ ge yuè de gōngzī yǒu duōshao?
   What's the monthly wage?

4. 工业 **gōngyè** industry
   这里 工业 污染 很 严重。
   Zhèlǐ gōngyè wūrǎn hěn yánzhòng.
   Industrial pollution is quite serious here.

5. 工厂 **gōngchǎng** factory
   这家 工厂 生产 运动鞋。
   Zhè jiā gōngchǎng shēngchǎn yùndòngxié.
   This factory manufactures sport shoes.

The second horizontal stroke is slightly longer.   3 strokes

一	丁	工								

97

作　**zuò**　do, make

The character combines *person* 亻 with 乍 which represents the idea of a cut being made by a person, and so means *to apply work to* or *make*.

Radical: 亻 'upright person'　　　**Index # 19**

Character components: 亻 + 乍　　　**Character configuration:**

Compounds, sentences and meanings

1. 作　**zuò**　work
   这 本 小说 是她的 成名 之作。
   Zhè běn xiǎoshuō shì tāde chéngmíng zhī zuò.
   This novel is the work that made her famous.

2. 作家　**zuòjiā**　writer
   我 从小 就 想 当 作家。
   Wǒ cóngxiǎo jiù xiǎng dāng zuòjiā.
   I've wanted to be a writer since I was small.

3. 作文　**zuòwén**　essay
   这 是 一 篇 小学生 的 作文。
   Zhè shì yì piān xiǎoxuéshēng de zuòwén.
   This is an essay by a school child.

4. 作业　**zuòyè**　assignment
   今天 的 作业 还 没 做 呢。
   Jīntiān de zuòyè hái méi zuò ne.
   I haven't done today's assignment yet.

5. 作用　**zuòyòng**　intention
   他 说 那 句 话 有 什么 作用?
   Tā shuō nà jù huà yǒu shénme zuòyòng?
   What was his intention in saying that?

The top horizontal is longer than those below it.　　　**7 strokes**

ノ	亻	亻	亻	竹	作	作						

Full form

医 yī cure, treat

醫

The simplified form takes the top left component of the full form as it is often the case in simplification.

Radical: 匚 '3-sided frame (open at the right)' **Index # 13**

Character components: 匚 + 矢 **Character configuration:** ⬚

Compounds, sentences and meanings

1. 医 yī cure, treat
   中医 把他的 病 医好。
   Zhōngyī bǎ tāde bìng yīhǎo.
   The Chinese doctor cured him.

2. 医生 yīshēng doctor
   他 是 内科 医生, 不 做 手术。
   Tā shì nèikē yīshēng, bú zuò shǒushù.
   He's a physician, he does not operate.

3. 医务所 yīwùsuǒ clinic
   今天 医务所 有 很多 人。
   Jīntiān yīwùsuǒ yǒu hěnduō rén.
   There are lots of people in the clinic today.

4. 医院 yīyuàn hospital
   请问, 到 医院 怎么 走?
   Qǐngwèn, dào yīyuàn zěnme zǒu?
   Excuse me, how do you get to the hospital?

5. 医科 yīkē medical courses in general
   她 在 大学 念 医科。
   Tā zài dàxué niàn yīkē.
   She studies medicine at university.

The second stroke is made up of vertical and horizontal lines. 7 strokes

一	匚	匚	医	医	医	医					

shēng birth, life

The character depicts a *growing plant.*

Radical: 丿 'downward-left stroke'

Index # 4

Character component: 生

Character configuration: ☐

Compounds, sentences and meanings

1. **生** shēng give birth to
   我 家 的 猫 生 了 三 只 小猫。
   Wǒ jiā de māo shēngle sān zhī xiǎomāo.
   Our cat gave birth to three kittens.

2. **生日** shēngrì birthday
   今天 是 谁 的 生日?
   Jīntiān shì shéide shēngrì?
   Whose birthday is it today?

3. **生词** shēngcí new word
   我 今天 学了 五 个 生词。
   Wǒ jīntiān xuéle wǔ ge shēngcí.
   I've learnt five new words today.

4. **大学生** dàxuéshēng university student
   美国 大学生 很 自由。
   Měiguó dàxuéshēng hěn zìyóu.
   American students have a lot of freedom.

5. **生产** shēngchǎn manufacture
   这 家 工厂 生产 运动鞋。
   Zhè jiā gōngchǎng shēngchǎn yùndòngxié.
   This factory manufactures sport shoes.

The bottom horizontal stroke is the longest.											5 strokes
丿	乍	仁	牛	生							

100

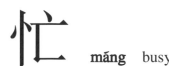

máng busy

The character combines *heart* 忄 with the phonetic 亡 to indicate the activities related to *being busy.*

Radical: 忄 'upright heart'   **Index # 33**

Character components: 忄 + 亡   **Character configuration:** ⊞

Compounds, sentences and meanings

1. **忙** **máng** busy
   我 最近 很 忙。
   Wǒ zuìjìn hěn máng.
   I've been very busy lately.

2. **忙着** **mángzhe** busy with something
   他 正 忙着 做饭 呢。
   Tā zhèng mángzhe zuòfàn ne.
   He's busying himself preparing the meal.

3. **忙人** **mángrén** busy person
   他 是 个 大 忙人。
   Tā shì ge dà mángrén.
   He's a very busy man.

4. **忙碌** **mánglù** be busy
   她 忙碌了 一个 上午， 结果 把 饭菜
   Tā mánglùle yī ge shàngwǔ, jiéguǒ bǎ fàncài
   做好。
   zuòhǎo.
   She was busy all morning, and eventually got the cooking done.

5. **帮忙** **bāngmáng** help
   他 来 找人 帮忙。
   Tā lái zhǎo rén bāngmáng.
   He came for help.

The last stroke is a vertical bend.   6 strokes

丶	丶	忄	忙	忙	忙						

Quiz 10 (91–100)

A. Look at the 16-character grid and CIRCLE words or phrases. They can be written horizontally or vertically. Look at the circled characters in the Key if unsure. COPY the word or phrase next to the grid and write the pinyin and meaning.

			Word or phrase		Pinyin	Meaning

狗	比	医	猫	(i)	大	小		dàxiǎo	size
大	小	生	学	(ii)					
工	岁	很	忙	(iii)					
作	女	里	男	(iv)					

B. Refer to the characters in the 16-character grid above and CONVERT the pinyin phrases into characters and check the English meaning in the Key.

(i)	Nǐ jiějie zuò shénme gōngzuò?									
(ii)	Tāde gōngzuò máng bumáng?									
(iii)	Nǐ gēge bǐ nǐ dà jǐ suì?									
(iv)	Nǐ mèimei bǐ nǐ xiǎo jǐ suì?									

C. Match the Chinese words with their English meaning.

(i)

小 shí — age in years
大 shēng — competition
岁 shù — hour
比 jiào — everybody
比不上 — compare
比 sài — puppy
小狗 — not as good as
大 jiā — loudly

(ii)

工 zī — help
生 cí — cook
医生 — do business
做 cài — wage/salary
bāng 忙 — new words
做 shēngyì — university student
工作 — doctor
大学生 — work

114

CHARACTER BUILDING 2 (51—100)

A. Memorize the following radicals and their English names. As a review exercise, write the pinyin spelling and meaning.

1. [一] 'horizontal stroke'

   哥 (_____) _____ ; 两 (_____) _____ .

2. [丿] 'downward-left stroke'

   生 (_____) _____ ; 九 (_____) _____ ;

   么 (_____) _____ .

3. [讠] 'word'

   谢 (_____) _____ ; 谁 (_____) _____ ;

   语 (_____) _____ ; 说 (_____) _____ ;

   认 (_____) _____ ; 识 (_____) _____ .

4. [八] 'eight'

   八 (_____) _____ ; 弟 (_____) _____ .

5. [亻] 'upright person'

   们 (_____) _____ ; 作 (_____) _____ ;

   体 (_____) _____ ; 做 (_____) _____ .

6. [阝] 'right ear-lobe'

   那 (_____) _____ ; 都 (_____) _____ ;

7. [氵] '3 drops of water'

   没 (_____) _____ ; 汉 (_____) _____ ;

8. [宀] 'roof'

   家 (_____) _____ ; 字 (_____) _____ ;

9. [辶] 'movement'

   这 (_____) _____ ; 还 (_____) _____ .

10. [小] 'small'

    小 (_____) _____ ; 少 (_____) _____ ;

11. [口] 'mouth'

    口 (_____) _____ ; 只 (_____) _____ ;

    兄 (_____) _____ ; 名 (_____) _____ .

12. [犭] 'animal'

    狗 (_____) _____ ; 猫 (_____) _____ .

13. ［女］ 'female'

女 (＿＿＿＿＿) ＿＿＿＿＿＿ ； 妈 (＿＿＿＿＿) ＿＿＿＿＿＿ ；

她 (＿＿＿＿＿) ＿＿＿＿＿＿ ； 姐 (＿＿＿＿＿) ＿＿＿＿＿＿ ；

妹 (＿＿＿＿＿) ＿＿＿＿＿＿ .

14. ［子］ 'child'

子 (＿＿＿＿＿) ＿＿＿＿＿＿ ； 学 (＿＿＿＿＿) ＿＿＿＿＿＿ ；

孩 (＿＿＿＿＿) ＿＿＿＿＿＿ .

15. ［心］ 'heart'

怎 (＿＿＿＿＿) ＿＿＿＿＿＿ ； 您 (＿＿＿＿＿) ＿＿＿＿＿＿ ；

16. ［父］ 'father'

父 (＿＿＿＿＿) ＿＿＿＿＿＿ ； 爸 (＿＿＿＿＿) ＿＿＿＿＿＿ .

17. ［月］ 'moon/flesh'

有 (＿＿＿＿＿) ＿＿＿＿＿＿ ； 朋 (＿＿＿＿＿) ＿＿＿＿＿＿ .

B. Write the pinyin and meaning against the characters classified under the following radicals.

1. ［乛］ 'horizontal bend hook'   也   (＿＿＿＿＿) ＿＿＿＿＿＿
2. ［匚］ 'three-sided frame (open at the right)'   医   (＿＿＿＿＿) ＿＿＿＿＿＿
3. ［儿］ 'son'   儿   (＿＿＿＿＿) ＿＿＿＿＿＿
4. ［几］ 'how many'   几   (＿＿＿＿＿) ＿＿＿＿＿＿
5. ［力］ 'strength'   男   (＿＿＿＿＿) ＿＿＿＿＿＿
6. ［忄］ 'upright heart'   忙   (＿＿＿＿＿) ＿＿＿＿＿＿
7. ［工］ 'work'   工   (＿＿＿＿＿) ＿＿＿＿＿＿
8. ［巾］ 'napkin'   师   (＿＿＿＿＿) ＿＿＿＿＿＿
9. ［山］ 'hill'   岁   (＿＿＿＿＿) ＿＿＿＿＿＿
10. ［彳］ 'double upright person'   很   (＿＿＿＿＿) ＿＿＿＿＿＿
11. ［木］ 'tree'   样   (＿＿＿＿＿) ＿＿＿＿＿＿
12. ［比］ 'compare'   比   (＿＿＿＿＿) ＿＿＿＿＿＿
13. ［立］ 'erect'   亲   (＿＿＿＿＿) ＿＿＿＿＿＿
14. ［母］ 'mother'   母   (＿＿＿＿＿) ＿＿＿＿＿＿
15. ［老］ 'old'   老   (＿＿＿＿＿) ＿＿＿＿＿＿
16. ［身］ 'body'   身   (＿＿＿＿＿) ＿＿＿＿＿＿
17. ［里］ 'inside'   里   (＿＿＿＿＿) ＿＿＿＿＿＿

C. Write the pinyin and meaning against the characters which share the following
   components. (Note that these components are not necessarily used as radicals.)

1. ［子］ 子 (_____) _____ ; 学 (_____) _____ ;
          字 (_____) _____ ; 孩 (_____) _____ ;
          好 (_____) _____ .

2. ［儿］ 儿 (_____) _____ ; 兄 (_____) _____ .

3. ［也］ 也 (_____) _____ ; 她 (_____) _____ .
          他 (_____) _____ .

REVIEW 2 (51–100)

The following are words classified under parts of speech. Write the pinyin and meaning.

Pronouns	我们 (_____) _____ ;	我们的 (_____) _____ :
	你们 (_____) _____ ;	你们的 (_____) _____ ;
	他们 (_____) _____ ;	他们的 (_____) _____ ;
	她们 (_____) _____ ;	她们的 (_____) _____ .
Demostrative pronouns	这 (_____) _____ ,	这些 (_____) _____ ;
	这儿 (_____) _____ ;	这里 (_____) _____ ;
	那 (_____) _____ ;	那些 (_____) _____ ;
	那儿 (_____) _____ ;	那里 (_____) _____ ;
Interrogative pronouns	谁的 (_____) _____ ;	哪儿 (_____) _____ ;
	哪里 (_____) _____ ;	怎么 (_____) _____ ;
	怎样 (_____) _____ ;	怎么样 (_____) _____ ;
	几 (_____) _____ ;	几个 (_____) _____ .
Nouns	父亲 (_____) _____ ;	母亲 (_____) _____ ;
	父母 (_____) _____ ;	哥哥 (_____) _____ ;
	姐姐 (_____) _____ ;	弟弟 (_____) _____ ;
	妹妹 (_____) _____ ;	兄弟 (_____) _____ ;
	姐妹 (_____) _____ ;	家 (_____) _____ ;
	国家 (_____) _____ ;	大家 (_____) _____ ;
	人家 (_____) _____ ;	
	孩子 (_____) _____ ;	儿子 (_____) _____ ;
	女儿 (_____) _____ ;	身体 (_____) _____ ;
	老师 (_____) _____ ;	医生 (_____) _____ ;
	学生 (_____) _____ ;	狗 (_____) _____ ;
	猫 (_____) _____ ;	岁 (_____) _____ ;
	工作 (_____) _____ .	

Verbs	有 (_____) _____ ;	没有 (_____) _____ ;
	谢 (_____) _____ ;	做 (_____) _____ ;
Adjectives	男 (_____) _____ ;	女 (_____) _____ ;
	大 (_____) _____ ;	小 (_____) _____ ;
	忙 (_____) _____ .	
Adverbs	很 (_____) _____ ;	比 (_____) _____ .
Conjunctions	还 (_____) _____ ;	也 (_____) _____ ;
	都 (_____) _____ .	
Numbers	两 (_____) _____ .	
Classifiers	口 (_____) _____ ;	只 (_____) _____ .

Noun phrases	中国人口 (_____) _____ ;
	美国人口 (_____) _____ ;
	英国人口 (_____) _____ ;
	小学生 (_____) _____ ;
	中学生 (_____) _____ ;
	大学生 (_____) _____ ;
	好学生 (_____) _____ .
	好朋友 (_____) _____ ;
	老朋友 (_____) _____ ;
	男朋友 (_____) _____ ;
	女朋友 (_____) _____ .

WORD/SENTENCE PUZZLE 2

Find and CIRCLE words, phrases or sentences hidden in the puzzle. They can be found horizontally from left to right or vertically. The lines across and down are indicated by numbers. Write the meaning next to the pinyin. The first one is done for you.

ACROSS (left to right)

2. Nǐ yǒu jǐ ge xiōngdì jiěmèi? *How many brothers and sisters do you have?*
   _____

5. Tā shuō Hànyǔ bǐ wǒ shuō de hǎo.
   _____

7. (i)   búshì
   _____

7. (ii) liǎng ge gōngzuò
   _____

9. nánhái
   _____

10. hěnduō xiǎoxuésheng hé zhōngxuésheng
   _____

12. Zhè zhī gǒu hěn dà.
   _____

13. xiǎomāo
   _____

DOWN

1. Tā fùmǔ shēntǐ hěn hǎo. _____
3. Nǐ huì shuō Hànyǔ bú huì? _____
4. nǚxuéshēng _____
6. Wǒ yǒu liǎng zhī māo hé yì zhī gǒu. _____
8. èrdì _____
9. (i) nánshēng _____
9. (ii) dàxiǎo _____
10. xiǎomèi _____

	1	2	3	4	5	6	7	8	9	10
1	名	哪	写	您	不	说	十	二	儿	小
2	们	谢	你	有	几	个	兄	弟	姐	妹
3	亲	妈	会	哪	七	医	里	多	吗	师
4	还	爸	说	是	会	字	我	名	语	么
5	他	说	汉	语	比	我	说	的	好	老
6	父	家	语	哥	忙	有	姓	学	妈	九
7	母	口	不	是	语	两	个	工	作	人
8	身	怎	会	英	多	只	少	汉	问	请
9	体	字	也	女	样	猫	名	这	男	孩
10	很	多	小	学	生	和	中	学	生	叫
11	好	识	写	生	您	一	多	吗	她	岁
12	认	那	友	少	这	只	狗	很	大	写
13	会	朋	我	名	都	狗	谁	他	小	猫

101

现

xiàn   appear

Full form

現

The character combines *king* 王 and *see* 见 to suggest the idea that when the king appears everyone is *watching*.

Radical: 王 'king'   **Index # 79**

or 见 'see'   **Index # 93**

Character components: 王 + 见   **Character configuration:** ▯▯

Compounds, sentences and meanings

1. **现 xiàn** appear
   他 脸上 现出了 笑容。
   Tā liǎnshang xiànchūle xiàoróng.
   A smile appears on his face.

2. **现在 xiànzài** now
   现在 几 点 了?
   Xiànzài jǐ diǎn le?
   What's the time now?

3. **现金 xiànjīn** cash (literally, ready money)
   你 可以 给 现金 吗?
   Nǐ kěyǐ gěi xiànjīn ma?
   Can you pay cash?

4. **现成 xiànchéng** ready-made
   定做 衣服 太 贵 了, 买 现成 的 吧。
   Dìngzuò yīfu tài guì le, mǎi xiànchéng de ba.
   It's too expensive to tailor-made clothes, let's buy ready-made ones.

5. **表现 biǎoxiàn** behavior
   他 今天 的 表现 很 好。
   Tā jīntiān de biǎoxiàn hěn hǎo.
   He's behaving very well today.

The last stroke is a vertical-bend hook.							8 strokes
一	二	王	王	扝	玑	现	现

102

 **zài**   at

The character signifies grass coming out of the *ground* 土 . It came to mean *exist*.

Radical: 土 'earth'   **Index # 40**

Character components: 一 + 丨 + 土   **Character configuration:**

Compounds, sentences and meanings

1. **在 zài** at
   你 住 在 哪里?
   Nǐ zhù zài nǎlǐ?
   Where do you live?

2. **在家 zài jiā** at home
   我 今天 晚上 不 在家。
   Wǒ jīntiān wǎnshang bú zài jiā.
   I won't be home tonight.

3. **在内 zàinèi** included
   连 我 在内 一共 是 八个 人。
   Lián wǒ zàinèi yígòng shì bā ge rén.
   Including me, there arc altogether eight people.

4. **在外 zàiwài** excluded
   这 是 饭钱，服务费 在外。
   Zhè shì fànqián, fúwùfèi zàiwài.
   That's the price of the meal exclusive of service charge.

5. **实在 shízài** really
   我 实在 不 知道。
   Wǒ shízài bù zhīdao.
   I really don't know.

The bottom horizontal stroke is slightly longer.   **6 strokes**

一	ナ	才	右	在	在						

 **diǎn** dot

The four dots of fire in the left component, *black* 黑 of the full form 點, are moved over to the right component, *occupy* 占, to give the simplified form 点.

Radical: 灬 '4 dots of fire'   **Index # 71**

Character components: 占 + 灬   **Character configuration:**

Compounds, sentences and meanings

1. **点 diǎn** a little
   他 今天 好 点 了。
   Tā jīntiān hǎo diǎn le.
   He's a bit better today.

2. **五点零七分 wǔ diǎn líng qī fēn** 5:07
   现在 五 点 零 七 分。
   Xiànzài wǔ diǎn líng qī fēn.
   It's now seven minutes past five.

3. **晚点 wǎndiǎn** behind schedule
   飞机 晚点 了。
   Fēijī wǎndiǎn le.
   The plane is late.

4. **点菜 diǎncài** choose dishes from a menu
   可以 点菜 了。
   Kěyǐ diǎncài le.
   We're ready to order now.

5. **点头 diǎntóu** nod one's head
   他 已经 点头 了。
   Tā yǐjīng diǎntóu le.
   He's already ok'd it.

Note the way the dots are drawn.									9 strokes

zhōng clock

The full form represented the old idea of a bell made of *metal* 金 as big as a *boy* 童 which was used to tell time. The phonetic 中 is used in simplification.

Radical: 钅 'metal'   **Index # 122**

Character components: 钅 + 中   **Character configuration:** ▭

Compounds, sentences and meanings

1. 钟 **zhōng** clock
   送 礼物 千万 不要 送 钟。
   Sòng lǐwù qiānwàn búyào sòng zhōng.
   When buying a gift, be sure that it is not a clock.
   (Note that the homonym of sòng zhōng is sòngzhōng 'attend upon a dying person'.)

2. 点钟 **diǎnzhōng** o'clock
   他 上午 十 点钟 来。
   Tā shàngwǔ shí diǎnzhōng lái.
   He's coming here at 10 a.m.

3. 一刻钟 **yī kèzhōng** 15 minutes, a quarter of an hour
   我 等了 一 刻钟。
   Wǒ děngle yī kèzhōng.
   I waited for a quarter of an hour.

4. 钟头 **zhōngtóu** hour
   我 看了 三 个 钟头 电视。
   Wǒ kànle sān ge zhōngtóu diànshì.
   I've spent three hours watching television.

5. 钟情 **zhōngqíng** be deeply in love
   他们 两 个 一见 钟情。
   Tāmen liǎng ge yī jiàn zhōngqíng.
   They fell in love at first sight.

The fifth stroke is a vertical tick.   **9 strokes**

ノ	𠂉	𠂢	钅	钅	钅	钔	钔	钟			

fēn   divide

The character combines 八 *cut in two* and 刀 *knife* to give the meaning *divide*.

Radical: 八 'eight'   **Index # 17**
or   刀 'knife'   **Index # 30**
Character components: 八 + 刀   **Character configuration:**

Compounds, sentences and meanings

1. **分** fēn   divide
   这 药 分 三 次 吃。
   Zhè yào fēn sān cì chī.
   This medicine is to be taken in three separate doses.

2. **分钟** fēnzhōng   minute
   我 五 分钟 就 回来。
   Wǒ wǔ fēnzhōng jiù huílai.
   I'll be back in five minutes.

3. **分别** fēnbié   difference
   有 什么 分别?
   Yǒu shénme fēnbié?
   What's the difference?

4. **分辨** fēnbiàn   distinguish
   很 难 分辨 谁 是 谁 非。
   Hěn nán fēnbiàn shéi shì shéi fēi.
   It's hard to tell who is right and who is wrong.

5. **百分之三十** bǎifēnzhīsānshí   30%
   房租 涨了 百分之三十。
   Fángzū zhǎngle bǎifēnzhīsānshí.
   Rent has gone up 30 per cent.

Leave a gap between the top two strokes.							4 strokes
ノ	八	分	分				

了　le　[particle]

The character is generally used after a verb to indicate the completion of an action. It is also used to indicate the emergence of a new situation.

Radical: 乛 'horizontal bend'　　　　**Index # 5**

Character component: 了　　　　**Character configuration:** ☐

Compounds, sentences and meanings

1. 了　le　(new situation).
   现在 几 点 了?
   Xiànzài jǐ diǎn le?
   What's the time now?

2. 了　le　(new situation)
   下 雨 了。
   Xiàyǔ le.
   It's starting to rain.

3. 了　le　(completed action).
   我 学了 一百 二十 个 汉字。
   Wǒ xuéle yībǎi-èrshí ge Hànzì.
   I've learnt 120 Chinese characters.

The last stroke ends with a hook.　　　　2 strokes

乛	了										

107

半 bàn half

The character depicted a *cow* 牛 being split ˋˊ in *half*. It suggests dividing goods and generally means *a half*.

Radical: 八 **'eight'** **Index # 17**
or 十 **'ten'** **Index # 11**
Character component: 半 **Character configuration:**

Compounds, sentences and meanings

1. **半** **bàn** half
 从 这里 去 要 半（个）小时。
 Cóng zhèlǐ qù yào bàn (ge) xiǎoshí.
 It'll take half an hour from here.

2. **一半** **yībàn** half
 这 箱 桔子 有 一半 坏了。
 Zhè xiāng júzi yǒu yībàn huàile.
 Half of this box of oranges is rotten.

3. **一倍半** **yībèibàn** 150%
 这里 的 房价 十 年 内 增加了 一倍半。
 Zhèlǐ de fángjià shí nián nèi zēngjiāle yībèibàn.
 Property values have increased one and a half times over the last ten years.

4. **半新不旧** **bànxīn-bújiù** showing signs of wear (literally, no longer new)
 他 穿着 一 身 半新不旧 的衣服。
 Tā chuānzhe yì shēn bànxīn-bújiù de yīfu.
 The clothes he was wearing, though not shabby, were far from new.

5. **半天** **bàntiān** a long time (literally, half the day)
 我们 谈了 半天 也 没 结果。
 Wǒmen tánle bàntiān yě méi jiéguǒ.
 We discussed the matter for a long time but did not come to any conclusion.

The bottom horizontal stroke is longer. **5 strokes**

吃　chī　eat

The character combines *mouth* 口 and *beg* 乞 to suggest the result of soliciting food. It means *to eat*.

Radical:　口 'mouth'　　　　　　**Index # 50**

Character components:　口 + 乞　　　**Character configuration:**

Compounds, sentences and meanings

1. **吃**　chī　eat
   我　每天　都　吃个　苹果。
   Wǒ měitiān dōu chī ge píngguǒ.
   I eat an apple every day.

2. **吃饭**　chīfàn　have a meal
   我们　什么　时候　吃饭?
   Wǒmen shénme shíhou chīfàn?
   When do we eat?

3. **吃得下**　chīdexià　be able to eat
   我　吃得下　两　碗　饭。
   Wǒ chīdexià liǎng wǎn fàn.
   I can eat two bowls of rice.

4. **吃不下**　chībuxià　not able to eat
   我　吃不下　两　碗　饭。
   Wǒ chībuxià liǎng wǎn fàn.
   I can't eat two bowls of rice.

5. **吃苦**　chīkǔ　bear hardships (literally, eat bitterness)
   他　小时候　吃了　不少　苦。
   Tā xiǎoshíhou chīle bùshǎo kǔ.
   He suffered a great deal in his childhood.

The last stroke is a horizontal-bend-hook.　　　　　　**6 strokes**

丨	口	口	口	吃	吃						

zǎo early

The character depicted the *sun* 日 shining on the grass early in the morning. From this, it came to mean *early*.

Radical: 日 'sun'   **Index # 90**

Character components: 日 + 十   **Character configuration:**

Compounds, sentences and meanings

1. 早 **zǎo** early
   我 早 知道 了。
   Wǒ zǎo zhīdao le.
   I knew that long ago.

2. 早饭 **zǎofàn** breakfast
   我 早饭 吃 点儿 水果。
   Wǒ zǎofàn chī diǎnr shuǐguǒ.
   I eat fruit for my breakfast.

3. 早上 **zǎoshang** morning
   早上 好!
   Zǎoshang hǎo!
   Good morning!

4. 早晨 **zǎochén** early morning
   早晨 空气 清新。
   Zǎochén kōngqì qīngxīn.
   The air is fresh early in the morning.

5. 早日 **zǎorì** at an early date
   祝 你 早日 恢复 健康。
   Zhù nǐ zǎorì huīfú jiànkāng.
   I hope you'll get well soon.

The bottom horizontal stroke is longer.   6 strokes

丶	丿	曰	日	旦	早								

fàn   meal

The character combines *eat* 饣 and the phonetic 反 to give the meaning of *cooked rice* or *meal*.

Radical: 饣 'food'   **Index # 59**

Character components: 饣 + 反   **Character configuration:**

Compounds, sentences and meanings

1. 饭 fàn meal
   饭 前 洗手。
   Fàn qián xǐshǒu.
   Wash your hands before meals.

2. 饭菜 fàncài food
   这 个 饭馆 的 饭菜 做得 不错。
   Zhè ge fànguǎn de fàncài zuòde búcuò.
   The food in this restaurant is quite good.

3. 饭馆儿 fànguǎnr restaurant
   学校 对面 有 一家 饭馆儿。
   Xuéxiào duìmiàn yǒu yī jiā fànguǎnr.
   There's a restaurant opposite the school.

4. 饭店 fàndiàn hotel
   我 住 在 北京 饭店。
   Wǒ zhù zài Běijīng Fàndiàn.
   I'm staying at Beijing Hotel.

5. 米饭 mǐfàn boiled rice
   我 平常 吃 两 碗 米饭。
   Wǒ píngcháng chī liǎng wǎn mǐfàn.
   I usually eat two bowls of rice.

The second stroke is a horizontal hook.   **7 strokes**

ノ	⺈	饣	饣	饣	饭	饭					

Quiz 11 (101–110)

A. Look at the 16-character grid and CIRCLE words or phrases. They can be written horizontally or vertically. Look at the circled characters in the Key if unsure. COPY the word or phrase next to the grid and write the pinyin and meaning.

					Word or phrase			Pinyin	Meaning
工	忙	作	吃	(i)	现	在		xiànzài	now
少	多	了	早	(ii)					
现	在	分	饭	(iii)					
几	点	钟	半	(iv)					

B. Refer to the characters in the 16-character grid above and CONVERT the pinyin phrases into characters and check their English meaning in the Key.

(i)	Xiànzài jǐ diǎnzhōng le?									
(ii)	Xiànzài liùdiǎnbàn le.									
(iii)	Nǐmen jǐ diǎn chī zǎofàn?									
(iv)	Wǒmen qīdiǎnbàn chī zǎofàn.									

C. Match the Chinese words with their English meaning.

(i)

现 jīn	minute
biǎo 现	quarter hour
分钟	cash
一 kè 钟	behavior
两点钟	hour
钟 tóu	2 o'clock
在家	difference
分 biē	at home

(ii)

一半	half
半 tiān	early morning
吃苦	food
吃不下	bear hardship
早 chén	boiled rice
饭 guǎnr	a long time
饭 cài	unable to eat
mǐ 饭	restaurant

130

时 shí time

Full form

時

The full form combines *sun* 日 with *temple* 寺 to represent a place where people used to keep track of *time*. In simplification *inch* 寸 replaces 寺 to give the idea of *an inch of the sun*.

Radical: 日 'sun'

Index # 90

Character components: 日 + 寸

Character configuration:

Compounds, sentences and meanings

1. 时 **shí** time
   大夫 说 要 按时 吃药。
   Dàifu shuō yào ànshí chīyào.
   The doctor said to take the medicine at the right time.

2. 时间 **shíjiān** time
   没有 时间 了，我们 得 走 了。
   Méiyǒu shíjiān le, wǒmen děi zǒu le.
   There's no time, we must be going.

3. 时候 **shíhou** time
   现在 什么 时候 了?
   Xiànzài shénme shíhou le?
   What's the time now?

4. 时机 **shíjī** opportunity
   他 在 等待 时机。
   Tā zài děngdài shíjī.
   He is waiting for an opportunity.

5. 时髦 **shímáo** fashionable
   她 喜欢 穿 时髦 的 服装。
   Tā xǐhuan chuān shímáo de fúzhuāng.
   She likes to wear fashionable clothes.

The last stroke ends with a hook.   **7 strokes**

丨	冂	冃	日	旷	时	时					

112

候 hòu time; wait

The character combines *person* 亻, *vertical stroke* 丨 and *expect* 矦 to suggest an expectant atmosphere in which something is about to happen.

Radical: 亻 'upright person'　　　　**Index # 19**

Character components: 亻 + 丨 + 矦　　**Character configuration:**

Compounds, sentences and meanings

1. 候 hòu wait
   请 稍 候 一会儿。
   Qǐng shāo hòu yīhuǐr.
   Please wait a moment.

2. 时候 shíhou time
   现在 什么 时候 了?
   Xiànzài shénme shíhou le?
   What's the time now?

3. 有时候 yǒu shíhou sometimes
   我 有 时候 去 看 电影。
   Wǒ yǒu shíhou qù kàn diànyǐng.
   Sometimes I go to see a movie.

4. 气候 qìhòu climate
   他 不 适应 这里 的 气候。
   Tā bú shìyìng zhèlǐ de qìhòu.
   He's not used to the climate here.

5. 问候 wènhòu give regards to
   请 代 我 问候 你 父母。
   Qǐng dài wǒ wènhòu nǐ fùmǔ.
   Please send my regards to your parents.

Remember to write the third stroke.　　　　**10 strokes**

丿 亻 亻 伫 伫 伫 候 候 候 候

shàng   above; go up

The bottom line represents the surface while the strokes above indicate something *above* the surface.

Radical: 一 'horizontal stroke'　　**Index # 2**

Character component: 上

Character configuration:

Compounds, sentences and meanings

1. 上　**shàng**　most recent, last
   上　星期三　我　有　事儿。
   Shàng Xīngqīsān wǒ yǒu shìr.
   I was busy last Wednesday.

2. 上　**shàng**　go to
   你　上　哪儿去?
   Nǐ shàng nǎr qù?
   Where are you going?

3. 上面　**shàngmian**　above
   书　上面　有　我的 名字。
   Shū shàngmiàn yǒu wǒde míngzi.
   My name is written on the book.

4. 上午　**shàngwǔ**　a.m.
   今天　上午　风　很　大。
   Jīntiān shàngwǔ fēng hěn dà.
   It's quite windy this morning.

5. 上学　**shàngxué**　go to school
   小孩 已经 五 岁了,该　上学　了。
   Xiǎohái yǐjīng wǔ suì le, gāi shàngxué le.
   The child is already five, she/he should be going to school.

The top horizontal stroke is shorter.　　　**3 strokes**

丨	卜	上									

114

xià   below

The bottom line represents the surface while the strokes below indicate something *below* the surface.

Radical: 一 'horizontal stroke'   **Index # 2**

Character component: 下   **Character configuration:** ☐

Compounds, sentences and meanings

1. 下   **xià**   next
   下 星期三 我 有 事儿。
   Xià Xīngqīsān wǒ yǒu shìr.
   I'll be busy next Wednesday.

2. 下面   **xiàmian**   below
   图表 下面 有 说明。
   Túbiǎo xiàmiàn yǒu shuōmíng.
   There are captions below the chart.

3. 下班   **xiàbān**   get off work
   你 今天 几点 下班?
   Nǐ jīntiān jǐ diǎn xiàbān?
   When will you be finishing work today?

4. 下午   **xiàwǔ**   afternoon
   下午 有 雷阵雨。
   Xiàwǔ yǒu léizhènyǔ.
   There'll be thunderstorms in the afternoon.

5. 下雨   **xiàyǔ**   rain
   外面 下雨。
   Wàimian xiàyǔ.
   It's raining outside.

End the last stroke firmly.   **3 strokes**

一	丁	下									

wǔ noon

The character combines the component 𠂉 and the character 十 which indicates *center* to give the idea that when the sun is right in the center, it's *noon*.

Radical: 丿 'downward-left stroke'   **Index # 4**

Character components: 丿 + 干   **Character configuration:** ☐

Compounds, sentences and meanings

1. 午 **wǔ** noon
   午 前 就是 中午 一点 之前。
   Wǔ qián jiùshì zhōngwǔ yīdiǎn zhīqián.
   Forenoon is before 1:00 p.m.

2. 中午 **zhōngwǔ** noon
   我 跟 他 约好 中午 见面。
   Wǒ gēn tā yuēhǎo zhōngwǔ jiànmiàn.
   I've arranged to meet with him at noon.

3. 午饭 **wǔfàn** lunch
   今天 午饭 吃 什么?
   Jīntiān wǔfàn chī shénme?
   What's for lunch today?

4. 午睡 **wǔshuì** afternoon nap
   中国人 有 午睡 的 习惯。
   Zhōngguórén yǒu wǔshuì de xíguàn.
   Chinese people have a habit of taking an afternoon nap.

5. 午间 **wǔjiān** afternoon (adjective)
   现在 播送 的 是 午间 新闻。
   Xiànzài bōsòng de shì wǔjiān xīnwén.
   We are now broadcasting the afternoon news.

The bottom horizontal stroke is longer.   **4 strokes**

丿	𠂉	上	午								

晚 **wǎn** late, evening

The character combines *sun* 日 and *exempt* 免 to suggest that when one is free from the scorching sun, it is *evening*. By extension, it gives the idea of *late*.

Radical: 日 'sun'

Index # 90

Character components: 日 + 免

Character configuration:

Compounds, sentences and meanings

1. 晚 **wǎn** late
   现在 去 还 不 晚。
   Xiànzài qù hái bù wǎn.
   It's still not too late to go.

2. 晚上 **wǎnshang** evening
   今天 晚上 我 请客。
   Jīntiān wǎnshang wǒ qǐngkè.
   I'm buying dinner tonight.

3. 晚饭 **wǎnfàn** evening meal
   今天 晚饭 很 丰盛。
   Jīntiān wǎnfàn hěn fēngshèng.
   Tonight's dinner is sumptuous.

4. 晚班 **wǎnbān** evening shift
   这个 工作 需要 上 晚班。
   Zhè ge gōngzuò xūyào shàng wǎnbān.
   This job involves working night shifts.

5. 晚点 **wǎndiǎn** behind schedule (train/bus/plane/ferry)
   飞机 晚点 了。
   Fēijī wǎndiǎn le.
   The plane is late.

The last stroke is a vertical-bend-hook.   **12 strokes**

| 丨 | 冂 | 冂 | 日 | 日′ | 日″ | 旷 | 昣 | 晓 | 晚 | 晚 | 晚 | | |

起  qǐ rise

The character combines *walk* 走 and the phonetic 己 to suggest the action of *rising*.

Radical: 走 'walk'

Index # 156

Character components: 走 + 己

Character configuration:

Compounds, sentences and meanings

1. **起** **qǐ** get out of bed
   早睡 早起 对 身体 好。
   Zǎo-shuì zǎo-qǐ duì shēntǐ hǎo.
   Early to bed and early to rise is good for the health.

2. **起床** **qǐchuáng** get out of bed
   今天 我 六点半 起床。
   Jīntiān wǒ liùdiǎnbàn qǐchuáng.
   I got up at 6:30 today.

3. **起动** **qǐdòng** start
   汽车 起动，请 抓好 扶手。
   Qìchē qǐdòng, qǐng zhuāhǎo fúshǒu.
   The bus is starting, please hold on to the handrail.

4. **起码** **qǐmǎ** at least
   这个 工作 起码要 三个 月 才 能
   Zhè ge gōngzuò qǐmǎ yào sān ge yuè cái néng
   完成。
   wánchéng.
   This job will take at least three months.

5. **一起** **yìqǐ** together
   跟 我 一起去 看 电影 吧。
   Gēn wǒ yìqǐ qù kàn diànyǐng ba.
   Let's see a movie together.

The last stroke is a vertical-bend-hook.   **10 strokes**

一	十	土	圡	走	走	走	起	起	起			

118

床

chuáng   bed

The character signifies something made of *wood* 木 and is placed under the roof of a big house 广. Thus, it means *bed*.

Radical: 广 'broad'   **Index # 36**
or   木 'tree'   **Index # 81**
Character components: 广 + 木   **Character configuration:**

Compounds, sentences and meanings

1. 床 chuáng bed
   房间 里 放着 两 张 床。
   Fángjiān li fàngzhe liǎng zhāng chuáng.
   There are two beds in the room.

2. 床上 chuángshang in bed
   我 喜欢 躺 在 床上 看书。
   Wǒ xǐhuan tǎng zài chuángshang kànshū.
   I like to read in bed.

3. 床单 chuángdān bed sheet
   该 换 床单 了。
   Gāi huàn chuángdān le.
   The bedsheets need changing.

4. 单人床 dānrénchuáng single bed
   我 觉得 单人床 太 窄。
   Wǒ juéde dānrénchuáng tài zhǎi.
   I find that single beds are too narrow for me.

5. 双人床 shuāngrénchuáng double bed
   我 喜欢 睡 双人床。
   Wǒ xǐhuan shuì shuāngrénchuáng.
   I like to sleep on a double bed.

The last stroke tapers off.   **7 strokes**

丶 一 广 广 斤 床 床

138

跑 **pǎo** run

The character combines *foot* 足 and the phonetic 包 to suggest the action of *running*.

Radical: 足 'foot'

Index # 164

Character components: 足 + 包

Character configuration:

Compounds, sentences and meanings

1. 跑 **pǎo** run
   她 跑得 很 快。
   Tā pǎode hěn kuài.
   She can run very fast.

2. 跑步 **pǎobù** jogging
   他 每天 早晨 都 跑步。
   Tā měitiān zǎochén dōu pǎobù.
   He jogs every morning.

3. 跑道 **pǎodào** runway
   飞机 正在 跑道 上 行驶。
   Fēijī zhèngzài pǎodào shang xíngshǐ.
   The plane is taxiing on the runway.

4. 赛跑 **sàipǎo** race
   他 经常 参加 长距离 赛跑。
   Tā jīngcháng cānjiā chángjùlí sàipǎo.
   He often takes part in long-distance races.

5. 长跑 **chángpǎo** long-distance running
   我 参加了 五千 米 的 长跑。
   Wǒ cānjiāle wǔqiān mǐ de chángpǎo.
   I took part in a 5000 meter race.

The seventh stroke is a tick.　　　　　　　　　　　　　**12 strokes**

丶	口	口	甲	𤼑	𧾷	足	趴	趵	跑	跑	跑

bù step

The character can be thought of as *foot* 止 and *few* 少, indicating the distance of one walking *stride*. Note that the lower part of the character 少 loses the right dot.

Radical: 止 'stop'

Index # 88

Character components: 止 + 少

Character configuration:

Compounds, sentences and meanings

1. **步　bù**　step
   只 有 几 步 路 了。
   Zhǐyǒu jǐ bù lù le.
   It's only a few steps away.

2. **步骤　bùzhòu**　step, stage
   她 有 步骤 地 进行 工作。
   Tā yǒu bùzhòu de jìnxíng gōngzuò.
   She carries out the work systematically.

3. **脚步　jiǎobù**　footstep
   走路 时 请 放 轻 脚步。
   Zǒulù shí qǐng fàng qīng jiǎobù.
   Please walk softly.

4. **进步　jìnbù**　make progress
   你 写 汉字 很 有 进步。
   Nǐ xiě Hànzì hěn yǒu jìnbù.
   You are making great progress in your Chinese character writing.

5. **止步　zhǐbù**　out of bounds
   游人 止步。
   Yóurén zhǐbù
   No visitors.

The last stroke sweeps down to left.　　　　　　　　　　**7 strokes**

丨	上	止	止	牛	耂	步					

Quiz 12 (111–120)

A. Look at the 16-character grid and CIRCLE words or phrases. They can be written horizontally or vertically. Look at the circled characters in the Key if unsure. COPY the word or phrase next to the grid and write the pinyin and meaning.

		Word or phrase			**Pinyin**	**Meaning**
起	时	跑	步	起 床	qǐchuáng	get ouf of bed
床	晚	上	早			
工	现	午	下			
在	候	里	分			

B. Refer to the characters in the 16-character grid above and CONVERT the pinyin phrases into characters and check their English meaning in the Ley.

(i)	Nǐ shénme shíhou qǐchuáng?								
(ii)	Wǒ qīdiǎnzhōng qǐchuáng.								
(iii)	Nǐ pǎo bu pǎobù?								
(iv)	Pǎo, yǒu shíhou pǎo.								

C. Match the Chinese words with their English meaning.

(i)

时 jiān	timetable
时 kèbiǎo	climate
什么时候	time
qì 候	what time
有时候	lunch
上午	afternoon
下午	a.m.
午饭	sometimes

(ii)

下 yǔ	improve
下 bān	evening meal
jìn 步	go to school
午 shuì	race
上学	together
sài 跑	raining
晚饭	finish work
一起	afternoon nap

今 jīn present

The top part of the character suggests convergence from three directions and the lower part suggests everlasting. It came to mean *present time*.

Radical: 人 'person'

Index # 18

Character components: 人 + 丶 + 乛

Character configuration:

Compounds, sentences and meanings

1. **今** jīn   now, the present
   他 说 从 今 以后 要 认真 学习。
   Tā shuō cóng jīn yǐhòu yào rènzhēn xuéxí.
   He said he will study conscientiously from now on.

2. **今天** jīntiān   today
   今天 会 下雨 吗?
   Jīntiān huì xiàyǔ ma?
   Will it rain today?

3. **今晚** jīnwǎn   tonight
   我 今晚 不 在家。
   Wǒ jīnwǎn bú zài jiā.
   I won't be home tonight.

4. **今年** jīnnián   this year
   我 今年 刚 开始 学 中文。
   Wǒ jīnnián gāng kāishǐ xué Zhōngwén.
   I just started learning Chinese this year.

5. **今后** jīnhòu   from now on
   希望 我们 今后 能 多 交流 经验。
   Xīwàng wǒmen jīnhòu néng duō jiāoliú jīngyàn.
   I hope we can have more exchange of experiences from now on.

今 is easily confused with 令.   **4 strokes**

丿	人	仒	今								

tiān day, sky

The character combines the characters 一 and 大 to suggest something very big and above the head of people — *the sky*.

Radical: 一 'horizontal stroke'   **Index # 2**
or   大 'big'   **Index # 43**
Character components: 一 + 大   **Character configuration:** ▢

Compounds, sentences and meanings

1. 天 **tiān** day
   天 不 早 了。
   Tiān bù zǎo le.
   It's getting late.

2. 天才 **tiāncái** genius
   这 孩子 有 音乐 天才。
   Zhè háizi yǒu yīnyuè tiāncái.
   This child has musical talent.

3. 天气 **tiānqì** weather
   今天 天气 真 好。
   Jīntiān tiānqì zhēn hǎo.
   The weather is really good today.

4. 天然 **tiānrán** nature
   我 喜欢 天然 景色。
   Wǒ xǐhuan tiānrán jǐngsè.
   I like natural scenery.

5. 天真 **tiānzhēn** innocent, naive
   你 要 相信 这样 的 话，那 就 太
     天真 了。
   Nǐ yào xiāngxìn zhèyàng de huà, nà jiù tài
     tiānzhēn le.
   If you believe that sort of talk, you're really naive.

The third stroke does not protrude over the top horizontal stroke.   **4 strokes**

一	二	于	天						

明 míng bright

The character combines *sun* 日 and *moon* 月 to express the idea of *brightness*.

Radical: 日 'day'

Index # 90

Character components: 日 + 月

Character configuration:

Compounds, sentences and meanings

1. **明** **míng** bright, clear
   你 有 没有 问明 他的 来意?
   Nǐ yǒu méiyǒu wènmíng tāde láiyì?
   Have you specifically asked him his reasons for coming?

2. **明白** **míngbai** understand
   我 不 明白 你的 意思。
   Wǒ bù míngbai nǐde yìsi.
   I don't understand what you mean.

3. **明天** **míngtiān** tomorrow
   对不起 我 明天 没有 空儿。
   Duìbuqǐ, wǒ míngtiān méiyǒu kòngr.
   Sorry, I'll be busy tomorrow.

4. **明显** **míngxiǎn** obvious
   这 很 明显 是 一个 借口。
   Zhè hěn míngxiǎn shì yí ge jièkǒu.
   This is evidently a pretext.

5. **明知** **míngzhī** know perfectly well
   你 明知 他 不 高兴， 为什么 还要
   Nǐ míngzhī tā bù gāoxìng, wèishénme hái yào
   说。
   shuō.
   You know quite well that he won't be happy to hear this, so why do you still say it?

The last stroke ends with a hook.											8 strokes
丨	冂	月	日	日丿	明	明	明				

月

yuè month

The character is a pictograph which represents the crescent *moon*.

Radical: 月 'moon/flesh'   **Index # 103**

Character component: 月

Character configuration: ☐

Compounds, sentences and meanings

1. 月 **yuè** month
   我的 月 收入 是 五 千 元。
   Wǒde yuè shōurù shì wǔ qiān yuán.
   My monthly income is ¥5000.

2. 这个月 **zhè ge yuè** this month
   这 个 月 我 比较 忙。
   Zhè ge yuè wǒ bǐjiào máng.
   I'm quite busy this month.

3. 上个月 **shàng ge yuè** last month
   我们 上 个 月 去 旅行 了。
   Wǒmen shàng ge yuè qù lǚxíng le.
   We went for a holiday last month.

4. 下个月 **xià ge yuè** next month
   我们 下 个 月 就 放假 了。
   Wǒmen xià ge yuè jiù fàngjià le.
   We'll be on holiday next month.

5. 月亮 **yuèliang** moon
   今晚 的 月亮 很 圆。
   Jīnwǎn de yuèliang hěn yuán.
   The moon is round tonight.

The last stroke ends with a hook.   **4 strokes**

丿 丌 月 月

 **rì** day

The character is a pictograph which represents the shape of the *sun*.

Radical: 日 'sun'

Index # 90

Character component: 日

Character configuration:

Compounds, sentences and meanings

1. 日 **rì** day
   十月 二十五日 是 我的 生日。
   Shíyuè-èrshíwǔrì shì wǒde shēngrì.
   October 25th is my birthday.

2. 日期 **rìqī** date
   你 忘了 填上 你的 出生 日期。
   Nǐ wàngle tiánshàng nǐde chūshēng rìqī.
   You forgot to fill in your date of birth.

3. 日记 **rìjì** diary
   我 没有 记日记的 习惯。
   Wǒ méiyǒu jì rìjì de xíguàn.
   I don't have a habit of keeping a diary.

4. 日常 **rìcháng** daily
   这些 都 是 日常 必须 用 的 东西。
   Zhèxiē dōu shì rìcháng bìxū yòng de dōngxi.
   These are all the daily needs.

5. 日本 **Rìběn** Japan
   你 去过 日本 没有?
   Nǐ qùguo Rìběn méiyǒu?
   Have you been to Japan?

The sealing stroke is written last.   **4 strokes**

丨	冂	日	日								

126

年

nián year

The character combines the idea of *rice plant* 禾 and *person bent over* 人, to represent the *yearly* harvest.

Radical: 丿 'downward-left stroke'　　**Index # 4**

Character component: 年

Character configuration: ☐

Compounds, sentences and meanings

1. 年　**nián**　year
你 是 哪 年 去 美国 的?
Nǐ shì nǎ nián qù Měiguó de?
Which year did you go to America?

2. 去年　**qùnián**　last year
我 是 去年 开始 学 跳舞 的。
Wǒ shì qùnián kāishǐ xué tiàowǔ de.
I started learning to dance last year.

3. 年纪　**niánjì**　age
你 多 大 年纪 了?
Nǐ duō dà niánjì le?
How old are you?

4. 年轻　**niánqīng**　young
这 位 教授 看起来 很 年轻。
Zhè wèi jiàoshòu kànqilai hěn niánqīng.
This professor looks quite young.

5. 拜年　**bàinián**　pay a New Year visit
去 朋友 家 拜年 最好 别 忘了 带 礼物。
Qù péngyou jiā bàinián zuìhǎo bié wàngle dài lǐwù.
When paying New Year visits to friends, don't forget to bring along some gifts.

The lowest horizontal stroke is the longest.　　**6 strokes**

丿 𠂉 𠂇 𠂉 年 年

147

空 kōng/kòng empty; leisure time

The character combines *hole* 穴 and *work* 工 to suggest a room which encloses space. From this came the meaning of *emptiness*. By extension, it means *sky*.

Radical: 穴 'cave'　　　　　　　　　　　**Index # 110**

Character components: 穴 + 工　　　　　**Character configuration:**

Compounds, sentences and meanings

1. 空 **kōng** empty
   屋里 是 空 的,一个 人 也 没有。
   Wūli shì kōng de, yí ge rén yě méiyǒu.
   The room is empty; there's no one there.

2. 空气 **kōngqì** air
   城里 空气 污染 很 严重。
   Chéngli kōngqì wūrǎn hěn yánzhòng.
   Air pollution is very serious in the city.

3. 空调 **kōngtiáo** air conditioning
   进来, 外面 很 热,屋里 有 空调。
   Jìnlai, wàimian hěn rè, wūli yǒu kōngtiáo.
   Come in, it's hot outside, there's air conditioning inside the room.

4. 空儿 **kòngr** free time
   今天 下午 我 有 空儿。
   Jīntiān xiàwǔ wǒ yǒu kòngr.
   I'm free this afternoon.

5. 空闲 **kòngxián** leisure time
   等 你 空闲 的 时候, 我们
   Děng nǐ kòngxián de shíhou, wǒmen
   聊聊天。
   liáoliaotiān.
   The next time when you're free, let's chat.

The bottom horizontal stroke is longer.　　　　　　　　　8 strokes

丶	丷	宀	宁	穴	灾	空	空				

128

kàn   see, watch

The character expresses the idea of putting *hand* 手 above *eyes* 目 in order to *see* clearly.

Radical: 目 'eyes'

Index # 118

Character components: 手 + 目

Character configuration:

Compounds, sentences and meanings

1. **看   kàn**   see, look at
   你 对 这 件 事 怎么 看?
   Nǐ duì zhè jiàn shì zěnme kàn?
   What's your view on this matter?

2. **看电影   kàn diànyǐng**   see a movie
   今晚 我 去 看 电影。
   Jīnwǎn wǒ qù kàn diànyǐng.
   I'm going to see a movie tonight.

3. **看书   kànshū**   read books
   我 喜欢 看书。
   Wǒ xǐhuan kànshū.
   I like to read.

4. **看见   kànjiàn**   see
   我 今天 在 车站 看见 她。
   Wǒ jīntiān zài chēzhàn kànjiàn tā.
   I saw her at the bus stop today.

5. **看来   kànlái**   it seems
   看来 他 还 没 拿定 主意。
   Kànlái tā hái méi nádìng zhǔyi.
   It looks as if he hasn't made up his mind.

The first stroke travels from right to left.   **9 strokes**

一	二	三	手	禾	看	看	看	看					

电 **diǎn** electricity

The character depicted a flash of *lightning*. The full form has *rain* 雨 on top to indicate that rain and lightning come together. From lightning *electricity* is derived.

Radical: ∟ 'vertical-bend-hook'   **Index # 5**

Character components: 日 + ∟   **Character configuration:** ☐

Compounds, sentences and meanings

1. 电 **diǎn** electricity
   电门 有 毛病, 电了 我 一下。
   Diǎnmén yǔ máobìng, diǎnle wǒ yíxià.
   There was something wrong with the switch and I got a shock.

2. 电影 **diànyǐng** movie
   我 喜欢 看 中国 电影。
   Wǒ xǐhuan kàn Zhōngguó diànyǐng.
   I like to see Chinese movies.

3. 电视 **diànshì** television
   今晚 电视 有 什么 好 节目?
   Jīnwǎn diànshì yǒu shénme hǎo jiēmù?
   Are there any good programs on TV tonight?

4. 电脑 **diànnǎo** computer
   现在 电脑 在 中国 很 普及。
   Xiānzài diànnǎo zài Zhōngguó hěn pǔjí.
   Computers are now common in China.

5. 电话 **diànhuà** telephone
   今晚 请 给 我 回 个 电话。
   Jīnwǎn qǐng gěi wǒ huí ge diànhuà.
   Please give me a call tonight.

The horizontal lines are equally spaced.   **5 strokes**

㇀	冂	冃	日	电							

130

影

 yǐng   shadow

The character combines *sun* 日, *feathery* 彡 and the phonetic 京 to give the meaning of *shadow*.

Radical: 彡 'feathery'

Index # 55

Character components: 日 + 京 + 彡

Character configuration: ⊟

Compounds, sentences and meanings

1. **影** **yǐng** shadow
   听说 他 是 回来了,可是 还 没 看见
   Tīngshuō tā shì huílai le, kěshì hái méi kànjiàn
   他的 影儿。
   tāde yǐngr.
   I heard that he's back, but I haven't seen any sign of him yet.

2. **影迷** **yǐngmí** movie fan
   他 喜欢 看 电影, 是 个 影迷。
   Tā xǐhuan kàn diànyǐng, shì ge yǐngmí.
   He's fond of movies, he's a movie fan.

3. **影印** **yǐngyìn** photocopy
   请 给 我 影印 两 份。
   Qǐng gěi wǒ yǐngyìn liǎng fèn.
   Please photocopy two copies for me.

4. **影响** **yǐngxiǎng** influence, effect
   吸烟 影响 健康。
   Xīyān yǐngxiǎng jiànkāng.
   Smoking affects health.

5. **合影** **héyǐng** take a photo together
   我们 照 个 合影 留念, 好 吗?
   Wǒmen zhào ge héyǐng liúniàn, hǎo ma?
   Let's take a photo together to mark the occasion, shall we?

The last three strokes slant downward, then left.   **15 strokes**

丶	冂	冋	日	旦	昰	昙	景	景	景	景	景	影
影	影											

A. Look at the 16-character grid and CIRCLE words or phrases. They can be written horizontally or vertically. Look at the circled characters in the Key if unsure. COPY the word or phrase next to the grid and write the pinyin and meaning.

					Word or phrase			**Pinyin**	**Meaning**
日	今	晚	吃		今	晚		jīnwǎn	tonight
明	天	月	看						
有	空	儿	电						
做	作	生	影						

B. Refer to the characters in the 16-character grid above and CONVERT the pinyin phrases into characters and check their English meaning in the Key.

(i)	Jīntiān shì Jiǔyuè-shíwǔrì.										
(ii)	Míngtiān shì wǒde shēngrì.										
(iii)	Jīnwǎn nǐ yǒu kòngr ma?										
(iv)	Wǒmen kàn diànyǐng zěnmeyàng?										

C. Match the Chinese words with their English meaning.

(i)

qù 年	understand
天 cái	date
天 qì	obvious
明 bai	talent
明 xiǎn	diary
日 qī	weather
日 jì	next month
下个月	last year

(ii)

年 qīng	read
空 qì	television
空 tiáo	computer
看 shū	young
看 jiàn	air
电 nǎo	photocopy
电 shì	air-conditioning
影 yìn	see

131

昨

zuó   yesterday

The character combines *sun* 日 and the phonetic 乍 to suggest the meaning of *yesterday*.

Radical: 日 'sun'

Index # 90

Character components: 日 + 乍

Character configuration:

Compounds, sentences and meanings

1. **昨天**   **zuótiān**   yesterday
   他 昨天 才 来过。
   Tā zuótiān cái láiguo.
   He came only yesterday.

2. **昨天的**   **zuótiān de**   yesterday's
   这 是 昨天 的 报。
   Zhè shì zuótiān de bào.
   This is yesterday's newspaper.

3. **昨日**   **zuórì**   yesterday
   他 昨日 才 来过。
   Tā zuórì cái láiguo.
   He came only yesterday.

4. **昨晚**   **zuówǎn**   last night
   昨晚 雨 下得 很 大,你 知道 吗?
   Zuówǎn yǔ xiàde hěn dà, nǐ zhīdao ma?
   It rained heavily last night, did you know?

5. **昨夜**   **zuóyè**   last night
   昨夜 雨 下得 很 大,你 知道 吗?
   Zuóyè yǔ xiàde hěn dà, nǐ zhīdao ma?
   It rained heavily last night, did you know?

The top horizontal stroke is longer than those below it.								9 strokes			
丨	冂	日	日	旷	昨	昨	昨	昨			

153

132

去 qù go

The character is the figure of a rice-container with a lid. Since the container becomes empty after the rice has been eaten, the character came to mean *to be gone*.

Radical: 厶 'private'   Index # 23
or   土 'earth'   Index # 40
Character components: 土 + 厶   **Character configuration:**

Compounds, sentences and meanings

1. **去 qù** go
   假期你到哪儿去玩儿？
   Jiàqī nǐ dào nǎr qù wánr?
   Where are you going during the holidays?

2. **去处 qùchù** place to go
   这是一个风景优美的去处。
   Zhè shì yí ge fēngjǐng yōuměi de qùchù.
   This is a scenic place to visit.

3. **去世 qùshì** (of grown-ups) die
   我父亲三年前去世了。
   Wǒ fùqin sān nián qián qùshì le.
   My father passed away three years ago.

4. **去年 qùnián** last year
   我是去年开始学跳舞的。
   Wǒ shì qùnián kāishǐ xué tiàowǔ de.
   I started learning to dance last year.

5. **拿去 náqù** take away
   谁把我的字典拿去了？
   Shéi bǎ wǒde zìdiǎn náqù le?
   Who's taken my dictionary?

The second horizontal stroke is longer.   5 strokes

一 十 土 去 去

xīng star

The character combines *sun* 日 and *seedling* 生 , a reference to emerging light. This then took on the meaning of *star*.

Radical: 日 'sun'　　　　　　　　**Index # 90**

Character components: 日 + 生

Character configuration:

Compounds, sentences and meanings

1. 星　**xīng**　star
   今晚 月 明 星 稀。
   Jīnwǎn yuè míng xīng xī.
   The moon is bright and the stars are sparse tonight.

2. 星期　**xīngqī**　week
   今天 星期几?
   Jīntiān xīngqījǐ?
   What day of the week is it today?

3. 这个星期　**zhè ge xīngqī**　this week
   这 个 星期 工作 比较 轻松。
   Zhè ge xīngqī gōngzuò bǐjiào qīngsōng.
   The workload is easy this week.

4. 上星期　**shàng xīngqī**　last week
   上 星期 我 度假 去了。
   Shàng xīngqī wǒ dùjià qù le.
   Last week I was on holiday.

5. 下星期　**xià xīngqī**　next week
   下 星期 我 比较 忙。
   Xià xīngqī wǒ bǐjiào máng.
   I'll be rather busy next week.

The *sun* component 日 should be written squarish.　　　**9 strokes**

丶	冖	冂	日	尸	臼	早	星	星				

期

qī   period of time

The character combines *month* 月 and the phonetic 其 to suggest *a period of time*.

Radical: 月 'moon/flesh'   **Index # 103**
or   其 'secondly'   **Index # 171**
Character components: 其 + 月   **Character configuration:** ⊟

Compounds, sentences and meanings

1. **期** qī period
   第一期 工程 已经 完成 了。
   Dìyī qī gōngchéng yǐjīng wánchéng le.
   The first phase of the project has been completed.

2. **期间** qījiān course
   他在 住院 期间 看了 很多 小说。
   Tā zài zhùyuàn qījiān kànle hěnduō xiǎoshuō.
   While in hospital, he read many novels.

3. **假期** jiàqī holiday
   假期你 有 什么 计划?
   Jiàqī nǐ yǒu shénme jìhuà?
   What plans do you have for your holidays?

4. **学期** xuéqī semester
   这个学期 功课 比较 轻松。
   Zhè ge xuéqī gōngkè bǐjiào qīngsōng.
   There's not much work this semester.

5. **到期** dàoqī expire
   我的 签证 下个月 到期。
   Wǒde qiānzhèng xià ge yuè dàoqī.
   My visa expires next month.

The third last stroke ends with a hook.   12 strokes

| 一 | 十 | 卄 | 廿 | 甘 | 其 | 其 | 其 | 期 | 期 | 期 | 期 | |

135

mǎi   every

The character combines *hairpin* ⼍ and *mother* 母 to give the idea of bearing children repeatedly. It came to mean *every*.

Radical: 母 'mother'

Index # 108

Character components: ⼍ + 母

Character configuration:

Compounds, sentences and meanings

1. 每 **měi**   every, each
   每 到 北京, 我 总 要 去 逛 一下
   Měi dào Běijīng, wǒ zǒng yào qù guàn yíxià
   长城。
   Chángchéng.
   Every time I am in Beijing, I have to visit the Great Wall.

2. 每每 **měiměi**   often
   他们 常 在一起, 每每 一谈 就 是
   Tāmen cháng zài yìqǐ, měiměi yì tán jiù shì
   半天。
   bàntiān.
   They often get together, and when they did, they'd talk for hours.

3. 每天 **měitiān**   everyday
   我 母亲 每天 都 去散步。
   Wǒ mǔqin měitiān dōu qù sànbù.
   My mother goes for a walk every day.

4. 每年 **měinián**   every year
   我 每年 都 去 旅行。
   Wǒ měinián dōu qù lǚxíng.
   I go for a trip every year.

5. 每个星期 **měi ge xīngqī**   every week
   她 每个 星期 都 请客。
   Tā měi ge xīngqī dōu qǐngkè.
   She entertains guests every week.

每 can be confused with 母.

7 strokes

ノ	⼍	仁	句	每	每	每					

136

进 *jìn* enter

Full form

進

The full form combines *movement* 辶 and *bird* 隹 to suggest rapid advance like a bird flying. It means *progress*.

Radical: 辶 'movement'

Index # 38

Character components: 辶 + 井

Character configuration:

Compounds, sentences and meanings

1. 进 jìn enter
   请 进!
   Qǐng jìn!
   Please come in!

2. 进来 jìnlai enter
   让 他 进来。
   Ràng tā jìnlai.
   Let him come in.

3. 进步 jìnbù make progress
   你 写 汉字 很 有 进步。
   Nǐ xiě Hànzì hěn yǒu jìnbù.
   You are making great progress in your Chinese character writing.

4. 进出口 jìnchūkǒu import & export
   她 在 一家 进出口 公司 工作。
   Tā zài yī jiā jìnchūkǒu gōngsī gōngzuò.
   She works in an import and export company.

5. 进行 jìnxíng be in progress
   工作 进行得 怎么样?
   Gōngzuò jìnxíngde zěnmeyàng?
   How are you getting on with your work?

The left vertical stroke slants to the left.

7 strokes

一	二	尹	井	丼	讲	进					

城

chéng city

The character combines *soil* 土 and the phonetic 成 to suggest the ancient idea of a walled city. It means *city*.

Radical: 土 'earth'   **Index # 40**

Character components: 土 + 成   **Character configuration:** ⊞

Compounds, sentences and meanings

1. 城 **chéng** city
   城里 的 商店 比较 高档。
   Chéngli de shāngdiàn bǐjiào gāodǎng.
   The shops in the city sell better quality goods.

2. 城乡 **chéngxiāng** town and country
   在 中国, 城乡 的 差别 很 大。
   Zài Zhōngguó, chéngxiāng de chābié hěn dà.
   There is quite a large difference between urban and rural areas in China.

3. 城市 **chéngshì** city
   上海 是 中国 最大的 城市。
   Shànghǎi shì Zhōngguó zuìdàde chéngshì.
   Shanghai is the largest city in China.

4. 进城 **jìnchéng** go to the city
   我 坐 地铁 进城。
   Wǒ zuò dìtiě jìnchéng.
   I take the subway to get to the city.

5. 长城 **Chángchéng** Great Wall of China
   我 终于 登上了 长城。
   Wǒ zhōngyú dēngshangle Chángchéng.
   I finally climbed the Great Wall of China.

The third stroke slants upward.   **9 strokes**

一	十	土	圠	圹	坊	城	城	城			

138   **Full form**

 mǎi   buy

The full form combines *net* ⺲ and *shells* 貝. Since shells were used for money, netting lots of shells meant being able to *buy* things.

Radical: 　 一 'horizontal-hook'　　　　**Index # 5**

Character components: 一 + 头　　　**Character configuration:** ▢

Compounds, sentences and meanings

1. 买 **mǎi** buy
   我 买了〈汉英 词典〉。
   Wǒ mǎile *Hànyīng Cídiǎn*.
   I've bought the Chinese-English Dictionary.

2. 买得起 **mǎideqǐ** can afford
   两百 元 不 太 贵, 我 买得起。
   Liǎngbǎi yuán bú tài guì, wǒ mǎideqǐ.
   ¥200 is not too much to pay, I can afford it.

3. 买不起 **mǎibuqǐ** can't afford
   五百 元 太 贵 了, 我 买不起。
   Wǔbǎi yuán tài guì le, wǒ mǎibuqǐ.
   ¥500 is too much, I can't afford it.

4. 买卖 **mǎimài** business (literally, buying and selling)
   我 父亲 是 做 买卖 的。
   Wǒ fùqin shì zuò mǎimài de.
   My father is a businessman.

5. 买不到 **mǎibudào** out of stock
   这 种 皮包 现在 买不到 了。
   Zhè zhǒng píbāo xiànzài mǎibudào le.
   You can't buy this kind of briefcase now.

End the last stroke firmly.　　　　　　　　**6 strokes**

一	亠	乛	三	买	买						

160

139

东

dōng east

Full form

東

The full form combines *tree* 木 and *sun* 日 to represent the morning sun rising in the *east* behind some tree branches.

Radical: 一 'horizontal stroke'

Index # 2

Character components: 一 + 乚 + 小

Character configuration: ☐

Compounds, sentences and meanings

1. 东 **dōng** east
   我 住 在 城 东。
   Wǒ zhù zài chéng dōng.
   I live in the eastern part of the city.

2. 东边 **dōngbian** east
   太阳 从 东边 升起来。
   Tàiyáng cóng dōngbian shēngqilai.
   The sun rises in the east.

3. 东南亚 **Dōngnányà** South-East Asia
   东南亚 有 很多 华人。
   Dōngnányà yǒu hěnduō Huárén.
   There are many Chinese in South-East Asia.

4. 东西 **dōngxi** thing (literally, east west)
   她 买 东西 去了。
   Tā mǎi dōngxi qù le.
   She's out shopping.

5. 房东 **fángdōng** landlord
   他 是 我的 房东。
   Tā shì wǒde fángdōng.
   He is my landlord.

The second stroke is a downward-left bend. **5 strokes**

一	十	左	夯	东							

140

西 **xī** west

The pictograph of a bird in a nest. A bird returns to its nest when the sun sets in the *west*.

Radical: 西 'west'   **Index # 139**

Character component: 西

Character configuration: ☐

Compounds, sentences and meanings

1. **西　xī**　west
   夕阳 西下。
   Xīyáng xī xià.
   The sun sets in the west.

2. **西方　Xīfāng**　the West
   澳大利亚是 西方 国家。
   Àodàlìyà shì Xīfāng guójiā.
   Australia is a Western country.

3. **西餐　Xīcān**　Western food
   你 喜欢 吃　中餐　还是 西餐?
   Nǐ xǐhuan chī Zhōngcān háishi Xīcān?
   Do you prefer Chinese or Western food?

4. **西药　Xīyào**　Western medicine
   在　中国　哪里可以 买到 西药?
   Zài Zhōngguó nǎli kěyǐ mǎidào Xīyào?
   Where can one buy Western medicine in China?

5. **西式　Xīshì**　Western style
   西式 快餐 在 北京 很 流行。
   Xīshì kuàicān zài Běijīng hěn liúxíng.
   Western style fast food is very popular in Beijing.

The inside right stroke bends.　　　　　　　　　　**6 strokes**

一	厂	冂	丏	西	西							

Quiz 14 (131–140)

A. Look at the 16-character grid and CIRCLE words or phrases. They can be written horizontally or vertically. Look at the circled characters in the Key if unsure. COPY the word or phrase next to the grid and write the pinyin and meaning.

星	每	都	做
期	昨	晚	买
了	去	天	东
进	城	里	西

	Word or phrase			Pinyin	Meaning
(i)	星	期		xīngqī	week
(ii)					
(iii)					
(iv)					

B. Refer to the characters in the 16-character grid above and CONVERT the pinyin phrases into characters and check their English meaning in the Key.

(i)	Zuótiān wǒ jìnchéng le.								
(ii)	Nǐ jìnchéng zuò shénme le?								
(iii)	Wǒ qù mǎi dōngxi le.								
(iv)	Měi Xīngqīliù wǒ dōu jìnchéng.								

C. Match the Chinese words with their English meaning.

(i)

jiā 期	in progress
去 chù	holiday
dào 期	go to the city
进 lai	city
进步	expire
进 xíng	come in
进城	place to go
城 shì	improvement

(ii)

买不起	thing
买卖	Western meal
东 nányà	can't afford
东 bian	business
东西	Western-style
西 fāng	east side
西 cān	South-East Asia
西 shì	the West

shāng commerce

The first two strokes of the character make up the radical while the rest is made up of two dots, the 3-sided frame and what goes inside it. The character looks like the face of a *merchant*.

Radical: 亠 'top of 六'　　　　　　　　**Index # 6**

Character components: 亠 + 丷 + 冂 + 口　　　**Character configuration:** ⊞

Compounds, sentences and meanings

1. **商 shāng** commerce
   中国　正在　发展　工商　企业。
   Zhōngguó zhèngzài fāzhǎn gōngshāng qǐyè.
   China is developing its industrial and commercial enterprises.

2. **商人 shāngrén** merchant
   现在　中国　商人　的 地位 提高 了。
   Xiànzài Zhōngguó shāngrén de dìwèi tígāo le.
   Nowadays the status of merchants in China is higher.

3. **商店 shāngdiàn** shop
   商店　几 点　开门？
   Shāngdiàn jǐ diǎn kāimén?
   What time does the shop open?

4. **商业 shāngyè** commerce
   上海　是 一个　商业　城市。
   Shànghǎi shì yí ge shāngyè chéngshì.
   Shanghai is a commercial city.

5. **商量 shāngliang** discuss
   我　有事儿要　跟 你　商量。
   Wǒ yǒu shìr yào gēn nǐ shāngliang.
   I have something to discuss with you.

The sixth stroke ends with a hook.　　　　**11 strokes**

| ` | 亠 | 六 | 立 | 产 | 肖 | 冎 | 肖 | 商 | 商 | 商 | | |

店 diàn shop

The character combines *broad* 广 and *arrange* 占 to suggest a place where objects are arranged and sold, i.e. a *shop*.

Radical: 广 'broad'　　　　　　　　　**Index # 36**

Character components: 广 + 占　　　　**Character configuration:**

Compounds, sentences and meanings

1. **店　diàn**　shop
   他 开了一个 什么 店？
   Tā kāile yī ge shénme diàn?
   What shop did he run?

2. **书店　shūdiàn**　bookshop
   书店 里 有 很多 人。
   Shūdiàn li yǒu hěnduō rén.
   There are lots of people in the bookshop.

3. **文具店　wénjùdiàn**　stationery shop
   附近 有 没有 文具店？
   Fùjìn yǒu méiyǒu wénjùdiàn?
   Is there a stationery shop nearby?

4. **服装店　fúzhuāngdiàn**　boutique
   这 家 服装店 的 衣服 很 特别。
   Zhè jiā fúzhuāngdiàn de yīfu hěn tèbié.
   The clothes in this boutique are quite special.

5. **店员　diànyuán**　shop assistant
   店员 的 服务 态度 很 热情。
   Diànyuán de fúwù tàidu hěn rèqíng.
   The shop assistants are very friendly.

占 can be confused with 古 .　　　　　　　　　　　**8 strokes**

、	二	广	广	庁	庄	店	店				

143

 máo   hair

The character represents an animal's furry tail held upright. It means *hair*.

Radical: 毛 'hair'

Index # 97

Character component: 毛

Character configuration: ☐

Compounds, sentences and meanings

1. 毛　máo　hair
   这 猫 长 得 一 身 好 毛。
   Zhè māo zhǎngde yī shēn hǎo máo.
   This cat has a fine coat of fur.

2. 毛衣　máoyī　woolen sweater
   今天 比较 冷，要 穿 毛衣。
   Jīntiān bǐjiào lěng, yào chuān máoyī.
   Today is quite cold, you need to wear a sweater.

3. 毛笔　máobǐ　writing brush
   我 会 用 毛笔 写字。
   Wǒ huì yòng máobǐ xiězì.
   I can write with a brush.

4. 毛病　máobìng　problem
   复印机 有 点 毛病。
   Fùyìnjī yǒu diǎn máobìng.
   There's something wrong with the photocopier.

5. 一毛（钱）　yī máo (qián)　ten cents
   报纸 一块 五毛 （钱） 一 份。
   Bàozhǐ yīkuài-wǔmáo (qián) yí fēn.
   The newspaper is $1.50 a copy.

Note the difference between 毛 and 手.　　　　4 strokes

⺊	⺒	三	毛								

144

 **yī** clothes

The character represents the figure of putting the neckbands together and means *garment*..

Radical: 衣 **'clothes'**

Index # 132

Character components: 亠 + 衣

Character configuration:

Compounds, sentences and meanings

1. **衣 yī** clothing
   老百姓 最 关心 的是 衣食住行。
   Lǎobǎixìng zuì guānxīn de shì yī-shí-zhù-xíng.
   Ordinary people are mainly concerned with clothing, food, shelter and transportation — the basic necessities of life.

2. **毛衣 máoyī** woolen sweater
   今天 比较 冷, 要 穿 毛衣。
   Jīntiān bǐjiào lěng, yào chuān máoyī.
   Today is quite cold, you need to wear a sweater.

3. **衣服 yīfu** clothes
   外边 冷, 多 穿 些 衣服。
   Wàibiān lěng, duō chuān xiē yīfu.
   It's cold outside. Put on more clothes.

4. **衣料 yīliào** material for clothing
   这 种 衣料 适合 做 裙子。
   Zhè zhǒng yīliào shìhé zuò qúnzi.
   This type of material is suitable for making skirts.

5. **衣架 yījià** coat hanger
   这里 有 没有 衣架?
   Zhèlǐ yǒu méiyǒu yījià?
   Are there any clothes hangers here?

The last stroke tapers off.   **6 strokes**

丶	亠	宀	犭	衣	衣				

145

 件　　**jiàn**　[classifier]; document

The character combines *person* 亻 and *cattle* 牛 to suggest a person counting cattle. It refers to a *unit in counting*.

Radical: 亻 'upright person'　　　　**Index # 19**

Character components: 亻 + 牛　　　　**Character configuration:**

Compounds, sentences and meanings

1. **件**　**jiàn**　classifier
   这 件 衣服 很 好看。
   Zhè jiàn yīfu hěn hǎokàn.
   This garment is very pretty.

2. **软件**　**ruǎnjiàn**　software
   这 是 盗版 软件，我 不要。
   Zhè shì dàobǎn ruǎnjiàn, wǒ bú yào.
   This is a pirated software, I don't want it.

3. **零件**　**língjiàn**　part
   新 的 零件 太 贵了, 买 二手 的 吧。
   Xīn de língjiàn tài guì le, mǎi èrshǒu de ba.
   New parts are too expensive, what if we buy second-hand ones?

4. **配件**　**pèijiàn**　fittings
   我们 需要 买 管子 配件。
   Wǒmen xūyào mǎi guǎnzi pèijiàn.
   We need to buy plumbing fittings.

5. **文件**　**wénjiàn**　document
   请 把 文件 放好，别 丢失了。
   Qǐng bǎ wénjiàn fànghǎo, biē diūshī le.
   Please put the document in a safe place, don't lose it.

The second horizontal stroke is longer.						6 strokes
丿	亻	亻	仁	仁	件	

146

qián money

Full form

The character combines *metal* 钅 and the phonetic 戋 to suggest the concept of *money*.

Radical: 钅 'metal'

Character components: 钅 + 戋

Index # 122

Character configuration:

Compounds, sentences and meanings

1. **钱** qián money
   你一个月的工资多少钱?
   Nǐ yí ge yuè de gōngzī duōshao qián?
   What's your monthly wage?

2. **钱包** qiánbāo wallet, purse
   他的钱包被贼抢了。
   Tāde qiánbāo bèi zéi qiǎng le.
   His wallet was snatched by a thief.

3. **有钱** yǒuqián wealthy
   她父母很有钱。
   Tā fùmǔ hěn yǒuqián.
   Her parents are very wealthy.

4. **零钱** língqián small change
   我要换点零钱。
   Wǒ yào huàn diǎn língqián.
   I want to get some small change.

5. **压岁钱** yāsuìqián money given to children
   during the Lunar New Year
   中国小孩过年都可以拿到
   Zhōngguó xiǎohái guònián dōu kěyǐ nádào
   很多压岁钱。
   hěnduō yāsuìqián.
   *Chinese children get quite a bit of gift money
   during the Lunar New Year.*

The last stroke appears at the top right corner.								10 strokes				
丿	𠂉	𠂒	𠂓	钅	钅	钅	钱	钱	钱			

百

bǎi   hundred

The character combines *one* 一 and *white* 白. It is believed that 白 once meant *hundred,* adding *one* 一 made it *one hundred.*

Radical:　一 'horizontal stroke'　　　　**Index # 2**

or　　　　白 'white'　　　　　　　　　**Index # 147**

Character components:　一 + 白　　　　**Character configuration:** ☐

Compounds, sentences and meanings

1. **百**　**bǎi**　hundred
   我 认识 两百 个 字。
   Wǒ rènshi liǎngbǎi ge zì.
   I know 200 characters.

2. **百分之百**　**bǎifēnzhībǎi**　absolutely (literally, 100%)
   这 是 百分之百 的　谎话!
   Zhè shì bǎifēnzhībǎi de huǎnghuà!
   That's an absolute lie!

3. **百分点**　**bǎifēndiǎn**　1% point
   银行 利息 增加了 半 个 百分点。
   Yínháng lìxī zēngjiāle bàn ge bǎifēndiǎn.
   Bank interest has increased by half a percentage point.

4. **百货**　**bǎihuò**　general merchandise
   这 是 一家 高档　的 百货 公司。
   Zhè shì yì jiā gāodǎng de bǎihuò gōngsī.
   This is an up-market department store.

5. **百万**　**bǎiwàn**　million (literally, a hundred ten thousands)
   她 想 嫁 给 百万 富翁。
   Tā xiǎng jià gěi bǎiwàn fùwēng.
   She wants to marry a millionaire.

The top horizontal stroke is longer.	6 strokes

一　丆　丆　百　百　百

147

170

Full form

块   **kuài**   classifier

塊

The character combines *earth* 土 and the phonetic 夬 to suggest the idea of a *lump* or *piece*. The full form uses a different phonetic.

Radical: 土 'earth'   **Index # 40**

Character components: 土 + 夬   **Character configuration:** ⊟

Compounds, sentences and meanings

1. **块 kuài** piece
   她 吃了 两 块 面包。
   Tā chīle liǎng kuài miànbāo.
   She ate two pieces of bread.

2. **鱼块 yúkuài** fish pieces
   我 要了 一个 糖醋 鱼块。
   Wǒ yàole yí ge tángcù yúkuài.
   I've ordered a plate of sweet and sour fish.

3. **一块钱 yí kuài qián** a dollar (literally, a piece of money)
   她 一个 月 的 工资 五百 块 钱。
   Tā yí ge yuè de gōngzī wǔbǎi kuài qián.
   Her monthly wage is 500 dollars.

4. **一块儿 yíkuàir** together
   你 有 兴趣 跟 我们 一块儿 去 吗?
   Nǐ yǒu xìngqù gēn wǒmen yíkuàir qù ma?
   Would you be interested in coming along with us?

5. **方块字 fāngkuàizì** square characters
   汉字 是 方块字,很 难 记。
   Hànzì shì fāngkuàizì, hěn nán jì.
   Chinese characters are square-shaped characters, so they are hard to remember.

The last stroke tapers off.   **7 strokes**

一	十	土	圠	圠	块	块					

biàn/pián   convenient; cheap

The character combines *person* 亻 and the phonetic 更 to give two meanings: *convenient* and *cheap*. By itself, it is used as an adverb in much the same way as *jiù* 就 .

Radical: 亻 'upright person'   **Index # 19**

Character components: 亻 + 更   **Character configuration:**

Compounds, sentences and meanings

1. **便   biàn**   then
   这 几 天 不 是 刮风， 便 是 下雨。
   Zhè jǐ tiān bú shì guāfēng, biàn shì xiàyǔ.
   During the last few days, if it was not windy, then it was raining.

2. **方便   fāngbiàn**   convenient
   什么 时候 方便， 什么 时候 来。
   Shénme shíhou fāngbiàn, shénme shíhou lái.
   Drop in whenever it's convenient.

3. **便利   biànlì**   convenient
   这里 交通 便利。
   Zhèlǐ jiāotōng biànlì.
   Transport is convenient here.

4. **便条   biàntiáo**   short note
   你 给 他 写 个 便条 吧。
   Nǐ gěi tā xiě ge biàntiáo ba.
   Why don't you write him a note?

5. **便宜   piányi**   cheap
   这里 的 东西 价钱 很 便宜。
   Zhèlǐ de dōngxi jiàqián hěn piányi.
   The things here are really inexpensive.

The second last stroke starts under the horizontal stroke.   **9 strokes**

ノ	亻	亻	伫	�	佰	佰	便	便				

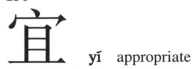

yí appropriate

The character combines *roof* 宀 and the phonetic 且 to suggest the meaning of *appropriate*. When combined with 便 it is pronounced in the neutral tone.

Radical: 宀 'roof'   **Index # 34**

Character components: 宀 + 且   **Character configuration:**

Compounds, sentences and meanings

1. 宜 **yí** appropriate
   老幼 咸宜。
   Lǎoyòu xiányí.
   Suitable for both young and old.

2. 不宜 **bùyí** not fitting
   对 孩子 不宜 要求 过 高。
   Duì háizi bùyí yāoqiú guò gāo.
   You shouldn't ask too much of a child.

3. 宜人 **yírén** pleasant
   这里 气候 宜人。
   Zhèlǐ qìhòu yírén.
   The weather's pleasant here.

4. 便宜 **piányi** inexpensive
   这里 的 东西 价钱 很 便宜。
   Zhèlǐ de dōngxi jiàqián hěn piányi.
   The things here are really inexpensive.

5. 适宜 **shìyí** appropriate
   游泳 对 老年人 很 适宜。
   Yóuyǒng duì lǎoniánrén hěn shìyí.
   Swimming is good for old people.

The last horizontal stroke is longer.   8 strokes

、	宀	宀	宁	宁	宁	宜	宜				

Quiz 15 (141–150)

A. Look at the 16-character grid and CIRCLE words or phrases. They can be written horizontally or vertically. Look at the circled characters in the Key if unsure. COPY the word or phrase next to the grid and write the pinyin and meaning.

	Word or phrase			Pinyin	Meaning
一 百 城 进	一	百		yībǎi	one hundred
钱 商 便 宜					
件 店 块 毛					
西 东 生 衣					

B. Refer to the characters in the 16-character grid above and CONVERT the pinyin phrases into characters and check their English meaning in the Key.

(i)	Chéngli shāngdiàn dōngxi guì ma?									
(ii)	Zhè jiàn máoyī hěn piányi.									
(iii)	Liǎngbǎi kuài qián yī jiàn, guì ma?									
(iv)	Wǒ mǎi liǎng jiàn, piányi diǎnr.									

C. Match the Chinese words with English meaning.

(i)

文 jù 店	clothes
文件	woolen sweater
shū 店	stationery shop
衣 fu	document
毛 bǐ	writing brush
毛衣	coat hanger
五毛 qián	book shop
衣 jià	50 cents

(ii)

便宜	wallet, purse
fāng 便	inexpensive
fāng 块字	commerce
百 huò	convenient
有钱	discuss
钱 bāo	merchandise
商 yè	well-off
商 liang	Chinese characters

174

CHARACTER BUILDING 3 (101–150)

A. Memorize each of the following radicals and their English names. As a review exercise, write the pinyin and English meaning.

1. [一]   'horizontal stroke'

    上 (_____) _____ ; 下 (_____) _____ ;

    东 (_____) _____ ; 百 (_____) _____ .

2. [丿]   'downward-left stroke'

    午 (_____) _____ ; 年 (_____) _____ .

3. [乛]   'horizontal hook'

    了 (_____) _____ ; 买 (_____) _____ .

4. [乚]   'vertical-bend hook'

    电 (_____) _____ ; 也 (_____) _____ .

5. [亠]   'top of 六 '

    商 (_____) _____ ; 六 (_____) _____ .

6. [八]   'eight'

    半 (_____) _____ ; 分 (_____) _____ ;

7. [人]   'people'

    人 (_____) _____ ; 今 (_____) _____ ;

    会 (_____) _____ ; 个 (_____) _____ .

8. [亻]   'upright person'

    候 (_____) _____ ; 件 (_____) _____ ;

    便 (_____) _____ ; 们 (_____) _____ .

9. [口]   'mouth'

    吃 (_____) _____ ; 哪 (_____) _____ ;

    名 (_____) _____ ; 吗 (_____) _____ .

10. [宀]   'roof'

    宜 (_____) _____ ; 字 (_____) _____ .

11. [广]   'broad'

    床 (_____) _____ ; 店 (_____) _____ .

12. [辶]   'movement'

    进 (_____) _____ ; 还 (_____) _____ ;

    这 (_____) _____ .

13. ［土］ 'earth'

在 (_____) _____ ；城 (_____) _____ ；

块 (_____) _____ .

14. ［日］ 'sun'

日 (_____) _____ ；早 (_____) _____ ；

明 (_____) _____ ；晚 (_____) _____ .

昨 (_____) _____ ；星 (_____) _____ ；

时 (_____) _____ .

15. ［月］ 'moon/flesh'

月 (_____) _____ ；期 (_____) _____ .

16. ［钅］ 'metal'

钟 (_____) _____ ；钱 (_____) _____ .

17. ［母］ 'mother'

每 (_____) _____ ；母 (_____) _____ .

B. Write the pinyin and meaning against the characters classified under the following radicals.

1. ［厶］ 'private'   去   (_____) _____

2. ［饣］ 'food'   饭   (_____) _____

3. ［大］ 'big'   天   (_____) _____

4. ［彡］ 'feathery'   影   (_____) _____

5. ［止］ 'stop'   步   (_____) _____

6. ［毛］ 'hair'   毛   (_____) _____

7. ［穴］ 'cave'   空   (_____) _____

8. ［衣］ 'clothing'   衣   (_____) _____

9. ［西］ 'west'   西   (_____) _____

10. ［目］ 'eye'   看   (_____) _____

11. ［足］ 'foot'   跑   (_____) _____

12. ［走］ 'walk'   起   (_____) _____

176

C. Write the pinyin and meaning against the characters which share the following components. (Note that these components are not necessarily used as radicals.)

1.　［工］　工（＿＿＿）＿＿＿＿；　空（＿＿＿）＿＿＿＿.

2.　［土］　去（＿＿＿）＿＿＿＿；　在（＿＿＿）＿＿＿＿.

3.　［木］　床（＿＿＿）＿＿＿＿；　样（＿＿＿）＿＿＿＿.

4.　［日］　早（＿＿＿）＿＿＿＿；　影（＿＿＿）＿＿＿＿.
　　　　　　星（＿＿＿）＿＿＿＿.

5.　［月］　期（＿＿＿）＿＿＿＿；　明（＿＿＿）＿＿＿＿.

6.　［且］　宜（＿＿＿）＿＿＿＿；　姐（＿＿＿）＿＿＿＿.

7.　［乍］　昨（＿＿＿）＿＿＿＿；　怎（＿＿＿）＿＿＿＿.

REVIEW 3 (101–150)

The following are words and phrases classified under parts of speech. Write the pinyin and meaning.

Interrogative　什么时候（＿＿＿＿＿）＿＿＿＿＿.
pronouns

Nouns	天（＿＿＿）＿＿＿＿；	日（＿＿＿）＿＿＿＿；
	星期（＿＿＿）＿＿＿＿；	月（＿＿＿）＿＿＿＿；
	年（＿＿＿）＿＿＿＿；	钱（＿＿＿）＿＿＿＿；
	床（＿＿＿）＿＿＿＿；	城（＿＿＿）＿＿＿＿；
	学期（＿＿＿）＿＿＿＿；	日期（＿＿＿）＿＿＿＿；
	商店（＿＿＿）＿＿＿＿；	东西（＿＿＿）＿＿＿＿；
	文件（＿＿＿）＿＿＿＿；	毛衣（＿＿＿）＿＿＿＿；
	电影（＿＿＿）＿＿＿＿；	空儿（＿＿＿）＿＿＿＿；
	小时（＿＿＿）＿＿＿＿；	分钟（＿＿＿）＿＿＿＿.

Verbs	吃（＿＿＿）＿＿＿＿；	买（＿＿＿）＿＿＿＿；
	看（＿＿＿）＿＿＿＿；	去（＿＿＿）＿＿＿＿；
	跑步（＿＿＿）＿＿＿＿；	起床（＿＿＿）＿＿＿＿.

Numbers	半（＿＿＿）＿＿＿＿；	百（＿＿＿）＿＿＿＿.

Classifiers	块（＿＿＿）＿＿＿＿；	毛（＿＿＿）＿＿＿＿；
	件（＿＿＿）＿＿＿＿.	

Adjectives	早 (_____) _____ ;	晚 (_____) _____ ;
	好吃 (_____) _____ ;	有钱 (_____) _____ ;
	便宜 (_____) _____ ;	空 (_____) _____ .

Time words	现在 (_____) _____ ;	昨天 (_____) _____ ;
(Adverbs)	今天 (_____) _____ ;	明天 (_____) _____ ;
	上午 (_____) _____ ;	下午 (_____) _____ ;
	早上 (_____) _____ ;	晚上 (_____) _____ ;
	每天 (_____) _____ ;	今年 (_____) _____ ;
	去年 (_____) _____ ;	明年 (_____) _____ ;
	有时候 (_____) _____ ;	
	上（个）星期 (_____) _____ ;	
	这（个）星期 (_____) _____ ;	
	下（个）星期 (_____) _____ ;	

| Adverbs | 一起 (_____) _____ ; 一块儿 (_____) _____ . |

| Prepositions | 在 (_____) _____ . |

| Particles | 了 (_____) _____ . |

WORD/SENTENCE PUZZLE 3

Find and CIRCLE words, phrases or sentences hidden in the puzzle. They can be found horizontally from left to right or vertically. The lines across and down are indicated by numbers. Write the meaning next to the pinyin. The first one is done for you.

ACROSS (left to right)

1. Jīntiān shì Jiǔyuè Èrshíwǔrì.   *Today is September 25th.*
3. Wǎnshang nǐ zuò shénme?   _____
5. Wǒmen měige Xīngqītiān dōu jìnchéng.   _____
8. Nǐ měitiān jǐ diǎn qǐchuáng?   _____
10. Míngtiān wǒ qù mǎi dōngxi.   _____

DOWN

1. Jīntiān wǎnshang wǒ yǒu kòng.   _____
2. Nǐ měitiān dōu qù pǎobù ma?   _____
4. Zuótiān nǐ qù kàn diànyǐng le ma?   _____
6. Dōngxi hěn piányi.   _____
8. (i)   Wǔbǎi kuài   _____
8. (ii) Shāngdiàn zài nǎr?   _____
10. Chéngli de máoyī duōshao qián?   _____

	1	2	3	4	5	6	7	8	9	10
1	今	天	是	九	月	二	十	五	日	人
2	天	名	姓	贵	朋	识	英	百	样	怎
3	晚	上	你	做	什	么	和	块	亲	吃
4	上	字	认	友	学	没	文	老	两	早
5	我	们	每	个	星	期	天	都	进	城
6	有	时	体	谢	期	年	父	医	母	里
7	空	男	小	昨	大	岁	比	饭	生	的
8	候	你	每	天	几	点	起	床	弟	毛
9	儿	每	子	你	身	还	女	妹	师	衣
10	明	天	我	去	买	东	西	猫	问	多
11	下	都	上	看	年	西	姐	商	只	少
12	贵	去	半	电	会	很	在	店	请	钱
13	中	跑	现	影	里	便	午	在	汉	忙
14	家	步	妈	了	爸	宜	分	哪	写	这
15	英	吗	美	吗	哪	谁	说	儿	狗	不

151

脑 **nǎo** brain

Full form

腦

The character combines *flesh* 月 and the phonetic 囟 to refer to the *brain*.

Radical: 月 'flesh/moon'

Index # 103

Character components: 月 + 囟

Character configuration:

Compounds, sentences and meanings

1. 脑 **nǎo** brain
   我 今天 用 脑 过度。
   Wǒ jīntiān yòng nǎo guòdù.
   I overtaxed my brain today.

2. 脑筋 **nǎojīn** brain
   多 动 脑筋 才 能 解决 问题。
   Duō dòng nǎojīn cái néng jiějué wèntí.
   By exercising one's brain more often, one can resolve problems.

3. 脑汁 **nǎozhī** brain
   我 绞尽 脑汁 也 想不出 解决 方法。
   Wǒ jiǎojìn nǎozhī yě xiǎngbuchū jiějué fāngfǎ.
   I racked my brain but I still couldn't work it out.

4. 电脑 **diànnǎo** computer
   她 刚 买了一台 电脑。
   Tā gāng mǎile yì tái diànnǎo.
   She just bought a computer.

5. 豆腐脑儿 **dòufu'nǎor** jellied beancurd
   我 喜欢 吃 豆腐 脑儿。
   Wǒ xǐhuan chī dòufu'nǎor.
   I'm fond of jellied beancurd.

The second last stroke is a vertical bend.							10 strokes			
丿	刀	月	月	月ˋ	肵	肵	肑	脑	脑			

152

台   **tái**   platform; [classifier]

The character combines *mouth* 口 and *private* 厶 to suggest the idea of *platform*. The whole character is used as a phonetic.

Radical: 厶 'private'   **Index # 23**

or   口 'mouth'   **Index # 50**

Character components: 厶 + 口   **Character configuration:**

Compounds, sentences and meanings

1. **台**   **tái**   classifier
   我 想 买 一 台 新 电脑。
   Wǒ xiǎng mǎi yì tái xīn diànnǎo.
   I want to buy a new computer.

2. **台阶**   **táijiē**   steps, stairs
   台阶 真 多, 把 我 累死了。
   Táijiē zhēn duō, bǎ wǒ lèisǐ le.
   There are so many steps, I'm dead tired.

3. **台湾**   **Táiwān**   Taiwan
   我 没 去过 台湾。
   Wǒ méi qùguo Táiwān.
   I haven't been to Taiwan.

4. **台北**   **Táiběi**   Taipei
   听说 台北 空气 污染 很 严重。
   Tīngshuō Táiběi kōngqì wūrǎn hěn yánzhòng.
   I've heard that air pollution in Taipei is really serious.

5. **台球**   **táiqiú**   billiards
   台球 在 中国 很 流行。
   Táiqiú zài Zhōngguó hěn liúxíng.
   Billiards are quite popular in China.

The top and bottom components are the same size.										5 strokes
厶	厶	台	台	台						

181

Full form

卖　mài　sell

賣

The simplified form combines *ten* 十 and *buy* 买 to suggest the idea of *sell*. Associate the extra component with the 4th tone to mark the meaning of *sell*.

Radical: 十 'ten'

Index # 11

Character components: 十 + 买

Character configuration:

Compounds, sentences and meanings

1. 卖　mài　sell
   这 台 电视机 怎么 卖? / 这 台 电视机
   Zhè tái diànshìjī zěnme mài? / Zhè tái diànshìjī
   卖 多少 钱?
   mài duōshao qián?
   How much is this TV set?

2. 卖力　màilì　exert all one's strength
   她 做事 很 卖力。
   Tā zuòshì hěn màilì.
   She puts in her best when she works.

3. 卖座　màizuò　draw large audiences
   (literally, seat seller)
   那部 电影 可 卖座 啦。
   Nà bù diànyǐng kě màizuò la.
   That movie drew audiences.

4. 卖弄　màinòng　show off one's cleverness
   他 喜欢 卖弄 小 聪明。
   Tā xǐhuan màinòng xiǎo cōngmíng.
   He likes to show off his smartness.

5. 买卖　mǎimài　business
   我 父亲 是 做 买卖 的。
   Wǒ fùqin shì zuò mǎimài de.
   My father is a businessman.

End the last stroke firmly.　　　　　　　　　**8 strokes**

一	十	士	击	吏	吏	卖	卖				

154

千 qiān   thousand

The character combines *person* 亻 and *one* 一 to represent many people in a crowd. It came to mean a *thousand*.

Radical: 丿 'downward-left stroke'   **Index # 4**

Character components: 丿 + 十   **Character configuration:** ☐

Compounds, sentences and meanings

1. 千 **qiān** thousand
   这 是 一千 块钱， 请 你 点一点。
   Zhè shì yīqiān kuài qián, qǐng nǐ diǎnyidiǎn.
   This is altogether 1000 dollars, please check it.

2. 千里 **qiānlǐ** a long distance (literally, a thousand miles)
   千里 之行， 始于足下。
   Qiānlǐ zhī xíng, shǐ yú zú xià.
   A thousand-li journey begins with the first step.

3. 千万 **qiānwàn** be sure to
   千万 要 小心 啊!
   Qiānwàn yào xiǎoxīn a!
   Do be careful!

4. 千方百计 **qiānfāng-bǎijì** in a thousand and one ways
   他 千方 百计地 请 好 大夫 看病。
   Tā qiānfāng-bǎijì de qǐng hǎo dàifu kànbìng.
   He goes all out to find good doctors to treat his illness.

5. 千篇一律 **qiān piān yī lǜ** following the same pattern
   那些 文章 千 篇 一律， 没有
   Nàxiē wénzhāng qiān piān yī lǜ, méiyǒu
   什么 新 东西。
   shénme xīn dōngxi.
   Those articles are like the rest; they offer nothing new.

The top stroke sweeps down to the left.	3 strokes

丿 二 千

万 wàn   ten thousand

Full form

萬

The full form depicted insects in grass which were counted in their tens of thousands. Thus the idea of *ten thousand*.

Radical: 一 'horizontal stroke'   **Index # 2**

Character component: 万

Character configuration: ☐

Compounds, sentences and meanings

1. **万 wàn** ten thousand
   买 一 辆 小 汽车 要 八 万 元。
   Mǎi yī liàng xiǎo qìchē yào bā wàn yuán.
   It costs ¥80,000 to buy a small car.

2. **百万 bǎiwàn** million
   她 想 嫁 给 百万 富翁。
   Tā xiǎng jià gěi bǎiwàn fūwēng.
   She wants to marry a millionaire.

3. **一千万 yī qiānwàn** 10 million
   北京 的 人口 超过 一千万。
   Běijīng de rénkǒu chāoguò yìqiānwàn.
   Beijing's population exceeds 10 million.

4. **万事 wànshì** all things
   万事 起头 难。
   Wànshì qǐtóu nán.
   Everything is difficult in the beginning.

5. **万一 wànyī** just in case
   万一 有 人 找 我, 就 请 他 留 个 条。
   Wànyī yǒu rén zhǎo wǒ, jiù qǐng tā liú ge tiáo.
   If someone looks for me, please ask him to leave a message.

The last stroke ends with a hook.   **3 strokes**

一	丁	万									

156

元　　yuán　　first; Chinese dollar

The character originally represented the figure of a person's head and neck, it symbolizes *origin* and *source*.

Radical: 二 'two'　　　　　　　　**Index # 10**

or 儿 'son'　　　　　　　　　　**Index # 21**

Character components: 二 + 儿　　**Character configuration:**

Compounds, sentences and meanings

1. 元　**yuán**　dollar
   买 一 辆 小 汽车 要 八 万 元。
   Mǎi yì liàng xiǎo qìchē yào bā wàn yuán.
   It costs ¥80,000 to buy a small car.

2. 美元　**Měiyuán**　American dollars
   一百 美元 兑换 九百 人民币。
   Yībǎi Měiyuán duìhuàn jiǔbǎi Rénmínbì.
   US$100 cxchangcs for ¥900.

3. 元旦　**Yuándàn**　New Year's Day
   一月 一号 是 元旦, 放假 一 天。
   Yīyuè-yīhào shì Yuándàn, fàngjià yì tiān.
   January 1st, being New Year's Day, is a holiday.

4. 公元　**Gōngyuán**　A.D., the Christian era
   公元 一九一二 年 民 国 建立。
   Gōngyuán yījiǔyī'èr nián Mín'guó jiànlì.
   In 1912, the Republic of China was established.

5. 公元前　**Gōngyuánqián**　B.C. (before the Christian era)
   公元前 二二一 年　秦始皇
   Gōngyuánqián èr'èryī'nián Qínshǐhuáng
   统一 中国。
   tǒngyī Zhōngguó.
   In 221 B.C. the Qin Emperor unified China.

The lower horizontal stroke is longer.　　　　　　　**4 strokes**

一　二　于　元

157

 太 **tài** too

The character combines *big* 大 and a dot to signify the idea of *bigger*. By extension, *super* and *excessive* were derived.

Radical: 大 'big'　　　　　　　**Index # 43**

Character components: 大 + 、　　　**Character configuration:** ☐

Compounds, sentences and meanings

1. **太　tài** too
   太 贵了,可以 便宜点儿 吗?
   Tài guì le, kěyǐ piányidiǎnr ma?
   It's too expensive! Can you make it cheaper?

2. **太阳　tàiyáng** the sun
   你 看, 太阳 出来了。
   Nǐ kàn, tàiyáng chūlai le.
   Look, the sun is out.

3. **太空　tàikōng** outer space
   美国 发明 太空梭。
   Měiguó fāmíng tàikōngsuō.
   The Americans invented the space shuttle.

4. **太平洋　Tàipíngyáng** the Pacific Ocean
   中国 在 太平洋 西边。
   Zhōngguó zài Tàipíngyáng xībian.
   China is situated at the west of the Pacific Ocean.

5. **太极拳　tàijíquán** Taichi
   我 会 打太极拳, 可是 打得 不 好。
   Wǒ huì dǎ tàijíquán, kěshì dǎde bù hǎo.
   I can do Taichi, but not very well.

The last stroke ends firmly.　　　　　**4 strokes**

一 ナ 大 太

186

就 jiù right away

The character combines *capital city* 京 and the phonetic 尤 to suggest the idea of *right away*.

Radical: 亠 'top of 六'

Index # 6

Character components: 京 + 尤

Character configuration:

Compounds, sentences and meanings

1. **就 jiù** as early as
   今天 我 七 点钟 就 来 了。
   Jīntiān wǒ qī diǎnzhōng jiù lái le.
   I was here as early as 7 o'clock today.

2. **就是 jiùshì** exactly
   就 是 嘛, 我 也 是 这么 想 的。
   Jiù shì ma, wǒ yě shì zhème xiǎng de.
   Precisely, that's just what I had in mind.

3. **就手 jiùshǒu** while you are at it
   就手 把 门 关上。
   Jiùshǒu bǎ mén guānshàng.
   Close the door behind you.

4. **就要 jiùyào** be going to
   火车 就要 开 了。
   Huǒchē jiùyào kāi le.
   The train is about to leave.

5. **就算 jiùsuàn** even if
   就算 你 等了 半 个 钟头, 也 不
   Jiùsuàn nǐ děngle bàn ge zhōngtóu, yě bù
   应该 发 这么 大 的 脾气 吧。
   yīnggāi fā zhème dà de píqi ba.
   Granted that you have waited for half an hour, still there is no reason to blow your top.

The second last stroke ends with a hook.

12 strokes

丶	二	亠	亡	古	亨	京	京	京	就	就	就

Full form

吧　ba　[particle]

罢

The character combines *mouth* 口 and the phonetic 巴 to indicate a *suggestion*.

Radical: 口 'mouth'

Index # 6

Character components: 口 + 巴

Character configuration:

Compounds, sentences and meanings

1. 吧　ba　*suggestion* [particle]
   我们 走 吧。
   Wǒmen zǒu ba.
   Let's go.

2. 就 ... 吧　jiù ... ba　*consent or approval*
   明天 就 明天 吧。
   Míngtiān jiù míngtiān ba.
   All right, let's make it tomorrow.

3. 会 ... 吧　huì ... ba　*confirmation*
   他 会 来吧?
   Tā huì lái ba?
   He'll come, won't he?

4. 好像是 ... 吧　hǎoxiàng shì ... ba　*doubt or uncertainty*
   他 好像 是 这么 说 的 吧。
   Tā hǎoxiàng shì zhème shuō de ba.
   It seems that's what he said.

5. ... 吧 , ... 吧 ,　...ba, ... ba,　*marking a pause*
   去吧, 不好; 不去吧, 也不好。
   Qù ba, bùhǎo; búqù ba, yě bùhǎo.
   If I go, it's no good; if I don't, it's no good either.

Finish the last stroke with a hook.　　　　　**7 strokes**

丨	丨	口	口	口	口	吧						

160

 líng   zero

The character 零 combines *rain* 雨 and the phonetic 令 to suggest *fragmentary*. It also means *zero*.

Radical: 雨 'rain'

Index # 172

Character components: 雨 + 令

Character configuration:

Compounds, sentences and meanings

1. 零 líng zero
   现在 六点 零 八分。
   Xiànzài liùdiǎn-líng-bāfēn.
   The time now is 6:08.

2. 零下 língxià below zero
   今天 气温 是 摄氏 零下 五度。
   Jīntiān qìwēn shì shèshì língxià wǔ dù.
   Today's temperature is 5°C below zero.

3. 零钱 língqián small change
   我 要 换 点 零钱。
   Wǒ yào huàn diǎn língqián.
   I want to get some small change.

4. 零碎 língsuì piecemeal
   我 还 有 点儿 零碎 事情 没有
   Wǒ hái yǒu diǎnr língsuì shìqing méiyǒu
   办完。
   bànwán.
   I still have some loose ends to tie up.

5. 零用钱 língyòngqián pocket money
   你 一个 月 给 孩子 多少 零用钱?
   Nǐ yí ge yuè gěi háizi duōshao língyòngqián?
   How much pocket money do you give your child a month?

Finish the last stroke firmly.   13 strokes

一	厂	产	币	币	币	雨	零	雾	雾	雾	零	零

Quiz 16 (151–160)

A. Look at the 16-character grid and CIRCLE words or phrases. They can written horizontally or vertically. Look at the encircled characters in the Key if unsure. COPY the word or phrase next to the grid and write the pinyin and meaning.

			Word or phrase	**Pinyin**	**Meaning**
元 太 贵 了			(i) 太 贵 了	Tài guì le!	It's too expensive!
千 卖 怎 买			(ii)		
电 万 么 东			(iii)		
脑 就 样 西			(iv)		

B. Refer to the characters in the 16-character grid above and CONVERT the pinyin phrases into characters and check their English meaning in the Key.

(i)	Zhè tái diànnǎo mài duōshao qián?										
(ii)	Yīwàn-èrqiān yuán.										
(iii)	Tài guì le, jiù yīwàn kuài ba.										
(iv)	Yīwàn-líng-bābǎi, zěnmeyàng?										

C. Match the Chinese words with their English meaning.

(i)

电脑	Taiwan
台 jiē	10 million
台 wān	just in case
卖 zuò	computer
卖 lì	exert one's strength
一千万	stairs
百万	draw large audiences
万一	million

(ii)

美元	A.D.
元 dàn	It's too expensive
gōng 元	American dollars
太 jíquán	New Year's Day
太贵了	small change
太 yáng	Taichi
zǒu 吧	sun
零钱	Let's go

190

dú   read

The full character combines *word* 言 and *sell* 賣 to suggest the idea of *to cut*. Thus it may mean punctuating a story at every clause and thus *to read*.

Radical: 讠 'word'

Index # 9

Character components: 讠 + 十 + 买

Character configuration:

Compounds, sentences and meanings

1. **读　dú**　read
   这 部　小说　值得 一读。
   Zhè bù xiǎoshuō zhíde yì dú.
   This novel is worth reading.

2. **读书　dúshū**　study
   他 读书 很　用功。
   Tā dúshū hěn yònggōng.
   He studies hard.

3. **读本　dúběn**　textbook
   这 是 一 本 汉语 读本。
   Zhè shì yì běn Hànyǔ dúběn.
   This is a Chinese reader.

4. **读者　dúzhě**　reader (of a book, newspaper, etc.)
   你 看了 今天　报上　的 读者 来信
   Nǐ kànle jīntiān bàoshang de dúzhě láixìn
   没有?
   méiyǒu?
   Have you read the letters to the editor in today's paper?

5. **阅读　yuèdú**　read
   我 来 图书馆　阅读 杂志。
   Wǒ lái túshūguǎn yuèdú zázhì.
   I came to the library to read magazines.

The last stroke ends firmly.

10 strokes

丶	讠	讠	计	读	读	读	读	读	读			

162

练

liàn　　practice

The full form combines *silk* 纟, *tie together* 柬 and *divide* `. It may represent raw silk glossed, selected and tied together. It means *practice*.

Radical: 纟 'silk'　　　　**Index # 68**

Character components: 纟 + 东

Character configuration:

Compounds, sentences and meanings

1. 练　liàn　practice
   我　下定　决心　练好　身体。
   Wǒ xiàdìng juéxīn liànhǎo shēntǐ.
   I've made up my mind to get fit.

2. 练习　liànxí　practice
   我　每天　练习　写　汉字。
   Wǒ měitiān liànxí xiě Hànzì.
   I practice writing Chinese characters every day.

3. 练习本　liànxíběn　workbook
   这　是　汉字　读写　练习本。
   Zhè shì Hànzì dú-xiě liànxíběn.
   This is a Chinese character reading workbook.

4. 练习题　liànxítí　exercise problems
   今天　的　作业　有　两　条　练习题我
   Jīntiān de zuòyè yǒu liǎng tiáo liànxítí wǒ
   不会 做。
   búhuì zuò.
   There are two exercise problems that I can't do in today's homework.

5. 练武　liànwǔ　practice martial arts
   我　每天　早晨　都　练武。
   Wǒ měitiān zǎochén dōu liànwǔ.
   I practice martial arts every morning.

Note the difference between 东 **and** 东.　　　　**8 strokes**

㇛	纟	纟	纟	纴	练	练	练					

163

习   **xí**   practice

 Full form

The full form represents the idea that a young bird flaps its wings many times, thus the meaning of *practice*.

Radical: 乛 'horizontal-vertical-hook'   **Index # 5**

Character component: 习

Character configuration:

Compounds, sentences and meanings

1. 习   **xí**   practice
   习 非 成 是。
   Xí fēi chéng shì.
   Accept what is wrong as right.

2. 习惯   **xíguàn**   habit
   我 习惯 早起。
   Wǒ xíguàn zǎoqǐ.
   I'm used to getting up early.

3. 习染   **xírǎn**   fall into a bad habit of
   青年人 很 容易 习染 抽烟。
   Qīngniánrén hěn róngyì xírǎn chōuyān.
   It's easy for young people to pick up the bad habit of smoking.

4. 习气   **xíqì**   bad habit
   中国 的 官僚 习气很 严重。
   Zhōngguó de guānliáo xíqì hěn yánzhòng.
   Bad bureaucratic habits prevail in China.

5. 习俗   **xísú**   custom
   中国人 有 赏月 的习俗。
   Zhōngguórén yǒu shǎngyuè de xísú.
   The Chinese people have the custom of enjoying the full moon.

The first stroke ends with a hook.   3 strokes

乛	习	习							

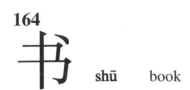

shū   book

Full form

The full form expresses the hand holding a brush writing a *book*. The cursive style of writing the character was adopted as the simplified form.

Radical: 乛 'horizontal-bend'   **Index # 5**

Character components: 乛 + 乛 + 丨 + 丶   **Character configuration:** ☐

Compounds, sentences and meanings

1. **书** shū   book
   这 是 一 本 教科书。
   Zhè shì yī běn jiàokēshū.
   This is a textbook.

2. **书包** shūbāo   school bag
   小孩 背着 书包 上学。
   Xiǎohái bēizhe shūbāo shàngxué.
   The children carry their school bags on their backs to go to school.

3. **书店** shūdiàn   book store
   马路 对面 有 一 家 书店。
   Mǎlù duìmiàn yǒu yī jiā shūdiàn.
   There is a book store across the road.

4. **书架** shūjià   bookshelf
   我 刚 买了 一 个 书架。
   Wǒ gāng mǎile yī ge shūjià.
   I just bought a bookshelf.

5. **书法** shūfǎ   calligraphy
   我 觉得 中国 书法 很 好看。
   Wǒ juéde Zhōngguó shūfǎ hěn hǎokàn.
   I think Chinese calligraphy is beautiful.

The second stroke ends with a hook.												4 strokes
乛	乛	书	书									

165

词　　cí　word

Full form

詞

The full form combines *speech* 言 and the phonetic 司 to give the idea of *word*.

Radical: 讠 'word'

Index # 9

Character components: 讠 + 司

Character configuration: ⊞

Compounds, sentences and meanings

1. 词　**cí**　new words
   调子 我 记得, 可是 词儿 我 忘 了。
   Diàozi wǒ jìde, kěshì cír wǒ wàng le.
   I remember the tune all right, but I've forgotten the words.

2. 词典　**cídiǎn**　dictionary
   这 本 词典 很 有用。
   Zhè běn cídiǎn hěn yǒuyòng.
   This dictionary is very useful.

3. 生词　**shēngcí**　new words
   这 篇 短文 生词 太 多。
   Zhè piān duǎnwén shēngcí tài duō.
   This narrative has too many new words.

4. 单词　**dāncí**　single word
   我 学 的 单词 不够 用。
   Wǒ xué de dāncí búgòu yòng.
   I haven't learnt enough words.

5. 词汇表　**cíhuìbiǎo**　glossary
   书 后面 有 词汇表。
   Shū hòumiàn yǒu cíhuìbiǎo.
   There's a glossary at the back of the book.

The second stroke is a horizontal-bend-lift.　　　　**7 strokes**

`	讠	订	订	词	词	词					

166

典　diǎn　standard

The character is a phonetic but used as a character. It means *standard* or *canon*.

Radical: 八 'eight'　　　　　　**Index # 17**

Character components: 曲 + 八　　**Character configuration:** ⊟

Compounds, sentences and meanings

1. 典　diǎn　ceremony
   校长　邀请 我 参加 五十 年
   Xiàozhǎng yāoqǐng wǒ cānjiā wǔshí nián
   校庆　盛典。
   xiàoqìng shēngdiǎn.
   The headmaster invited me to take part in the school's 50th anniversary ceremony.

2. 典礼　diǎnlǐ　ceremony
   校长　邀请　我 参加五十　年
   Xiàozhǎng yāoqǐng wǒ cānjiā wǔshí nián
   校庆　典礼。
   xiàoqìng diǎnlǐ.
   The headmaster invited me to take part in the school's 50th anniversary ceremony.

3. 典型　diǎnxíng　typical
   这 是 典型 的　中国　村庄。
   Zhè shì diǎnxíng de Zhōngguó cūnzhuāng.
   This is a typical Chinese village.

4. 词典　cídiǎn　dictionary
   这 本 词典 很 有用。
   Zhè běn cídiǎn hěn yǒuyòng.
   This dictionary is very useful.

5. 古典　gǔdiǎn　classical
   我 喜欢 古典 音乐。
   Wǒ xǐhuan gǔdiǎn yīnyuè.
   I like classical music.

The bottom horizontal stroke is longer.　　　　　**8 strokes**

丶	冂	冋	曲	曲	典	典	典						

běn root, base; [classifier]

The character represents a *tree* 木 with a line marked at the base, referring to the most important part. It means *foundation*. It is also used as *classifier* for books.

Radical: 木 'tree'　　　　　　　　**Index # 81**

Character components: 木 + 一　　　　**Character configuration:** ☐

Compounds, sentences and meanings

1. **本** **běn** classifier
   我 去 图书馆 借了 两 本 书。
   Wǒ qù túshūguǎn jièle liǎng běn shū.
   I went to the library and borrowed two books.

2. **本地** **běndì** local
   我 是 本地人。
   Wǒ shì běndìrén.
   I was born here.

3. **本行** **běnháng** one's own profession
   搞 电脑 是 我 的本行。
   Gǎo diànnǎo shì wǒde běnháng.
   Computers are my line of work.

4. **本来** **běnlái** original
   他 本来 身体 很 瘦弱。
   Tā běnlái shēntǐ hěn shòuruò.
   He used to be thin and weak.

5. **本领** **běnlǐng** ability
   他的 本领 很 大。
   Tāde běnlǐng hěn dà.
   He's very capable.

Make sure the bottom horizontal stroke is not too low.　　　　**5 strokes**

一	十	才	木	本					

它　tā　it

This character is a modern character. *It* can be thought of as a member of the household (it's under the roof) but it is an animal or thing, not a person.

Radical: 宀 'roof'

Index # 34

Character components: 宀 + 匕

Character configuration: ⊟

Compounds, sentences and meanings

1. **它** tā it (animal/thing)
   这 杯 牛奶 你 喝完 它。
   Zhè bēi niúnǎi nǐ hēwán tā.
   Drink up this glass of milk.

2. **它的** tāde its (animals/things)
   这 裙子 很 好看, 我 喜欢 它的颜色。
   Zhè qúnzi hěn hǎokàn, wǒ xǐhuan tāde yánsè.
   This skirt is pretty. I like its color.

3. **它们** tāmen they (animals/things)
   猫 狗 虽然 可爱, 但 它们 不会
   Māo gǒu suīrán kě'ài, dàn tāmen bùhuì
   说话。
   shuōhuà.
   Although cats and dogs are cute, they can't speak.

4. **其它** qítā other; else
   还有　什么 其它 事情 要 我们 做
   Háiyǒu shénme qítā shìqing yào wǒmen zuò
   吗?
   ma?
   Is there anything else you want us to do?

The last stroke sweeps from right to left.　　　　5 strokes

丶	宀	宀	宁	它					

169

帮

bāng help

Full form

幫

The full form denotes the trimming of an upper sole which kept the foot tightly in the shoe. To make the shoe moveable is to *assist* walking. The simplified form borrows the sound 邦 to combine with *napkin* 巾.

Radical: 巾 'napkin'

Character components: 邦 + 巾

Index # 52

Character configuration:

Compounds, sentences and meanings

1. **帮** **bāng** help
   我 帮 她 搬了 行李。
   Wǒ bāng tā bānle xíngli.
   I helped her with her luggage.

2. **帮助** **bāngzhù** help
   他 帮助 我 学 汉语。
   Tā bāngzhù wǒ xué Hànyǔ.
   He helps me to learn Chinese.

3. **帮手** **bāngshǒu** helper
   你 真 是 个 好 帮手。
   Nǐ zhēn shì ge hǎo bāngshǒu.
   You really are a good helper.

4. **帮忙** **bāngmáng** help
   我 要 请 她 帮忙。
   Wǒ yào qǐng tā bāngmáng.
   I'll ask her to help.

5. **帮倒忙** **bāngdàománg** make the matter worse with one's help
   请 小心 点儿, 别 给 我 帮倒忙
   Qǐng xiǎoxīn diǎnr, bié gěi wǒ bāngdàománg
   了。
   le.
   Please be careful, don't make things worse.

The fourth stroke sweeps down and tapers off.									9 strokes
一	二	三	丰	丰彡	邦	邦	帮	帮	

170

助 zhù assistance

The character combines *things piled up* 且 and *strength* 力 to represent the act of adding force to an object already under pressure. It means *help*.

Radical: 力 'strength'   **Index # 31**

Character components: 且 + 力   **Character configuration:** ⊟

Compounds, sentences and meanings

1. **助** zhù help
   感谢 你 助 我 一 臂 之 力。
   Gǎnxiè nǐ zhù wǒ yí bèi zhī lì.
   Thanks for lending me a helping hand.

2. **帮助** bāngzhù help
   他 帮助 我 学 汉语。
   Tā bāngzhù wǒ xué Hànyǔ.
   He helps me learn Chinese.

3. **助手** zhùshǒu assistant
   他 是 我的 助手。
   Tā shì wǒde zhùshǒu.
   He is my assistant.

4. **助兴** zhùxìng add to the fun
   给 大家 唱 支 歌 助助兴。
   Gěi dàjiā chàng zhī gē zhùzhuxìng.
   Sing us a song to liven things up.

5. **助学金** zhùxuéjīn grant-in-aid
   他 是 领 助学金 的 学生。
   Tā shì lǐng zhùxuéjīn de xuésheng.
   He is a grant-in-aid student.

The fifth stroke lifts slightly.   **7 strokes**

丨	冂	月	目	且	助	助					

Quiz 17 (161–170)

A. Look at the 16-character grid and CIRCLE words or phrases. They can be written horizontally or vertically. Look at the circled characters in the Key if unsure. COPY the word or phrase next to the grid and write the pinyin and meaning.

					Word or phrase			**Pronunciation**	**Translation**
帮	脑	卖	生	(i)	帮	助		bāngzhù	help
助	零	词	典	(ii)					
它	练	学	就	(iii)					
本	习	读	书	(iv)					

B. Refer to the characters in the 16-character grid above and CONVERT the pinyin phrases into characters and check their English meaning in the Key.

(i)	Zhè shì yī běn shénme shū?									
(ii)	Zhè búshì shū, yě búshì cídiǎn.									
(iii)	Zhè shì Hànzì dú-xiě liànxíběn.									
(iv)	Tā bāngzhù wǒ xué Hànzì.									

C. Match the Chinese words with their English meaning.

(i)

习 sú	calligraphy
练习本	dictionary
书店	custom
yuè 读	bookshelves
书 jià	workbook
书 fǎ	reading
生词	new words
词典	book store

(ii)

本 dì	skills
本 lǐng	assistant
本 lái	typical
帮助	local
助手	help
典 xíng	reading text
读书	study
读本	originally

前

qián   in front of, ahead

The character represents a slow advance forward by bringing the rear foot up to the heel of the front foot before taking a step. It means *forward*.

Radical: 八 'eight'   **Index # 17**

Character components: 丷 + 月 + 刂   **Character configuration:** ⬒

Compounds, sentences and meanings

1. 前 **qián**   forward, ahead
   我们 应该 往 前 看。
   Wǒmen yīnggāi wǎng qián kàn.
   We should look ahead.

2. 前面 **qiánmian**   in front of, ahead
   前面 有 座位。
   Qiánmiàn yǒu zuòwèi.
   There are seats in the front.

3. 前边 **qiánbian**   in front of, ahead
   前边 有 座位 吗?
   Qiánbian yǒu zuòwèi ma?
   Are there seats in the front?

4. 前天 **qiántiān**   day before yesterday
   前天 他 来过 这里。
   Qiántiān tā láiguo zhèlǐ.
   He came here the day before yesterday.

5. 前途 **qiántú**   future prospect
   你的 工作 很 有 前途。
   Nǐde gōngzuò hěn yǒu qiántú.
   Your work has great potential.

The last stroke ends with a hook.   **9 strokes**

丶	丷	丷	产	斺	肖	肖	前	前						

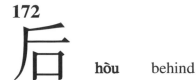

后 hòu behind

The full form 後 refers to someone who is walking slowly and thus *falling behind*. In simplification, the homonym *queen* 后 is used instead.

Radical: 丿 'downward-left-stroke'　　　　**Index # 4**

or　　口 'mouth'　　　　　　　　　　　**Index # 50**

Character components: 厂 + 口　　　　　**Character configuration:**

Compounds, sentences and meanings

1. **后** **hòu** back
   屋后 养着 很多 花儿。
   Wūhòu yǎngzhe hěnduō huār.
   There are flowers growing at the back of the house.

2. **后面** **hòumian** at the back, behind
   后面 还 有 座位。
   Hòumian hái yǒu zuòwèi.
   There are still some seats at the back.

3. **后天** **hòutiān** day after tomorrow
   后天 你 有 没有 空儿?
   Hòutiān nǐ yǒu méiyǒu kòngr?
   Are you free the day after tomorrow?

4. **后果** **hòuguǒ** consequence
   后果 不堪 设想。
   Hòuguǒ bùkān shèxiǎng.
   The consequences would be too ghastly to contemplate.

5. **以后** **yǐhòu** afterwards
   以后 你 会 有 机会 去 的。
   Yǐhòu nǐ huì yǒu jīhuì qù de.
   You will have a chance to go later.

The first two strokes are written separately.　　　　**6 strokes**

丿	厂	厂	斥	后	后						

173

面   miàn   face

The pictograph is a face with a nose. It means *face* or *surface*.

Radical: 一 'horizontal stroke'   **Index # 2**

Character components: 一 + ′ + 囬   **Character configuration:** ⊟

Compounds, sentences and meanings

1. 面 **miàn** face
   她 常常 面 带 笑容。
   Tā chángcháng miàn dài xiàoróng.
   She often has a smile on her face.

2. 面貌 **miànmào** features
   他们 的 面貌 十分 相似。
   Tāmen de miànmào shífēn xiāngsì.
   They look very much alike.

3. 面熟 **miànshú** look familiar
   这 人 看着 面熟。
   Zhè rén kànzhe miànshú.
   That person looks familiar.

4. 面积 **miànji** area
   这 套 房子 的 使用 面积 是 五十
   Zhè tào fángzi de shǐyòng miànji shì wǔshí
   平方 公尺。
   píngfāng gōngchǐ.
   The usable area of this apartment is 50 square meters.

5. 面子 **miànzi** face
   他 是老板， 给他留 点 面子 吧。
   Tā shì lǎobǎn, gěi tā liú diǎn miànzi ba.
   He is our boss, show some respect.

Note the difference between 面 and 而.   **9 strokes**

一	丆	广	丙	而	面	面	面	面			

páng   next to

The character combines *standing* 立 and the phonetic 方 to suggest the idea that while standing on a fixed locality, one is conscious of direction. It means *adjacent to*.

Radical: 方 'direction'

Index # 74

Character components: 产 + 方

Character configuration:

Compounds, sentences and meanings

1. 旁 **páng** other
   旁 的 还 要 什么?
   Páng de hái yào shénme?
   Do you want anything else?

2. 旁边 **pángbiān** next to
   坐 在 我 旁边 吧。
   Zuò zài wǒ pángbiān ba.
   Why don't you sit next to me?

3. 两旁 **liǎngpáng** both sides
   马路 两旁 种了 很多 树。
   Mǎlù liǎngpáng zhòngle hěnduō shù.
   There are lots of trees planted on both sides of the road.

4. 旁观者 **pángguānzhě** onlooker
   旁观者 清。
   Pángguānzhě qīng.
   The spectator sees most clearly.

5. 旁听 **pángtīng** be a visitor in a school class
   我 明天 旁听 你的 课可以 吗?
   Wǒ míngtiān pángtīng nǐde kè kěyǐ ma?
   May I sit in on your lecture tomorrow?

The last stroke ends with a hook.   **10 strokes**

丶	一	亠	六	亠	产	立	立	旁	旁			

175

边 biān side

Full form

邊

The full form combines *movement* 辶 and 臱 to represent the *edge* and means *borderline*. In simplification, 力 is used to replace 臱.

Radical: 辶 'movement'　　**Index # 38**

Character components: 力 + 辶

Character configuration: ⌐

Compounds, sentences and meanings

1. 边 **biān** side
   马路 两 边 种了 很多 树。
   Mǎlù liǎng biān zhòngle hěnduō shù.
   There are lots of trees planted on both sides of the road.

2. 边...边 **biān ... biān** as ... as
   他 边 唱歌 边 跳舞。
   Tā biān chànggē biān tiàowǔ.
   He sings as he dances.

3. 上边 **shàngbian** above
   大桥 上边 走 汽车。
   Dàqiáo shàngbian zǒu qìchē.
   The upper deck of the bridge is for cars.

4. 外边 **wàibian** outside
   请 到 外边 抽烟。
   Qǐng dào wàibian chōuyān.
   Please go outside to smoke.

5. 海边 **hǎibiān** seaside
   夏天 很多 人 到 海边 游泳。
   Xiàtiān hěnduō rén dào hǎibiān yóuyǒng.
   In summer, many people go to the seaside to swim.

辶 is written in 3 strokes.　　5 strokes

フ	力	力	边	边								

206

duì   opposite; correct

The full form combines 丵 and 寸 to give the idea of *symmetry*. The simplified form replaces 丵 with 又 which also functions as a radical.

Radical: 又 'again'   **Index # 24**
or   寸 'inch'   **Index # 46**
Character components: 又 + 寸   **Character configuration:**

Compounds, sentences and meanings

1. 对 duì   correct
   这 件 事 你 做得 很 对。
   Zhè jiàn shì nǐ zuòde hěn duì.
   You did the right thing.

2. 对面 duìmiàn   opposite
   他 家 就 在 我 家 对面。
   Tā jiā jiù zài wǒ jiā duìmiàn.
   His house is opposite mine.

3. 对不起 duìbuqǐ   I'm sorry
   对不起，给 你 添 麻烦 了。
   Duìbuqǐ, gěi nǐ tiān máfan le.
   Sorry to have given you so much trouble.

4. 对手 duìshǒu   opponent
   他 不是 你的 对手。
   Tā búshì nǐde duìshǒu.
   He's no match for you.

5. 对于 duìyú   with regard to, about
   对于 他的 工作 我 没有 什么
   Duìyú tāde gōngzuò wǒ méiyǒu shénme
   意见。
   yìjiàn.
   I have no complaints about his work.

End the second stroke firmly.   **5 strokes**

フ	又	双	对	对							

院 yuàn courtyard

The character combines *earth-mound* 阝 and the phonetic 完 to give the meaning of a large *building* with an earthern wall around it, e.g schools and hospitals.

Radical: 阝 **'left-ear lobe'**   **Index # 27**

Character components: 阝 + 完   **Character configuration:** ⬚

Compounds, sentences and meanings

1. **院** **yuàn** courtyard
   院里 种了 几颗 果树。
   Yuànli zhòngle jǐ kē guǒshù.
   There are some fruit trees in the courtyard.

2. **院子** **yuànzi** courtyard
   我 家 有 个 院子，孩子们 可以 在那儿
   Wǒ jiā yǒu ge yuànzi, háizimen kěyǐ zài nàr
   玩儿。
   wánr.
   My house has a yard for the children to play in.

3. **医院** **yīyuàn** hospital
   医院 对面 是 公园。
   Yīyuàn duìmiàn shì gōngyuán.
   Opposite the hospital is a park.

4. **住院** **zhùyuàn** stay in hospital
   他 住了 两 个 星期 的 院。
   Tā zhùle liǎng ge xīngqī de yuàn.
   He was hospitalized for two weeks.

5. **电影院** **diànyǐngyuàn** cinema
   这 是 新开 的 电影院。
   Zhè shì xīnkāi de diànyǐngyuàn.
   This is a new cinema.

The last stroke ends with a hook.   **9 strokes**

了	阝	阝`	阝`	阼	阼	陀	院	院			

校 **jiào/xiào** check; school

The character combines *tree* 木 and the phonetic 交 to give the idea of distinguishing right from wrong. It is pronounced *jiào* (*to check*) and *xiào* (*school*).

Radical: 木 'tree'　　　　　　　　　　**Index # 81**

Character components: 木 + 交　　　　**Character configuration:**

Compounds, sentences and meanings

1. 校　**jiào**　check, proofread
   先 校 错字, 然后 校 标点 符号。
   Xiān jiào cuòzì, ránhou jiào biāodiǎn fúhào.
   First proofread for typos, then correct the punctuation.

2. 校对　**jiàoduì**　check, proofread
   校对 汉字 时, 要 注意 笔顺。
   Jiàoduì Hànzì shí, yào zhùyì bǐshùn.
   When proofreading Chinese characters, pay attention to the stroke order.

3. 学校　**xuéxiào**　school
   这 个 学校 有 一百 年 的 历史。
   Zhè ge xuéxiào yǒu yībǎi nián de lìshǐ.
   This school has a 100-year history.

4. 校园　**xiàoyuán**　campus
   校园 进行 绿化 已经 一 年 了。
   Xiàoyuán jìnxíng lǜhuà yǐjīng yì nián le.
   The greening of our campus has been under way for a year.

5. 母校　**mǔxiào**　Alma Mater
   悉尼 大学 是 我的 母校。
   Xīní Dàxué shì wǒde mǔxiào.
   Sydney University is my Alma Mater.

The second stroke sweeps to the left.　　　　　　　　　　**10 strokes**

一	十	才	木	术	杧	栌	栌	栌	校			

gōng public

The character was derived from *divide* 八 and *private property* 厶 to give the idea of making private property *public*.

Radical: 八 'eight'

Index # 17

Character components: 八 + 厶

Character configuration:

Compounds, sentences and meanings

1. 公 **gōng** official business
   我 今天 因 公 外出。
   Wǒ jīntiān yīn gōng wàichū.
   Today I'm going on offical business.

2. 公共 **gōnggòng** public
   公共 场所 不准 抽烟。
   Gōnggòng chǎngsuǒ bùzhǔn chōuyān.
   No smoking in public places.

3. 公里 **gōnglǐ** kilometer
   我 家离 学校 一公里。
   Wǒ jiā lí xuéxiào yì gōnglǐ.
   My house is one kilometer from the school.

4. 公斤 **gōngjīn** kilogram
   买 一 公斤 桔子。
   Mǎi yì gōngjīn júzi.
   Give me [buy] a kilogram of oranges.

5. 公升 **gōngshēng** liter
   买 四十 公升 汽油。
   Mǎi sìshí gōngshēng qìyóu.
   Give me [buy] 40 liters of gasoline.

Leave a gap between the first two strokes.　　　　　**4 strokes**

ノ	八	公	公									

180

yuán garden; park

The full form combines *surround* 口 and *ample room* 袁 to mean 'a wide fenced area such as an orchard or a garden.' The phonetic 袁 is replaced by 元 in simplification.

Radical: 口 '4-sided frame'　　　　　　**Index # 51**

Character components: 口 + 元　　　　**Character configuration:** ⬜

Compounds, sentences and meanings

1. 园　**yuán**　garden
   我 家 园子 种了 几颗 果树。
   Wǒ jiā yuánzi zhòngle jǐ kē guǒshù.
   There are a few fruit trees in my garden.

2. 公园　**gōngyuán**　park
   假日里 很多 人 到 公园 去 玩儿。
   Jiàrìli, hěnduō rén dào gōngyuán qù wánr.
   On holidays, many people go to the park to enjoy themselves.

3. 花园　**huāyuán**　(flower) garden
   我 家 前面 有 一个 小 花园。
   Wǒ jiā qiánmiàn yǒu yí ge xiǎo huāyuán.
   There's a small garden in front of our house.

4. 苹果园　**píngguǒyuán**　apple orchard
   这里 一带 都 是 苹果园。
   Zhèlǐ yídài dōu shì píngguǒyuán.
   There are apple orchards around here.

5. 动物园　**dòngwùyuán**　zoo
   北京 动物园 有 大熊猫。
   Běijīng dòngwùyuán yǒu dàxióngmāo.
   There are pandas in Beijing Zoo.

The sealing stroke is written last.　　　　　　**7 strokes**

丨	冂	冂	冃	冈	园	园						

A. Look at the 16-character grid and CIRCLE words or phrases. They can be written horizontally or vertically. Look at the circled characters in the Key if unsure. COPY the word or phrase next to the grid and write the pinyin and meaning.

			Word or phrase			Pinyin	Meaning
			(i) 前 边			qiánbian	in front of, ahead

院	前	对	父
旁	边	母	面
公	后	校	园
西	家	生	学

(i) 前 边 qiánbian in front of, ahead
(ii)
(iii)
(iv)

B. Refer to the characters in the 16-character grid above and CONVERT the pinyin phrases into characters and check their English meaning in the Key.

(i)	Qiánmian shì yīyuàn.									
(ii)	Xuéxiào hòumian shì gōngyuán.									
(iii)	Diànyǐngyuàn zài nǎr?									
(iv)	Diànyǐngyuàn zài xuéxiào duìmiàn.									

C. Match the Chinese words with their English meaning.

(i)
前面	outside
后面	above, on top of
两旁	seaside
hǎi 边	ahead, in front of
上边	I'm sorry
wài 边	opposite
对不起	behind, at the back
对面	on both sides

(ii)
前天	afterwards
后天	cinema
yǐ 后	the day after tomorrow
医院	park
电影院	the day before yesterday
学校	hospital
面子	respect, 'face'
公园	school

181

离 lí depart

Full form

離

The full form combines *bird* 隹 and the phonetic 离 to suggest the idea of escaping or *to separate*. The simplified form retains only the phonetic part.

Radical: 亠 'top of 六'   **Index # 6**

Character components: 亠 + 凶 + 禸   **Character configuration:** ⬚

Compounds, sentences and meanings

1. 离 lí distance from
   公园 离 学校 有 一 公里。
   Gōngyuán lí xuéxiào yǒu yì gōnglǐ.
   The park is one kilometer from the school.

2. 离婚 líhūn divorce
   离婚 以后 他 就 没有 再 结婚。
   Líhūn yǐhòu tā jiù méiyǒu zài jiēhūn.
   He hasn't remarried since his divorce.

3. 离开 líkāi depart
   离开 北京，她 坐 火车 去 西安。
   Líkāi Běijīng, tā zuò huǒchē qù Xī'ān.
   Departing Beijing, she took the train to Xian.

4. 离别 líbié bid farewell
   我 离别 故乡 已经 十 年 了。
   Wǒ líbié gùxiāng yǐjīng shí nián le.
   It's been ten years since I left my hometown.

5. 离题 lítí digress from the subject
   发言 不要 离题。
   Fāyán búyào lítí.
   Please keep to the subject when you speak.

End the last stroke firmly.   **10 strokes**

丶	亠	亣	文	立	卤	卨	离	离	离			

远 yuǎn far

Full form

遠

The full form combines *movement* 辶 and the phonetic 袁 which carries the idea of *ample room*. Thus it means *ample distance* or *far*. In simplification, the simpler phonetic 元 is used.

Radical: 辶 'movement'
Character components: 元 + 辶

Index # 38
Character configuration:

Compounds, sentences and meanings

1. 远 **yuǎn** far
   公园 离 学校 有 多 远?
   Gōngyuán lí xuéxiào yǒu duō yuǎn?
   How far is the park from the school?

2. 远处 **yuǎnchù** distant point or place
   我 看见 几个 人 从 远处 走来。
   Wǒ kànjiàn jǐ ge rén cóng yuǎnchù zǒulái.
   I saw a few people coming towards me from a distance.

3. 远近 **yuǎnjìn** distance
   这 两 条 路 远近 差不多。
   Zhè liǎng tiáo lù yuǎnjìn chàbuduō.
   The distance is about the same by either road.

4. 远大 **yuǎndà** long-range, lofty
   年青人 应该 有 远大 的 理想。
   Niánqīngrén yīnggāi yǒu yuǎndà de lǐxiǎng.
   Young people ought to have lofty ideals.

5. 长远 **chángyuǎn** long-term
   从 长远 的 观点 看 问题。
   Cóng chángyuǎn de guāndiǎn kàn wèntí.
   Look at problems from a long-term view.

The last stroke of 元 ends with a hook.   **7 strokes**

一	二	亍	元	远	远	远							

直 zhí straight

The character combines *direct* 十, *eye* 目 and *hidden* 一, suggesting the idea of taking a *direct* look at something concealed.

Radical: 十 'ten'

Index # 11

Character components: 十 + 且

Character configuration:

Compounds, sentences and meanings

1. **直　zhí**　straight
   这里的街道 又 宽 又 直。
   Zhèlǐ de jiēdào yòu kuān yòu zhí.
   The streets are wide and straight.

2. **一直　yìzhí**　all the way
   你 从 这儿一直 走 就是了。
   Nǐ cóng zhèr yìzhí zǒu jiù shì le.
   Go straight ahead and you'll be there.

3. **直到　zhídào**　until
   我 直到 昨晚 才 接到 通知。
   Wǒ zhídào zuówǎn cái jiēdào tōngzhī.
   I was not informed until last night.

4. **直接　zhíjiē**　direct
   你 应该 直接 跟 我 说。
   Nǐ yīnggāi zhíjiē gēn wǒ shuō.
   You should speak to me directly.

5. **直来直去　zhílái-zhíqù**　blunt, frank and outspoken
   她 是 个 直来 直去 的人，说话
   Tā shì ge zhílái-zhíqù de rén, shuōhuà
   有口 无心。
   yǒukǒu-wúxīn.
   She's a blunt woman, often speaking sharply but she means well.

The three short horizontals are in the middle.　　　　**8 strokes**

一　十　广　亍　古　育　直　直

往 **wǎng** toward

The character combines *slow pace* 彳 and *to go to* 主 to give the meaning of *proceeding in a certain direction* or *toward*.

Radical: 彳 **'double-person'**　　　　　**Index # 54**

Character components: 彳 + 主　　　　**Character configuration:**

Compounds, sentences and meanings

1. 往　**wǎng**　toward
   你 往　东　走 去 就 是 了。
   Nǐ wǎng dōng zǒu qù jiù shì le.
   Go east and you'll get there.

2. 往往　**wǎngwǎng**　often
   这里 春天　往往　刮 大 风。
   Zhèlǐ chūntiān wǎngwǎng guā dà fēng.
   It's often windy here in spring.

3. 往常　**wǎngcháng**　habitually in the past
   她　往常　不 这样。
   Tā wǎngcháng bù zhèyàng.
   She wasn't like that before.

4. 往返　**wǎngfǎn**　journey there and back.
   往返 要 多 长　时间?
   Wǎngfǎn yào duō cháng shíjiān?
   How long does it take to get there and back?

5. 往来　**wǎnglái**　contact, dealings
   他们　两 家人 往来 很 密切。
   Tāmen liǎng jiā rén wǎnglái hěn mìqiè.
   The two families are in close contact.

Note the difference between 往 and 住.						8 strokes					
✂	✂	彳	彳	往	往	往	往				

 **zǒu** walk

The character depicts a person *running*, taking long strides and with arms outstretched.

Radical: 走 **'walk'**　　　　　　**Index # 156**

Character components: 土 + 止　　　**Character configuration:** ⊟

Compounds, sentences and meanings

1. 走　**zǒu**　walk
   一直 往 前 走。
   Yīzhí wǎng qián zǒu.
   Go straight ahead.

2. 走路　**zǒulù**　go on foot
   你们 是 坐车 去 还是 走路 去?
   Nǐmen shì zuòchē qù háishi zǒulù qù?
   Will you go there by bus or on foot?

3. 走运　**zǒuyùn**　be in luck
   祝 你 走运!
   Zhù nǐ zǒuyùn!
   Good luck!

4. 走失　**zǒushī**　wander away
   我们 一起 出去 的, 半路 上 她 走失 了。
   Wǒmen yìqǐ chūqu de, bànlù shàng tā zǒushī le.
   We went out together and she got lost on the way.

5. 走动　**zǒudòng**　stretch one's legs
   坐了 一 整天 了, 出去 走动 走动 吧。
   Zuòle yì zhěngtiān le, chūqu zǒudòng zǒudòng ba.
   Wc've been sitting all day long. Let's go out and stretch our legs.

The second horizontal is longer.　　　　　**7 strokes**

一	十	土	丰	击	走	走					

186

过 guò pass; cross

過

The full form combines *movement* 辶 and the phonetic 咼 to suggest the idea of *surpassing* or *to pass the limit*.

Radical: 辶 'movement'

Index # 38

Character components: 寸 + 辶

Character configuration:

Compounds, sentences and meanings

1. 过 **guò** pass, cross
   过 两 条 街 就 是。
   Guò liǎng tiáo jiē jiù shì.
   Cross two streets and you are there.

2. 过敏 **guòmǐn** allergy
   我 对 牛奶 过敏。
   Wǒ duì niúnǎi guòmǐn.
   I'm allergic to milk.

3. 过去 **guòqù** formerly
   他 比 过去 瘦 多 了。
   Tā bǐ guòqù shòu duō le.
   He's much thinner than he used to be.

4. 过时 **guòshí** out of date
   这 件 衣服 早 就 过时 了。
   Zhè jiàn yīfu zǎo jiù guòshí le.
   This garment is long out of fashion.

5. 不过 **búguò** but, however
   爸爸 的 身体 还 不错，不过 有点儿
   Bàba de shēntǐ hái búcuò, búguò yǒudiǎnr
   胖。
   pàng.
   My dad's heath is quite good, but he is a bit overweight.

End the third last stroke firmly.							6 strokes					
一	寸	寸	寸	讨	过							

条

tiáo [classifier]

條

The simplified form combines *tree* 木 and 夂, which is the figure of a hand holding a stick. It also means an *item*.

Radical: 夂 'top of 冬'   **Index # 57**
or   木 'tree'   **Index # 81**
Character components: 夂 + 朩   **Character configuration:**

Compounds, sentences and meanings

1. 条 **tiáo**   classifier
   过 了 这 条 街 就 是。
   Guòle zhè tiáo jiē jiù shì.
   You're there after you pass this street.

2. 条件 **tiáojiàn**   condition
   这里 的 工作 条件 还 不错。
   Zhèlǐ de gōngzuò tiáojiàn hái búcuò.
   The working conditions here are quite okay.

3. 条理 **tiáolǐ**   orderliness
   她 工作 很 有 条理。
   Tā gōngzuò hěn yǒu tiáolǐ.
   She is a methodical worker.

4. 便条 **biàntiáo**   short note
   你 给 他 写 个 便条 吧。
   Nǐ gěi tā xiě ge biàntiáo ba.
   Why don't you write him a note?

5. 面条 **miàntiáo**   noodles
   北方人 一般 喜欢 吃 面条。
   Běifāngrén yībān xǐhuan chī miàntiáo.
   In North China, people prefer noodles.

The fifth stroke ends with a hook.   7 strokes

ノ	夂	夂	冬	乆	条	条					

街 jiē street

The character is made up of 彳, 圭 and 亍. The first and third components combine to mean *business firms* or *shops*. The addition of the middle component suggests that the shops line up to form a *street*.

Radical: 彳 **'double-person'** | **Index # 54**

Character components: 彳 + 圭 + 亍 | **Character configuration:**

Compounds, sentences and meanings

1. **街** **jiē** street
   这 条 街 很 宽。
   Zhè tiáo jiē hěn kuān.
   This street is very wide.

2. **街道** **jiēdào** residential district
   这里的 街道 很 干净。
   Zhèlǐ de jiēdào hěn gānjìng.
   This neighborhood is very clean.

3. **大街** **dàjiē** main street
   我们 去 逛 大街 怎么样?
   Wǒmen qù guàng dàjiē zěnmeyàng?
   How about if we stroll around the streets?

4. **上街** **shàngjiē** go shopping
   妈妈 上街 去了。
   Māma shàngjiē qù le.
   Mum has gone shopping.

5. **唐人街** **Tángrénjiē** Chinatown
   西方 国家 很多 城市 都 有
   Xīfāng guójiā hěnduō chéngshì dōu yǒu
   唐人街。
   Tángrénjiē.
   Many cities in the West have Chinatowns.

The seventh stroke is horizontal. | **12 strokes**

| ノ | ク | 彳 | 彳 | 彳 | 彳 | 徍 | 徍 | 街 | 街 | 街 | 街 | |

zài   again

The character looks like a set of scales which gives rise to the idea of *repetition*. It means *again*.

Radical: 一 'horizontal stroke'   **Index # 2**

Character components: 一 + 冉   **Character configuration:** ⊟

Compounds, sentences and meanings

1. 再 **zài**   again
   有 工夫， 请 再来 玩儿。
   Yǒu gōngfu, qǐng zài lái wánr.
   Please come again whenever you're free.

2. 再次 **zàicì**   once more
   再次 感谢 你们的 帮助。
   Zàicì gǎnxiè nǐmende bāngzhù.
   Thanks once again for your help.

3. 再见 **zàijiàn**   see you again, goodbye
   下 星期天 再见。
   Xià xīngqītiān zàijiàn.
   I'll see you next Sunday.

4. 再三 **zàisān**   again and again
   希望 你 再三 考虑 才 决定。
   Xīwàng nǐ zàisān kǎolǜ cái juédìng.
   I hope that you consider carefully before you make your decision.

5. 再说 **zàishuō**   what's more, besides
   现在 去 找 他 太 晚 了，再 说 我 路
   Xiànzài qù zhǎo tā tài wǎn le, zài shuō wǒ lù
   也 不 熟。
   yě bù shú.
   It's too late to go and see him now; besides, I don't quite know the way.

The bottom horizontal stroke is the longest.   **6 strokes**

一	厂	厃	冄	冉	再						

190

jiàn see

The character combines *eyes* 目 and *child* 儿 to give the idea of eyes on two legs or *see*. The simplified form has one of the legs extended into the eyes.

Radical: 见 'see'

Index # 93

Character component: 见

Character configuration: ☐

Compounds, sentences and meanings

1. 见　jiàn　see
   下午 他 要 来 见 你。
   Xiàwǔ tā yào lái jiàn nǐ.
   He's coming to see you this afternoon.

2. 见面　jiànmiàn　meet, see
   他们 经常 见面。
   Tāmen jīngcháng jiànmiàn.
   They see a lot of each other.

3. 见识　jiànshi　experience, knowledge
   多 旅游, 长 见识。
   Duō lǚyóu, zhǎng jiànshi.
   More travels will broaden your experience.

4. 见笑　jiànxiào　laugh at (me or us)
   我 刚 开始 学, 您 别 见笑。
   Wǒ gāng kāishǐ xué, nín bié jiànxiào.
   Don't laugh at me, I'm only a beginner.

5. 再见　zàijiàn　see you again
   下 星期天 再见。
   Xià xīngqītiān zàijiàn.
   I'll see you next Sunday.

The last stroke ends with a hook.

4 strokes

丨	冂	𠕁	见								

Quiz 19 (181–190)

A. Look at the 16-character grid and CIRCLE words or phrases. They can written horizontally or vertically. Look at the circled characters in the Key if unsure. COPY the word or phrase next to the grid and write down the pinyin and meaning.

两	条	街	离
习	就	一	远
边	过	直	再
往	前	走	见

	Word or phrase			Pinyin	Meaning
(i)	两	条	街	liǎng tiáo jiē	two streets
(ii)					
(iii)					
(iv)					

B. Refer to the characters in the 16-character grid above and CONVERT the pinyin phrases into characters and check their English meaning in the Key.

(i)	Qǐngwèn, qù yīyuàn zěnme zǒu?								
(ii)	Yìzhí wǎng qián zǒu.								
(iii)	Lí zhèr yuǎn ma?								
(iv)	Bù yuǎn, guò liǎng tiáo jiē jiù shì.								

C. Match the Chinese words with their English meaning.

(i)

离 kāi	long term
远 jìn	until
cháng 远	distance
直 dào	depart
往往	often
走 lù	out of fashion
走 yùn	lucky
过时	on foot

(ii)

面条	laugh at (me or us)
条 lǐ	again and again
再 cì	meet, see
再三	noodles
上街	go shopping
见面	once again
见识	methodical
见 xiào	experience, knowledge

 jìn   near

The character combines *movement* 辶 and the phonetic 斤 which carries the idea of an ax. It suggests a short distance within the arch of an ax.

Radical: 辶 'movement'

Index # 38

Character components: 斤 + 辶

Character configuration: ⌞

Compounds, sentences and meanings

1. 近 jìn near
   我 家 离 火车站 很 近。
   Wǒ jiā lí huǒchēzhàn hěn jìn.
   My house is near the rail station.

2. 近来 jìnlái recently
   近来他的 身体 不 太 好。
   Jìnlái tāde shēntǐ bú tài hǎo.
   He has been rather unwell recently.

3. 近视 jìnshì near-sighted
   她 有点 近视。
   Tā yǒudiǎn jìnshì.
   She is slightly short-sighted.

4. 近便 jìnbiàn close and convenient
   我们 找 个 近便 的 饭馆 吃
   Wǒmen zhǎo ge jìnbiàn de fànguǎn chī
   午饭 吧。
   wǔfàn ba.
   Let's have lunch at the nearest restaurant.

5. 附近 fùjìn nearby
   学校 附近 有 一个 公园。
   Xuéxiào fùjìn yǒu yí ge gōngyuán.
   There is a park near the school.

The last stroke tapers off.   7 strokes

´	厂	斤	斤	斤	近	近							

外

wài   outside

The character combines *crescent moon* 夕 and *divination* 卜. Tortoise shells, emptied of their contents, are used in fortune-telling. It means *outside*.

Radical: 卜 'divination'　　　　　　**Index # 14**

Character components: 夕 + 卜　　　**Character configuration:**

Compounds, sentences and meanings

1. 外　**wài**　outside
   这 是 意料 外 的 事。
   Zhè shì yìliào wài de shì.
   That's outside my expectation.

2. 外面　**wàimian**　outside
   今天 我们 要 在 外面 吃饭。
   Jīntiān wǒmen yào zài wàimian chīfàn.
   We are dining out today.

3. 外表　**wàibiǎo**　outward appearance
   不要 从 外表 看 人。
   Búyào cóng wàibiǎo kàn rén.
   Don't judge people by their outward appearances.

4. 外国人　**wàiguórén**　foreigner
   你 有 没有 外国人 居留证?
   Nǐ yǒu méiyǒu wàiguórén jūliúzhèng?
   Do you have a residence permit for foreigners?

5. 外人　**wàirén**　stranger, outsider
   别客气, 我 又 不是 外人。
   Bié kèqi, wǒ yòu búshì wàirén.
   Don't stand on ceremony, I'm no stranger.

End the last stroke firmly.　　　　　　　　　　　**5 strokes**

ノ	ク	夕	夘	外						

193

马

mǎ horse

Full form

馬

The full character was derived from a pictograph of a *horse* 馬, showing its four legs and a tail drooping downwards. The simplified form retains the general shape of the *horse*.

Radical: 马 'horse'

Index # 69

Character component: 马

Character configuration:

Compounds, sentences and meanings

1. 马 **mǎ** horse
   2002 年 是 马 年。
   Èrlínglíng'èrnián shì mǎ nián.
   2002 is the Year of the Horse.

2. 马路 **mǎlù** road
   过 马路 要 小心 车辆。
   Guò mǎlù yào xiǎoxīn chēliàng.
   Be careful of vehicles when crossing the road.

3. 马虎 **mǎhu** careless
   他 这 个 人 做事 比较 马虎。
   Tā zhè ge rén zuòshì bǐjiào mǎhu.
   He's a rather careless fellow.

4. 马上 **mǎshàng** at once
   你 马上 就 走 吗?
   Nǐ mǎshàng jiù zǒu ma?
   Are you leaving right away?

5. 马拉松 **Mǎlāsōng** marathon
   去年 我 参加了 马拉松 赛跑。
   Qùnián wǒ cānjiāle Mǎlāsōng sàipǎo.
   Last year I took part in the marathon race.

The last stroke ends in a straight line.   **3 strokes**

丁	马	马								

路

lù road

The character combines *foot* 足 and *each* 各 to suggest the idea that each is going on his or her own way or *road*.

Radical: 足 'foot'

Index # 164

Character components: 足 + 各

Character configuration:

Compounds, sentences and meanings

1. **路** lù route
   312路　公共汽车　去 大学。
   Sānyāo'èrlù gónggòngqìchē qù dàxué.
   Route 312 goes to the University.

2. **路标** lùbiāo road sign
   前面　有 路标。
   Qiánmiàn yǒu lùbiāo.
   There are road signs ahead.

3. **路上** lùshang en route
   路上　不要　耽搁。
   Lùshang búyào dān'ge.
   Don't waste any time on the way.

4. **路口** lùkǒu intersection
   在 路口 左　拐弯。
   Zài lùkǒu zuǒ guǎiwān.
   Turn left at the intersection.

5. **路线** lùxiàn route, itinerary
   请 你 说说　旅行 路线。
   Qǐng nǐ shuōshuo lǚxíng lùxiàn.
   Please tell me about the itinerary of the tour.

The seventh stroke slants upwards slightly.

13 strokes

丶	口	口	𧾷	𧾷	足	𧾷	𧿹	𧿹	政	路	路	路

能

néng possible

The character represents the pictograph of an animal with strong muscles. The sense of *capability* or *power* was derived from its features.

Radical: 厶 'private'　　　　　　**Index # 23**

Character components: 厶 + 月 + 匕 + 匕　　**Character configuration:**

Compounds, sentences and meanings

1. 能　**néng**　be capable of
   我 能 用 左手 写字。
   Wǒ néng yòng zuǒshǒu xiězì.
   I can write with my left hand.

2. 能够　**nénggòu**　be capable of
   她 能够 说 三 种 外国语。
   Tā nénggòu shuō sān zhǒng wàiguóyǔ.
   She can speak three foreign languages.

3. 能干　**nénggàn**　capable
   她 是 个 很 能干 的人。
   Tā shì ge hěn nénggàn de rén.
   She's a very capable person.

4. 能力　**nénglì**　ability
   她的 分析 能力 很 强。
   Tāde fēnxi nénglì hěn qiáng.
   She has strong analytical skills.

5. 能源　**néngyuán**　energy
   世界 正在 面临 能源 危机。
   Shìjiè zhèngzài miànlín néngyuán wēijī.
   The world is facing an energy crisis.

The seventh and ninth strokes sweep to the left.　　**10 strokes**

厶 厽 彳 台 台 台 台 能 能 能

 **yòng** use

The character represents a fence, which is something useful to have. Thus, the character came to mean *useful*.

Radical: 用 'use'

Index # 128

Character component: 用

Character configuration: ☐

Compounds, sentences and meanings

1. **用 yòng** use
   你 会 不 会 用 电脑?
   Nǐ huì bú huì yòng diànnǎo?
   Can you use a computer?

2. **用处 yòngchù** use
   抱怨 有 什么 用处?
   Bàoyuàn yǒu shénme yòngchù?
   What's the use of complaining?

3. **用功 yònggōng** hardworking
   学生 都 很 用功。
   Xuésheng dōu hěn yònggōng.
   The students are very hardworking.

4. **用力 yònglì** exert oneself physically
   他 用力 把 门 推开。
   Tā yònglì bǎ mén tuīkāi.
   He gave the door a hard push to open it.

5. **用心 yòngxīn** attentively
   学生 都 用心 听讲。
   Xuésheng dōu yòngxīn tīngjiǎng.
   The students listen attentively to the lecture.

The first stroke tapers off, the second stroke ends with a hook.　　　　5 strokes

丿	几	月	月	用							

 **zuǒ** left

The character represents the idea of the left hand with which the carpenter uses his square. Thus it means *left*.

Radical: 工 'work'　　　　　　　　　　**Index # 39**

Character components: ナ + 工

Character configuration: ⌐

Compounds, sentences and meanings

1. 左 **zuǒ** left
   在 前面 红绿灯 左 拐弯。
   Zài qiánmian hónglǜdēng zuǒ guǎiwān.
   Turn left at the lights.

2. 左边 **zuǒbian** the left
   房子 左边 有 一颗 大树。
   Fángzi zuǒbian yǒu yì kē dà shù.
   There's a big tree on the left side of the house.

3. 左手 **zuǒshǒu** left hand
   他 能 用 左手 写字。
   Tā néng yòng zuǒshǒu xiězì.
   He can write with his left hand.

4. 左撇子 **zuǒpiězi** left-handed person
   他 是 个 左撇子。
   Tā shì ge zuǒpiězi.
   He's left-handed.

5. 左右 **zuǒyòu** about (used after a numeral)
   他 说 八点 左右 到 这儿来。
   Tā shuō bādian zuǒyòu dào zhèr lái.
   He said he'll be here around 8:00.

Don't mistake 左 for 在. Note the difference between 左 and 在.　　　　**5 strokes**

一	ナ	左	左	左							

198

右 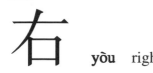 yòu right

The character combines *hand* 𠂇 and *mouth* 口 to suggest the idea that in the past, people preferred to use their *right* hand for eating.

Radical: 口 'mouth'   **Index # 50**

Character components: 𠂇 + 口   **Character configuration:**

Compounds, sentences and meanings

1. 右 yòu right
   在 中国 车辆 靠 右 走。
   Zài Zhōngguó chēliàng kào yòu zǒu.
   In China, traffic keeps to the right.

2. 右边 yòubian the right
   房子 右边 有 一棵 大树。
   Fángzi yòubian yǒu yì kē dà shù.
   There's a big tree on the right side of the house.

3. 右侧 yòucè right-hand side
   房子 右侧 种了 很多 花儿。
   Fángzi yòucè zhòngle hěnduō huār.
   There are flowers planted on the right-hand side of the house.

4. 右手 yòushǒu right hand
   大部分 人 用 右手 写字。
   Dàbùfēn rén yòng yòushǒu xiězì.
   Most people write with their right hand.

5. 左思右想 zuǒsī-yòuxiǎng think over from different angles (literally, think left and right)
   她躺 在 床上 左思右想, 一夜
   Tā tǎng zài chuángshang zuǒsī-yòuxiǎng, yí yè
   也 没 睡好。
   yě méi shuìhǎo.
   She lay awake all night, thinking about it over and over again.

Note the difference between 右 and 石.   5 strokes

一 ナ 才 右 右

231

shǒu hand

The character is derived from the shape of a *hand* with its five fingers extended.

Radical: 手 'whole hand'   **Index # 96**

Character component: 手   **Character configuration:**

Compounds, sentences and meanings

1. 手 **shǒu** hand
   这 是 手织 的 毛衣。
   Zhè shì shǒuzhī de máoyī.
   This is a hand-knitted sweater.

2. 手纸 **shǒuzhǐ** toilet paper
   厕所 没有 手纸 了。
   Cèsuǒ méiyǒu shǒuzhǐ le.
   There's no toilet paper in the lavatory.

3. 手气 **shǒuqì** luck at gambling
   我 今晚 打牌 的 手气 好得 出奇。
   Wǒ jīnwǎn dǎpái de shǒuqì hǎode chūqí.
   I've had a lot of luck at cards/mahjong tonight.

4. 手艺 **shǒuyì** craftsmanship
   那个 裁缝 的 手艺 很 好。
   Nà ge cáifeng de shǒuyì hěn hǎo.
   That tailor is very skilful.

5. 手续 **shǒuxù** formalities
   请 过来 这边 办 入境 手续。
   Qǐng guòlai zhèbian bàn rùjìng shǒuxù.
   Please come over here to go through the entry formalities.

The last stroke ends with a hook.   **4 strokes**

ノ	二	三	手								

200

只　　zhǐ　　only

The full form combines *ceremony* 礻 and the phonetic 氏 to suggest the idea of *only*. The simplified form uses 只, but is pronounced in the 3rd tone. See also *zhī* in character #90.

Radical: 口 'mouth'　　　　　　　　　**Index # 50**

or　　　　　八 'eight'　　　　　　　　**Index # 17**

Character components: 口 + 八　　　　**Character configuration:**

Compounds, sentences and meanings

1. 只　zhǐ　only
   我 只 想 问 一个 问题。
   Wǒ zhǐ xiǎng wèn yí ge wèntí.
   I only want to ask a question.

2. 只顾　zhǐgù　just think of
   你 别 只顾 自己。
   Nǐ bié zhǐgù zìjǐ.
   Don't just think of yourself.

3. 只是　zhǐshì　merely
   我 说 这 个 只是 开个 玩笑 罢丁。
   Wǒ shuō zhè ge zhǐshì kāi ge wánxiào ba le.
   I said it merely as a joke.

4. 只要 ... 就　zhǐyào ... jiù　if only
   只要 虚心，就 会 进步。
   Zhǐyào xūxīn, jiù huì jìnbù.
   If you are modest, you'll get on.

5. 只有　zhǐyǒu　be forced to
   如果 下 大雨，比赛 只有 延期。
   Rúguǒ xià dàyǔ, bǐsài zhǐyǒu yánqī.
   If it rains hard, we have to put off the match.

The last stroke ends firmly.　　　　　　　　　　　　　　　5 strokes

丶	冂	口	尸	只						

A. Look at the 16-character grid and CIRCLE words or phrases. They can be written horizontally or vertically. Look at the circled characters in the Key if unsure. COPY the word or phrase next to the grid and write the pinyin and meaning.

		Word or phrase	**Pinyin**	**Meaning**
能 过 右 手	(i)	右 手	yòushǒu	right hand
过 左 手 里	(ii)			
近 用 进 马	(iii)			
远 外 面 路	(iv)			

B. Refer to the characters in the 16-character grid above and CONVERT the pinyin phrases into characters and check their English meaning in the Key.

(i)	Xuéxiào lí zhèr yuǎn bu yuǎn?								
(ii)	Hěn jìn, guòle mǎlù jiù shì.								
(iii)	Nǐ néng yòng zuǒshǒu xiězì ma?								
(iv)	Bù néng, wǒ zhǐ néng yòng yòushǒu.								

C. Match the Chinese words with their English meaning.

(i)

附近	capable
近 lái	nearby
外面	outside
外国人	intersection
马 hu	foreigner
马上	immediately
路口	careless
能 gàn	recently

(ii)

用 chù	formalities
用 xīn	craftsmanship
左边	the left
右 cè	toilet paper
手 zhǐ	right side
手 yì	merely
手 xù	use
只是	attentively

CHARACTER BUILDING 4 (151–200)

A. Memorize the following radicals and their English names. As a review exercise, write the pinyin and meaning of each example.

1. ［一］ 'horizontal stroke'

    再 (＿＿＿＿) ＿＿＿＿＿＿ ；万 (＿＿＿＿) ＿＿＿＿＿＿ .

    面 (＿＿＿＿) ＿＿＿＿＿＿ .

2. ［丿］ 'downward-left stroke'

    千 (＿＿＿＿) ＿＿＿＿＿＿ ；后 (＿＿＿＿) ＿＿＿＿＿＿ ；

3. ［乛］ 'horizontal-bend-hook'

    习 (＿＿＿＿) ＿＿＿＿＿＿ ；书 (＿＿＿＿) ＿＿＿＿＿＿ ；

4. ［亠］ 'top of 六'

    离 (＿＿＿＿) ＿＿＿＿＿＿ ；就 (＿＿＿＿) ＿＿＿＿＿＿ .

5. ［讠］ 'word'

    读 (＿＿＿＿) ＿＿＿＿＿＿ ；词 (＿＿＿＿) ＿＿＿＿＿＿ ；

6. ⌊二⌋ 'two'

    二 (＿＿＿＿) ＿＿＿＿＿＿ ；元 (＿＿＿＿) ＿＿＿＿＿＿ ；

7. ⌈十⌉ 'ten'

    直 (＿＿＿＿) ＿＿＿＿＿＿ ；卖 (＿＿＿＿) ＿＿＿＿＿＿ ；

8. ⌈八⌉ 'eight'

    典 (＿＿＿＿) ＿＿＿＿＿＿ ；前 (＿＿＿＿) ＿＿＿＿＿＿ ；

    公 (＿＿＿＿) ＿＿＿＿＿＿ .

9. ［厶］ 'private'

    能 (＿＿＿＿) ＿＿＿＿＿＿ ；去 (＿＿＿＿) ＿＿＿＿＿＿ ；

10. ［又］ 'again'

    对 (＿＿＿＿) ＿＿＿＿＿＿ ；友 (＿＿＿＿) ＿＿＿＿＿＿ ；

11. ［力］ 'strength'

    助 (＿＿＿＿) ＿＿＿＿＿＿ ；男 (＿＿＿＿) ＿＿＿＿＿＿ ；

12. ［宀］ 'roof'

    它 (＿＿＿＿) ＿＿＿＿＿＿ ；字 (＿＿＿＿) ＿＿＿＿＿＿ ；

13. ［辶］ 'movement'

    远 (＿＿＿＿) ＿＿＿＿＿＿ ；过 (＿＿＿＿) ＿＿＿＿＿＿ ；

    边 (＿＿＿＿) ＿＿＿＿＿＿ ；近 (＿＿＿＿) ＿＿＿＿＿＿ ；

14. ［工］ 'work'

    工 (＿＿＿＿) ＿＿＿＿＿＿ ；左 (＿＿＿＿) ＿＿＿＿＿＿ ；

15. ［大］ 'big'

    太 (＿＿＿＿) ＿＿＿＿＿＿ ；天 (＿＿＿＿) ＿＿＿＿＿＿ ；

16. ［口］ 'mouth'
台 (＿＿＿＿＿) ＿＿＿＿＿＿＿ ; 右 (＿＿＿＿＿) ＿＿＿＿＿＿＿ .

17. ［囗］ 'four-sided frame'
园 (＿＿＿＿＿) ＿＿＿＿＿＿＿ ; 国 (＿＿＿＿＿) ＿＿＿＿＿＿＿ .

18. ［巾］ 'napkin'
帮 (＿＿＿＿＿) ＿＿＿＿＿＿＿ ; 师 (＿＿＿＿＿) ＿＿＿＿＿＿＿ ;

19. ［彳］ 'double-person'
往 (＿＿＿＿＿) ＿＿＿＿＿＿＿ ; 街 (＿＿＿＿＿) ＿＿＿＿＿＿＿ .

20. ［木］ 'wood'
本 (＿＿＿＿＿) ＿＿＿＿＿＿＿ ; 校 (＿＿＿＿＿) ＿＿＿＿＿＿＿ .

21. ［月］ 'moon/flesh'
脑 (＿＿＿＿＿) ＿＿＿＿＿＿＿ ; 期 (＿＿＿＿＿) ＿＿＿＿＿＿＿ ;

22. ［走］ 'walk'
走 (＿＿＿＿＿) ＿＿＿＿＿＿＿ ; 起 (＿＿＿＿＿) ＿＿＿＿＿＿＿ .

23. ［足］ 'foot'
路 (＿＿＿＿＿) ＿＿＿＿＿＿＿ ; 跑 (＿＿＿＿＿) ＿＿＿＿＿＿＿ .

B. Write the pinyin and meaning against the characters classified under the following radicals.

1. ［卜］ 'divination' 外 (＿＿＿＿＿) ＿＿＿＿＿＿＿
2. ［阝］ 'left ear-lobe' 院 (＿＿＿＿＿) ＿＿＿＿＿＿＿
3. ［夂］ 'top of 冬' 条 (＿＿＿＿＿) ＿＿＿＿＿＿＿
4. ［纟］ 'silk' 练 (＿＿＿＿＿) ＿＿＿＿＿＿＿
5. ［马］ 'horse' 马 (＿＿＿＿＿) ＿＿＿＿＿＿＿
6. ［方］ 'direction' 旁 (＿＿＿＿＿) ＿＿＿＿＿＿＿
7. ［手］ 'hand' 手 (＿＿＿＿＿) ＿＿＿＿＿＿＿
8. ［用］ 'use' 用 (＿＿＿＿＿) ＿＿＿＿＿＿＿
9. ［雨］ 'rain' 雨 (＿＿＿＿＿) ＿＿＿＿＿＿＿

C. Write the pinyin and meaning against the characters which share the following components. (Note that these components are not necessarily used as radicals.)

1. ［卖］ 卖 (＿＿＿＿＿) ＿＿＿＿＿＿＿ ; 读 (＿＿＿＿＿) ＿＿＿＿＿＿＿ ;
2. ［寸］ 对 (＿＿＿＿＿) ＿＿＿＿＿＿＿ ; 过 (＿＿＿＿＿) ＿＿＿＿＿＿＿ .
3. ［力］ 边 (＿＿＿＿＿) ＿＿＿＿＿＿＿ ; 助 (＿＿＿＿＿) ＿＿＿＿＿＿＿ .
4. ［月］ 脑 (＿＿＿＿＿) ＿＿＿＿＿＿＿ ; 明 (＿＿＿＿＿) ＿＿＿＿＿＿＿ ;
5. ［巴］ 吧 (＿＿＿＿＿) ＿＿＿＿＿＿＿ ; 爸 (＿＿＿＿＿) ＿＿＿＿＿＿＿ .
6. ［口］ 右 (＿＿＿＿＿) ＿＿＿＿＿＿＿ ; 名 (＿＿＿＿＿) ＿＿＿＿＿＿＿ .

REVIEW 4 (151–200)

The following are words and phrases classified under parts of speech. Write the pinyin and meaning of each example.

Pronouns   它   (_____) _____ ;   它们 (_____) _____ ;

Nouns   脑   (_____) _____ ; 电脑 (_____) _____ ;

           零钱   (_____) _____ ; 读本 (_____) _____ ;

           练习本 (_____) _____ ; 书   (_____) _____ ;

           书店   (_____) _____ ; 词   (_____) _____ ;

           生词   (_____) _____ ; 词典 (_____) _____ ;

           帮手   (_____) _____ ; 助手 (_____) _____ ;

           面子   (_____) _____ ; 医院 (_____) _____ ;

           电影院 (_____) _____ ; 学校 (_____) _____ ;

           校园   (_____) _____ ; 母校 (_____) _____ ;

           公里   (_____) _____ ; 公园 (_____) _____ ;

           远近   (_____) _____ ; 面条 (_____) _____ ;

           街   (_____) _____ ; 见识 (_____) _____ ;

           外国人 (_____) _____ ; 外人 (_____) _____ ;

           路   (_____) _____ ; 马路 (_____) _____ ;

           路口   (_____) _____ ; 手   (_____) _____ ;

Verbs   卖   (_____) _____ ; 读   (_____) _____ ;

           读书 (_____) _____ ; 练   (_____) _____ ;

           练习 (_____) _____ ; 学习 (_____) _____ ;

           帮   (_____) _____ ; 帮助 (_____) _____ ;

           帮忙 (_____) _____ ; 住院 (_____) _____ ;

           走   (_____) _____ ; 过   (_____) _____ ;

           上街 (_____) _____ ; 见   (_____) _____ ;

           见面 (_____) _____ ; 用   (_____) _____ .

Auxiliary verbs   能 (_____) _____ .

Numbers   零   (_____) _____ ; 千   (_____) _____ ;

           万   (_____) _____ ; 百万 (_____) _____ ;

           一千万 (_____) _____ .

Classifiers   台 (_____) _____ ; 元 (_____) _____ ;

           件 (_____) _____ ; 条 (_____) _____ .

237

Adjectives	远 (_____) _____ ;	直 (_____) _____ ;
	近 (_____) _____ ;	对 (_____) _____ ;
	过时 (_____) _____ .	

Location	前 (_____) _____ ;	后 (_____) _____ ;
words	前面 (_____) _____ ;	后面 (_____) _____ ;
	前边 (_____) _____ ;	两旁 (_____) _____ ;
	旁边 (_____) _____ ;	上边 (_____) _____ ;
	外边 (_____) _____ ;	对面 (_____) _____ ;
	外面 (_____) _____ ;	路上 (_____) _____ ;
	左 (_____) _____ ;	左边 (_____) _____ ;
	右 (_____) _____ ;	右边 (_____) _____ ;

| Time words | 前天 (_____) _____ ; | 后天 (_____) _____ ; |
| (Adverbs) | 以后 (_____) _____ . | |

Adverbs	千万 (_____) _____ ;	就 (_____) _____ ;
	一直 (_____) _____ ;	直到 (_____) _____ ;
	往往 (_____) _____ ;	再 (_____) _____ ;
	再三 (_____) _____ ;	马上 (_____) _____ ;
	只 (_____) _____ ;	只是 (_____) _____ ;

| Conjunction | 不过 (_____) _____ . |

| Prepositions | 离 (_____) _____ . |

| Particles | 吧 (_____) _____ . |

WORD/SENTENCE PUZZLE 4

Find and CIRCLE words, phrases or sentences hidden in the puzzle. They can be found horizontally from left to right or vertically. The lines across and down are indicated by numbers. Write down the meaning next to the pinyin. The first one is done for you.

ACROSS (left to right)

1. Tā búhuì yòng diànnǎo.   *She can't use a computer* _____

4. Wǒ jiā qiánmiàn yǒu yí ge dà shāngdiàn.   _____

7. (i)   zuǒbian   _____

7. (ii)   Nǐ jīntiān qù xuéxiào ma?   _____

8. zhùshǒu   _____

9. wàimian   _____

10. zìdiǎn   _____

238

12. Diànyǐngyuàn lí zhèr yuǎn bù yuǎn? _____

14. Chī miàntiáo. _____

DOWN

2. Wǒ néng yòng zuǒshǒu xiězì. _____

4. Yīyuàn pángbiān. _____

5. Qǐng nǐ bāngmáng. _____

6. Tā jiālǐ yǒu gǒu. _____

7. Míngtiān wǒmen zài nǎr jiànmiàn? _____

9. Duìbuqǐ! _____

10. Shāngdiàn zài xiàoyuán wàibian. _____

11. shūdiàn _____

	1	2	3	4	5	6	7	8	9	10	11
1	能	过	右	只	吧	她	不	会	用	电	脑
2	进	左	直	再	习	家	手	里	本	词	它
3	零	步	元	直	就	里	走	近	过	马	书
4	街	我	家	前	面	有	·	个	大	商	店
5	往	能	街	离	太	狗	钱	路	对	店	面
6	千	用	一	远	请	猫	明	毛	钟	在	现
7	卖	左	边	万	你	今	天	去	学	校	吗
8	助	手	走	见	帮	了	我	半	点	园	吃
9	工	写	公	作	忙	早	们	上	晚	外	面
10	台	字	典	生	时	下	在	候	午	边	跑
11	昨	月	子	医	饭	床	哪	人	对	日	空
12	星	电	影	院	离	这	儿	远	不	远	女
13	东	每	亲	旁	早	看	见	做	起	母	明
14	买	西	城	边	友	吃	面	条	父	期	进

201

 zhù   live

The character combines *person* 亻 and the phonetic 主 to suggest the idea of *to live* or *stay*.

Radical: 亻 'upright person'   **Index # 19**

Character components: 亻 + 主   **Character configuration:** ▯

Compounds, sentences and meanings

1. **住** zhù   to live, to stay
   你 住 在 哪儿?
   Nǐ zhù zài nǎr?
   Where do you live?

2. **住处** zhùchù   lodging
   你 找到 住处 没有?
   Nǐ zhǎodào zhùchù méiyǒu?
   Have you found accommodation?

3. **住户** zhùhù   household
   这儿 有 姓 陈 的 住户 吗?
   Zhèr yǒu xìng Chén de zhùhù ma?
   Is there anyone named Chen living here?

4. **住院** zhùyuàn   be hospitalized
   他 病了, 住了 两 天 院。
   Tā bìngle, zhùle liǎng tiān yuàn.
   He was sick and was hospitalized for two days.

5. **住宅** zhùzhái   one's residence
   这 是 我 住宅 的 电话。
   Zhè shì wǒ zhùzhái de diànhuà.
   This is my home phone number.

The left and right components don't meet.   **7 strokes**

| ノ | 亻 | 亻 | 亻 | 住 | 住 | 住 |

到

dào   arrive

The character combines *reaching* 至 and 刂 to suggest the idea of *reaching like a cut*. Thus it means *to arrive*.

Radical: 刂 'upright knife'   **Index # 15**

Character components: 至 + 刂

Character configuration: ▯▯

Compounds, sentences and meanings

1. 到 **dào** arrive
   火车 到站 了。
   Huǒchē dàozhàn le.
   The train has arrived at the station.

2. 到处 **dàochù** everywhere, anywhere
   烟头 不要 到处 乱 扔。
   Yāntóu búyào dàochù luàn rēng.
   Don't drop cigarette butts over the place.

3. 到底 **dàodǐ** finally
   你 到底 是 什么 意思?
   Nǐ dàodǐ shì shénme yìsi?
   What on earth do you mean?

4. 到家 **dàojiā** be excellent
   这 几个 汉字 写得 很 到家。
   Zhè jǐ ge Hànzì xiěde hěn dàojiā.
   These Chinese characters are remarkably well written.

5. 到期 **dàoqī** become due
   这 本 书 已经 到期了。
   Zhè běn shū yǐjīng dàoqī le.
   This book is due for return.

The sixth stroke goes upwards.   8 strokes

一	工	云	至	至	至	到	到				

203 从 cóng from

從

The full form represents the idea of *following another person*, and means *follow* or *obey*. The simplified form retains the same idea using just two persons.

Radical: 人 'person'

Index # 18

Character components: 人 + 人

Character configuration:

Compounds, sentences and meanings

1. **从 cóng** from
   你 从 哪儿来?
   Nǐ cóng nǎr lái?
   Where do you come from?

2. **从 ... 到 cóng ... dào** from ... to
   她 从 早 到 晚 都 想着 跳舞。
   Tā cóng zǎo dào wǎn dōu xiǎngzhe tiàowǔ.
   She thinks of dancing day and night.

3. **从来 cónglái** all along
   我 从来 没有 见过 他。
   Wǒ cónglái méiyǒu jiànguo tā.
   I've never seen him before.

4. **从前 cóngqián** formerly
   这 是 从前, 现在 不 一样 了。
   Zhè shì cóngqián, xiànzài bù yíyàng le.
   That was in the past, now it is different.

5. **从小 cóngxiǎo** from childhood
   我 从小 就 喜欢 运动。
   Wǒ cóngxiǎo jiù xǐhuan yùndòng.
   I love sports ever since I was a child.

The last stroke tapers off.   4 strokes

ノ	人	从	从								

zuò sit

The character depicts the figure of *two people* 人 + 人 sitting on the *ground* 土 . This gives rise to the idea of *to sit*.

Radical: 土 'earth'　　　　　　　　**Index # 40**

Character components: 人 + 人 + 土　　**Character configuration:**

Compounds, sentences and meanings

1. 坐 **zuò** sit
   请 坐。
   Qǐng zuò.
   Please sit down.

2. 坐火车 **zuò huǒchē** travel by train
   我 坐 火车 去 上海。
   Wǒ zuò huǒchē qù Shànghǎi.
   I'm traveling to Shanghai by train.

3. 坐位 **zuòwèi** seat
   请 回到 你的 坐位 上 去。
   Qǐng huídào nǐde zuòwèi shàng qù.
   Please return to your seat.

4. 坐不下 **zuòbuxià** have not enough seats for
   这 车 坐不下 这么 多 人。
   Zhè chē zuòbuxià zhème duō rén.
   This car can't seat so many people.

5. 坐班 **zuòbān** keep office hours
   我的 孩子 还 小, 不 适合 干 坐班 的
   工作。
   Wǒde háizi hái xiǎo, bù shìhé gàn zuòbān de
   gōngzuò.
   *My children are still small, it's not convenient
   for me to work in an office.*

The vertical stroke separates the two 人 components.　　　　**7 strokes**

ノ	人	人ノ	人人	亼	坐	坐					

地　**dì**　earth

The character combines *soil* 土 and the pictograph of a scorpion 也 to give the meaning of *earth*.

Radical: 土 'earth'

Index # 40

Character components: 土 + 也

Character configuration:

Compounds, sentences and meanings

1. **地** **dì** fields
   农民 在地里干活儿。
   Nóngmín zài dìli gānhuór.
   The peasants are working in the fields.

2. **地方** **dìfang** place, space
   这 个 地方 不错。
   Zhè ge dìfang búcuò.
   This is quite a nice place.

3. **地图** **dìtú** map
   你 有 没有 中国 地图？
   Nǐ yǒu méiyǒu Zhōngguó dìtú?
   Do you have a map of China?

4. **地下** **dìxià** on the ground
   你的 毛衣 掉 在 地下了。
   Nǐde máoyī diào zài dìxià le.
   Your sweater fell on the ground.

5. **地道** **dìdao** pure, typical
   他的 广州话 说得 真 地道。
   Tāde Guǎngzhōuhuà shuōde zhēn dìdao.
   He speaks Cantonese like a native.

The last stroke ends with a hook.　　　　　　　**6 strokes**

一	十	土	圫	坩	地							

206

铁　*tiě*　iron

Full form

鐵

The simplified form combines *metal* 钅 and the phonetic 失 to suggest the idea of *iron*. The use of this phonetic in simplification is arbitrary, probably for ease of writing.

Radical: 钅 'metal'　　　　**Index # 122**

Character components: 钅 + 失

Character configuration: ⊟

Compounds, sentences and meanings

1. 铁　*tiě*　iron
   这 是 铁 的 事实。
   Zhè shì tiě de shìshí.
   This is ironclad evidence.

2. 钢铁　*gāngtiě*　steel
   他 在 钢铁厂 工作。
   Tā zài gāngtiěchǎng gōngzuò.
   He works in a steelworks.

3. 铁路　*tiělù*　railway
   火车 在 铁路 上 走。
   Huǒchē zài tiělù shang zǒu.
   Trains travel on railway tracks.

4. 地铁　*dìtiě*　subway
   中国 很多 大 城市 都 有 地铁。
   Zhōngguó hěnduō dà chéngshì dōu yǒu dìtiě.
   Many big cities in China have subways.

5. 铁饭碗　*tiěfànwǎn*　iron rice-bowl
   现在 中国 没有 铁饭碗 了。
   Xiànzài Zhōngguó méiyǒu tiěfànwǎn le.
   There are no secure jobs in China now.

The fifth stroke is a vertical lift.　　　　**10 strokes**

ノ	ト	ヒ	钅	钅	钊	针	钎	铁	铁			

245

车　chē　vehicle

The full form depicts the two wheels and carriage of a *vehicle* viewed from above.

Radical: 车 'vehicle'

Index # 84

Character component: 车

Character configuration: ☐

Compounds, sentences and meanings

1. **车** **chē** vehicle
   路上 有 很多 车。
   Lùshang yǒu hěnduō chē.
   There are many vehicles on the road.

2. **车费** **chēfèi** (passenger's) fare
   到 颐和园 的 车费 多少?
   Dào Yíhéyuán de chēfèi duōshao?
   How much is the fare to the Summer Palace?

3. **火车** **huǒchē** train
   中国 的 火车 比较 慢。
   Zhōngguó de huǒchē bǐjiào màn.
   Trains in China are rather slow.

4. **公共气车** **gōnggòngqìchē** bus
   中国 的 公共汽车 很挤。
   Zhōngguó de gōnggòngqìchē hěn jǐ.
   Buses in China are packed.

5. **车祸** **chēhuò** traffic accident
   前面 好像 发生了 车祸。
   Qiánmian hǎoxiàng fāshēngle chēhuò.
   It seems that there's an accident ahead.

The last stroke doesn't meet the top horizontal stroke.　　4 strokes

一　七　车　车

北 běi north

The character depicts two people standing back to back, a reference to turning one's back to the direction of the *north*.

Radical: | 'vertical stroke'   **Index # 3**

Character components: ⺫ + 匕   **Character configuration:** ▯

Compounds, sentences and meanings

1. **北** **běi** north
   你 从 这儿 往 北 走。
   Nǐ cóng zhèr wǎng běi zǒu.
   Go north from here.

2. **北方** **běifāng** northern
   这 个 饭馆儿 做 的 是 北方菜。
   Zhè ge fànguǎnr zuò de shì běifāngcài.
   This restaurant serves northern Chinese cuisine.

3. **东北** **dōngběi** north-east
   大连市 在 中国 东北。
   Dàliánshì zài Zhōngguó dōngběi.
   The city of Dalian is in north-east China.

4. **北京** **Běijīng** Beijing
   2008 年 奥运会 在 北京 举办。
   Èrlínglíngbā'nián Àoyùnhuì zài Běijīng jǔbàn.
   The 2008 Olympic Games will be hosted by Beijing.

5. **北美洲** **Běiměizhōu** North America
   北美洲 包括 美国 和 加拿大。
   Běiměizhōu bāokuò Měiguó hé Jiā'nádà.
   North America includes the US and Canada.

The last stroke is a vertical-bend hook.   **5 strokes**

丨	十	⺫	⺭	北							

209

京 jīng capital

The character means *man-made high hill* to accommodate important people. It came to mean a *palace* or *capital*.

Radical: 亠 'top of 六'　　　　**Index # 6**

Character components: 亠 + 口 + 小　　　**Character configuration:** ⊟

Compounds, sentences and meanings

1. 京　jīng　capital
   从 外地 进 京 的 车辆 很多。
   Cóng wàidì jìn jīng de chēliàng hěnduō.
   Lots of vehicles come to the capital from other parts of the country.

2. 北京　Běijīng　Beijing
   2008 年 奥运会 在 北京 举办。
   Èrlínglíngbā nián Àoyùnhuì zài Běijīng jǔbàn.
   The 2008 Olympic Games will be hosted by Beijing.

3. 南京　Nánjīng　Nanjing (Nanking)
   南京 也 有 很多 名胜 古迹。
   Nánjīng yě yǒu hěnduō míngshèng gǔjī.
   There are also many scenic spots and historical sites in Nanjing.

4. 东京　Dōngjīng　Tokyo
   东京 是 日本 的 首都。
   Dōngjīng shì Rìběn de shǒudū.
   Tokyo is the capital of Japan.

5. 京剧　Jīngjù　Beijing opera
   我 没 看过 京剧。
   Wǒ méi kànguo Jīngjù.
   I've never watched Beijing opera.

The last stroke ends firmly.　　　　**8 strokes**

丶 亠 六 亩 亩 亭 亭 京

248

南 nán south

The character can be thought of as *ten* 十 houses with plants growing inside 冂 , a reference to villages in the *south*.

Radical: 十 'ten'

Index # 11

Character components: 十 + 冎

Character configuration:

Compounds, sentences and meanings

1. 南 **nán** south
   你 从 这儿 往 南 走。
   Nǐ cóng zhèr wǎng nán zǒu.
   Go south from here.

2. 南边 **nánbian** south side
   学校 南边 有 一个 公园。
   Xuéxiào nánbian yǒu yí ge gōngyuán.
   There is a park on the southern side of the school.

3. 南部 **nánbù** southern part
   广州 在 广东 省 南部。
   Guǎngzhōu zài Guǎngdōng shěng nánbù.
   Canton is in the south of Guangdong province.

4. 南方 **nánfāng** south of a country
   他 说话 带 南方 腔调。
   Tā shuōhuà dài nánfāng qiāngdiào.
   He speaks with a southern accent.

5. 南半球 **nánbànqiú** Southern Hemisphere
   澳大利亚在 南半球。
   Àodàlìyà zài Nánbànqiú.
   Australia is in the Southern Hemisphere.

Note the difference between 羊 and 半 in the bottom half of the character.   **9 strokes**

一	十	十	冇	内	南	南	南	南				

Quiz 21 (201–210)

A. Look at the 16-character grid and CIRCLE words or phrases. They can be written horizontally or vertically. Look at the circled characters in the Key if unsure. COPY the word or phrase next to the grid and write the pinyin and meaning.

	Word or phrase	Pinyin	Meaning
	怎 么 走		
怎 么 走 里	(i) 怎 么 走	zěnme zǒu	How do you get to ...?
中 到 下 车	(ii)		
国 坐 地 铁	(iii)		
城 住 从 上	(iv)		

B. Refer to the characters in the 16-character grid above and CONVERT the pinyin phrases into characters and check their English meaning in the Key.

(i)	Wǒ zhù zài chénglǐ.									
(ii)	Dào nǐ jiā zěnme zǒu?									
(iii)	Nǐ cóng zhèr zuò dìtiě.									
(iv)	Dào Zhōngguóchéng xiàchē jiù shì.									

C. Match the Chinese words with their English meaning.

(i)

从前	railroad
地 fang	train
地 tú	formerly
地下	place
铁路	subway
地铁	bus
huǒ 车	map
公 gòngqì 车	on the ground

(ii)

北京	the north
北 fāng	seat
到期	southern part
京 jù	Beijing
南 bù	expire
住 zhái	Beijing opera
坐 wèi	North America
北 Měizhōu	residence

211

来　lái　come

Full form

The character was derived from a pictograph of a barley plant. Barley was considered a gift from heaven. Thus, it came to mean *to come from* or *to come here*.

Radical: 一 'horizontal stroke'　　　**Index # 2**

Character components: 一 + 米

Character configuration: ☐

Compounds, sentences and meanings

1. 来　lái　come
   来 客人 了。
   Lái kèren le.
   The guests are here.

2. 来不及　láibují　there's not enough time
   今天 我们 来不及 去 看 他 了。
   Jīntiān wǒmen láibují qù kàn tā le.
   There's no time for us to go and see him today.

3. 来回　láihuí　a return journey
   来回 有 多 远?
   Láihuí yǒu duō yuǎn?
   How far is it there and back?

4. 来往　láiwǎng　come and go
   街上 来往 的 人 很多。
   Jiēshang láiwǎng de rén hěnduō.
   There are many people coming and going on the streets.

5. 从来　cónglái　all along, never
   我 从来 没有 见过 他。
   Wǒ cónglái méiyǒu jiànguo tā.
   I've never seen him before.

The bottom horizontal stroke is longer than the one above.						7 strokes

一	一	一	平	平	来	来					

jiǔ a long time

The character represents the figure of a person supported from the rear for a long time. It means *after a long time*.

Radical: 丿 'downward-left stroke'   **Index # 4**

Character component: 久   **Character configuration:** ☐

Compounds, sentences and meanings

1. **久** **jiǔ** for a long time
   我们 久 不 见面 了。
   Wǒmen jiǔ bú jiànmiàn le.
   We haven't seen each other for a long time.

2. **多久** **duō jiǔ** how long?
   你来了 多 久?
   Nǐ láile duō jiǔ?
   How long have you been here?

3. **久等** **jiǔděng** wait for a long time
   对不起 让 你 久等 了。
   Duìbuqǐ, ràng nǐ jiǔděng le.
   Sorry to have kept you waiting.

4. **久留** **jiǔliú** stay a long time
   我 有 要事 在 身, 不能 久留。
   Wǒ yǒu yàoshì zài shēn, bùnéng jiǔliú.
   I can't stay long because I have some important business to attend to.

5. **不久** **bùjiǔ** not very long time
   回家 不久 就 下 大雨 了。
   Huíjiā bùjiǔ jiù xià dàyǔ le.
   Not long after I came home, it rained.

The last stroke tapers off.   **3 strokes**

丿	夕	久									

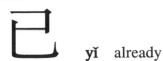

已　**yǐ**　already

This character *already* 已 looks similar to *self* 己 . The difference is it has a half-open gap on the top-left corner of the character while the latter is completely open.

Radical: 己 'self'　　　　　　　　**Index # 62**

Character component: 已

Character configuration: ☐

Compounds, sentences and meanings

1. **已　yǐ**　already
   天 已 黑 了。
   Tiān yǐ hēi le.
   It's already dark.

2. **已经　yǐjīng**　already
   问题 已经 解决 了。
   Wèntí yǐjīng jiějué le.
   The problem has already been solved.

3. **已往　yǐwǎng**　in the past
   已往 的 事 不要 再 提 了。
   Yǐwǎng de shì búyào zài tí le.
   Don't mention the past.

4. **而已　éryǐ**　that is all
   我 只 是 个 学生 而已。
   Wǒ zhǐ shì ge xuésheng éryǐ.
   I'm just a student, that is all.

已 and 己 are easily confused.　　　　　　　　　3 strokes

㇇	㇋	已									

214

经 jīng classics; pass through

The full form combines *silk* 糸 and 巠 to suggest *a thing that runs straight* or a *good example*. It means *classics*.

Radical: 纟 'silk'

Index # 68

Character components: 纟 + 圣

Character configuration:

Compounds, sentences and meanings

1. 经 jīng pass through
   他 经 新加坡 回 广州。
   Tā jīng Xīnjiāpō huí Guǎngzhōu.
   He returns to Guangzhou via Singapore.

2. 经常 jīngcháng frequently
   他 经常 上 图书馆 去。
   Tā jīngcháng shàng túshūguǎn qù.
   He goes to the library regularly.

3. 经过 jīngguò pass
   这 路 车 经过 动物园 吗?
   Zhè lù chē jīngguò dòngwùyuán ma?
   Does this bus go past the zoo?

4. 经理 jīnglǐ manager
   她 在 一家 饭馆 当 经理。
   Tā zài yì jiā fànguǎn dāng jīnglǐ.
   She works as a manager in a restaurant.

5. 经验 jīngyàn experience
   他的 经验 很 丰富。
   Tāde jīngyàn hěn fēngfù.
   He's got a lot of experience.

The final vertical stroke does not go through the upper horizontal stroke.   **8 strokes**

纟	纟	纟	纟	绉	绉	纺	经				

215

cháng/zhǎng   long; grow

Full form

The full form depicted a long-haired old man with a walking stick, referring to a *long passage of time*. Another meaning is *grow,* pronounced *zhǎng.*

Radical: 丿 'downward-left stroke'

Index # 4

Character component: 长

Character configuration:

Compounds, sentences and meanings

1. 长 **cháng**   long
   这 条 河 很 长。
   Zhè tiáo hé hěn cháng.
   This river is quite long.

2. 长江 **Chángjiāng**   the Yangtze river
   (literally, long river)
   长江 是 世界 第三 长 河。
   Chángjiāng shì shìjiè dìsān cháng hé.
   The Yangtze is the third longest river in the world.

3. 长处 **chángchù**   strong points
   她 有 很多 长处。
   Tā yǒu hěnduō chángchù.
   She has many good qualities.

4. 长大 **zhǎngdà**   grow up
   他们的 孩子 长大 了。
   Tāmende háizi zhǎngdà le.
   Their children have grown up.

5. 长辈 **zhǎngbèi**   elder, senior
   对 长辈 要 有 礼貌。
   Duì zhǎngbèi yào yǒu lǐmào.
   Show respect for one's elders.

Write the downward-right stroke last.   4 strokes

丿	⸗	长	长						

216

间　jiān　space

Full form

間

The character combines *gate* 门 and *sun* 日 to indicate light shining through a space between the gates. It means *space*.

Radical: 门 'door'

Index # 37

Character components: 门 + 日

Character configuration:

Compounds, sentences and meanings

1. 间　jiān　between, among
   朋友 之 间 不要 分得 太 清。
   Péngyou zhī jiān búyào fēnde tài qīng.
   Among friends, there should not be clear-cut distinctions.

2. 时间　shíjiān　time
   现在 是 北京 时间 二十点 整。
   Xiànzài shì Běijīng shíjiān èrshídiǎn zhěng.
   The time now is 20 hours Beijing time.

3. 中间　zhōngjiān　middle
   他是 我们 中间 最 年轻 的。
   Tā shì wǒmen zhōngjiān zuì niánqīng de.
   He's the youngest of us three.

4. 房间　fángjiān　room
   这 个 房间 又 大 又 亮。
   Zhè ge fángjiān yòu dà yòu liàng.
   This room is big and bright.

5. 夜间　yèjiān　at night
   很多 中国 城市 在 夜间 施工。
   Hěnduō Zhōngguó chéngshì zài yèjiān shīgōng.
   Many Chinese cities carry out construction work at night.

The initial dot stroke ends firmly to the right.　　　　7 strokes

丶	亻	门	门	问	间	间					

217

喜 xǐ happy

The upper part of 喜 represents a bowl filled with food. 口 of course means *mouth*. The idea of carrying food to the mouth means *rejoice*.

Radical: 士 'scholar' **Index # 41**
or 口 'mouth' **Index # 50**
Character components: 士 + 口 + 䒑 + 口 **Character configuration:**

Compounds, sentences and meanings

1. 喜 **xǐ** be happy
   笑 在 脸上， 喜在 心里。
   Xiào zài liǎnshang, xǐ zài xīnli.
   With a smile on your face and joy in your heart.

2. 喜爱 **xǐ'ài** be fond of
   我 喜爱 户外 活动。
   Wǒ xǐ'ài hùwài huódòng.
   I'm keen on outdoor activities.

3. 喜欢 **xǐhuan** be fond of
   我 喜欢 听 中国 音乐。
   Wǒ xǐhuan tīng Zhōngguó yīnyuè.
   I like Chinese music.

4. 欢喜 **huānxǐ** joyful
   一家 人 欢欢喜喜地 过 春节。
   Yī jiā rén huānhuānxǐxǐde guò Chūnjié.
   The whole family spent a joyful Chinese New Year.

5. 喜事 **xǐshì** happy event
   你 这么 高兴， 有 什么 喜事？
   Nǐ zhème gāoxìng, yǒu shénme xǐshì?
   You look so happy. What's the good news?

The short strokes in the middle do not protrude.   12 strokes

一 十 士 吉 吉 吉 吉 吉 壴 喜 喜 喜

257

欢

huān   happy

歡

The full form combines *food* 雚 and *open mouth* 欠 to suggest facing food *happily* with the mouth open. It means *happy*.

Radical: 欠 'owe'　　　　　　　　　Index # 104

or　　　　　 又 'again'　　　　　　Index # 24

Character components: 又 + 欠　　　**Character configuration:**

Compounds, sentences and meanings

1. 欢　huān　joyous

   大家 欢天喜地 地 过 圣诞节。

   Dàjiā huāntiān-xǐdì de guò Shēngdànjié.

   Everyone was having a very happy Christmas.

2. 欢喜　huānxǐ　joyful

   一家人　欢欢喜喜 地过 春节。

   Yī jiā rén huānhuānxǐxǐ de guò Chūnjié.

   The whole family spent a joyful Chinese New Year.

3. 欢聚　huānjù　happy reunion

   难得 有 机会 跟 老朋友　欢聚。

   Nándé yǒu jīhuì gēn lǎopéngyou huānjù.

   Old friends don't often get the chance to meet.

4. 欢乐　huānlè　happy

   国庆 的 时候，北京 一 片 欢乐 的
   景象。

   Guóqìng de shíhou, Běijīng yí piàn huānlè de jǐngxiàng.

   On National Day, Beijing is a scene of great joy.

5. 欢迎　huānyíng　welcome

   欢迎 你 到 北京 来。

   Huānyíng nǐ dào Běijīng lái.

   Welcome to Beijing.

Note the difference between 久 and 欠.　　　　　　　**6 strokes**

フ	又	又ノ	欢ノ	欢	欢								

219

lěng   cold

The character combines *icy cold* 冫 and the phonetic 令 to give the sensation of *very cold*.

Radical: 冫 'ice'   **Index # 7**

Character components: 冫 + 令   **Character configuration:** ⊟

Compounds, sentences and meanings

1. 冷 lěng   cold
   今天 真 冷。
   Jīntiān zhēn lěng.
   It's really cold today.

2. 冷静 lěngjìng   calm (of people)
   请 你 冷静 一点儿。
   Qǐng nǐ lěngjìng yìdiǎnr.
   Please calm down.

3. 冷水 lěngshuǐ   unboiled water
   喝 冷水 容易 得病。
   Hē lěngshuǐ róngyì débìng.
   If you drink unboiled water, you're likely to get sick.

4. 冷落 lěngluò   treat coldly
   不要 冷落了 客人。
   Búyào lěngluòle kèren.
   Don't leave the guest out in the cold.

5. 冷冰冰 lěngbīngbīng   cold in manner
   他 对 人 冷冰冰 的。
   Tā duì rén lěngbīngbīng de.
   He has a cold manner.

The second dot lifts and has no bend.						7 strokes
丶	冫	丷	汄	冰	冷	冷

220

冬 dōng winter

The character was derived from a pictograph of two bags hanging from a rope with the two dots below representing ice, indicating that it was *cold*.

Radical: 夂 'top of 冬'　　　　　　　**Index # 57**

Character components: 夂 + 冫　　　　**Character configuration:**

Compounds, sentences and meanings

1. 冬　dōng　winter
   这　种　鸟　在哪里 过冬?
   Zhè zhǒng niǎo zài nǎli guòdōng?
   Where do these birds go in winter?

2. 冬天　dōngtiān　winter
   上海　的　冬天　不下雪。
   Shànghǎi de dōngtiān bú xiàxuě.
   It doesn't snow in Shanghai in winter.

3. 冬季　dōngjì　winter
   上海　的　冬季 不下雪。
   Shànghǎi de dōngjì bú xiàxuě.
   It doesn't snow in Shanghai in winter.

4. 冬菇　dōnggū　dried mushrooms
   我　喜欢 吃 冬菇。
   Wǒ xǐhuan chī dōnggū.
   I like dried mushrooms.

5. 冬装　dōngzhuāng　winter fashion
   今年 的　冬装　好看极了。
   Jīnnián de dōngzhuāng hǎokànjíle.
   This year's winter fashions are very pretty.

The last two dots end firmly.											5 strokes
丿	夂	冬	冬	冬							

Quiz 22 (211–220)

A. Look at the 16-character grid and CIRCLE words or phrases. They can be written horizontally or vertically. Look at the circled characters in the Key if unsure. COPY the word or phrase next to the grid and down the pinyin and meaning.

	Word or phrase	Pinyin	Meaning

多	过	时	间
久	北	已	经
还	来	京	南
冬	喜	欢	长

(i)

多	久	

duō jiǔ	how much time?

(ii)

(iii)

(iv)

B. Refer to the characters in the 16-character grid above and CONVERT the pinyin phrases into characters and check their English meaning in the Key.

(i)	Nǐ lái Běijīng duō jiǔ le?								
(ii)	Yǐjīng hěn cháng shíjiān le.								
(iii)	Nǐ xǐhuan Bějing ma?								
(iv)	Hái hǎo, dōngtiān lěng yìdiǎnr.								

C. Match the Chinese words with their English meaning.

(i)

从来	grow up
来回	the Yangtze River
不久	all along
已经	pass through
经常	a return journey
经过	not long
长大	already
长 jiāng	often

(ii)

时间	be fond of
中间	happy
fáng 间	unboiled water
喜欢	time
欢喜	winter
欢 yíng	room
冷 shuǐ	middle
冬天	welcome

海 hǎi sea

The character combines *water* 氵 and *every* 每 to suggest the idea that water always returns to the *sea*.

Radical: 氵 '3 drops of water'   **Index # 32**

Character components: 氵 + 每   **Character configuration:**

Compounds, sentences and meanings

1. 海 **hǎi** sea
   台湾 四面 环海。
   Táiwān sìmiàn huánhǎi.
   Taiwan is surrounded by sea.

2. 海拔 **hǎibá** above sea level
   这里的 山 比较 高, 平均 海拔
   Zhèlǐ de shān bǐjiào gāo, píngjūn hǎibá
   四千 米。
   sìqiān mǐ.
   The mountains here are quite high, averaging 4000 meters above sea level.

3. 海边 **hǎibian** seaside
   我 常 去 海边 游泳。
   Wǒ cháng qù hǎibian yóuyǒng.
   I often go to the seaside to swim.

4. 海外 **hǎiwài** overseas
   他 是 海外 华侨。
   Tā shì hǎiwài Huáqiáo.
   He is an overseas Chinese.

5. 上海 **Shànghǎi** Shanghai
   她 是 上海人
   Tā shì Shànghǎirén.
   She's a native of Shanghai.

Write the horizontal stroke before the final two dots.											10 strokes
丶	丷	氵	汀	浐	汇	海	海	海	海		

夏　　xià　summer

The character was derived from a pictograph of a masked person dancing, perhaps in a *summer* festival.

Radical: 夊 'top of 冬'　　　　　　　　　**Index # 57**

Character components: 百 + 夊　　　　　　**Character configuration:**

Compounds, sentences and meanings

1. 夏　**xià**　summer
   这 种 树 冬 夏 常 青。
   Zhè zhǒng shù dōng xià cháng qīng.
   This type of trees is evergreen. (Literally, winter summer always green)

2. 夏天　**xiàtiān**　summer
   北京 的 夏天 比较 热。
   Běijīng de xiàtiān bǐjiào rè.
   Summer in Beijing is quite hot.

3. 夏令时　**xiàlìngshí**　daylight-saving
   明天 晚上 要 调 夏令时。
   Míngtiān wǎnshang yào tiáo xiàlìngshí.
   Adjust the clock for daylight-saving time tomorrow night.

4. 夏令营　**xiàlìngyíng**　summer camp
   这 个 暑假 我 参加了 夏令营。
   Zhè ge shǔjià wǒ cānjiāle xiàlìngyíng.
   This summer vacation I went to a summer camp.

5. 夏装　**xiàzhuāng**　summer fashion
   今年 的 夏装 很 好看。
   Jīnnián de xiàzhuāng hěn hǎokàn.
   The summer fashions this year are pretty.

Note the difference between 夊 and 又.　　　　　　**10 strokes**

| 一 | 一 | 丆 | 丙 | 丙 | 百 | 百 | 頁 | 夏 | 夏 | | | |

223

 rè　hot

Full form

The character combines *grasp* 执 and *fire* 灬 to suggest the sensation of heat. It means *hot*.

Radical: 灬 '4 dots of fire'

Index # 71

Character components: 执 + 灬

Character configuration:

Compounds, sentences and meanings

1. **热** **rè** heat up
   请 把 汤 热一热。
   Qǐng bǎ tāng rèyirè.
   Please heat up the soup.

2. **热带** **rèdài** the tropics
   新加坡 地 处 热带。
   Xīnjiāpō dì chǔ rèdài.
   Singapore is situated in the tropics.

3. **热点** **rèdiǎn** hot spot
   那 是 个 旅游 热点。
   Nà shì ge lǚyóu rèdiǎn.
   That is a hot spot for tourists.

4. **热情** **rèqíng** enthusiasm
   那个 服务员 对 顾客 很 热情。
   Nà ge fúwùyuán duì gùkè hěn rèqíng.
   That waiter is friendly to the customers.

5. ... **热** ... **rè** craze, fad
   卡拉 OK 热遍及 全 中国。
   Kǎlā'ōukēi-rè biànjí quán Zhōngguó.
   The karaoke craze has spread all over China.

The first dot goes to the left, the rest go to the right.　　　　　**10 strokes**

一	丁	扌	扎	执	执	执	热	热	热			

224

jiào   compare

The character combines *vehicle* 车 and *crossing* 交 possibly to suggest that careful *comparison* is necessary.

Radical: 车 'vehicle'   **Index # 84**

Character components: 车 + 交   **Character configuration:**

Compounds, sentences and meanings

1. 较 **jiào** relatively
   你的 汉语 有 较大 的 进步。
   Nǐde Hànyǔ yǒu jiàodà de jìnbù.
   You have made considerable progress in your Chinese.

2. 比较 **bǐjiào** comparatively
   我 最近 比较 忙。
   Wǒ zuìjìn bǐjiào máng.
   I've been rather busy recently.

3. 相较 **xiāngjiào** compare
   相较 实力, 我方 优于 对方。
   Xiānjiào shílì, wǒfāng yōuyú duìfāng.
   Using our strengths to compare, we are better than our opponent.

4. 较量 **jiàoliàng** measure one's strength with
   你 还是 别 跟 这 个 小伙子 较量 了。
   Nǐ háishì bié gēn zhè ge xiǎohuǒzi jiàoliàng le.
   You'd be better off not to test your strength against this young guy.

5. 较为 **jiàowéi** comparatively
   这 本 词典 较为 便宜。
   Zhè běn cídiǎn jiàowéi piányi.
   This dictionary is comparatively cheap.

The last stroke comes down from left to right.   **10 strokes**

一	土	吉	车	车`	车⸍	轩	轩⸍	轮	较			

225

常

cháng common

The character combines *jin* 巾 and the phonetic 尚 to mean *continue for a long time* or *often*.

Radical: 小 'small'   **Index # 49**
or   巾 'napkin'   **Index # 52**
Character components: 尚 + 口 + 巾   **Character configuration:** ▭

Compounds, sentences and meanings

1. 常 **cháng** constant
   这 种 树 冬 夏 常 青。
   Zhè zhǒng shù dōng xià cháng qīng.
   This type of trees is evergreen.

2. 常常 **chángcháng** often
   她 常常 工作 到 晚上
   Tā chángcháng gōngzuò dào wǎnshang
   十二点。
   shí'èrdiǎn.
   She often works until 12:00 midnight.

3. 常见 **chángjiàn** common
   这儿 春天 风沙 是 常见 的。
   Zhèr chūntiān fēngshā shì chángjiàn de.
   Dust storms are common here in spring.

4. 常识 **chángshí** general knowledge
   我的 科学 常识 不够。
   Wǒde kēxué chángshí búgòu.
   My general knowledge in science is weak.

5. 平常 **píngcháng** common
   这 种 情况 很 平常。
   Zhè zhǒng qíngkuàng hěn píngcháng.
   This sort of thing is quite common.

Write the short vertical stroke first, then the two side dots.   **11 strokes**

⺊	⺊	⺌	⺌	尚	尚	尚	常	常	常	常		

226

雨 **yǔ** rain

The character can be thought of as *heaven* 一 , *clouds* 冂 , and *rain falling* ⺢ . It means *rain.*

Radical: 雨 **'rain'**

Index # 172

Character components: 一 + 冂 + ⺢

Character configuration:

Compounds, sentences and meanings

1. **雨 yǔ** rain
   天气 预报 说 今天 有 雨。
   Tiānqì yùbào shuō jīntiān yǒu yǔ.
   Rain is forecast today.

2. **阵雨 zhènyǔ** showers
   今天 下午 有 阵雨。
   Jīntiān xiàwǔ yǒu zhènyǔ.
   There'll be showers this afternoon.

3. **下雨 xiàyǔ** rain
   天气 预报 说 今天 下雨。
   Tiānqì yùbào shuō jīntiān xiàyǔ.
   Rain is forecast today.

4. **雨季 yǔjì** rainy season
   五、六月 是 上海 的雨季。
   Wǔ、Liùyuè shì Shànghǎi de yǔjì.
   The time around May and June is the rainy season in Shanghai.

5. **雨伞 yǔsǎn** umbrella
   我 忘了 带 雨伞。
   Wǒ wàngle dài yǔsǎn.
   I forgot to bring my umbrella.

The dots come down firmly to the right. **8 strokes**

游

yóu swim; tour

遊

When the phonetic 斿 is combined with *water* 氵, it means *swim*. However, the same character is used as the simplified form for *tour* or *play* 遊 with the *movement* 辶 radical, as illustrated in examples 3, 4 and 5.

Radical: 氵 '3 drops of water' **Index # 32**

Character components: 氵 + 方 + 孚

Character configuration:

Compounds, sentences and meanings

1. 游 **yóu** swim
   这 条 河 太 宽， 我 游 不 过去。
   Zhè tiáo hé tài kuān, wǒ yóu bu guòqu.
   This river is too wide, I can't swim across it.

2. 游泳 **yóuyǒng** swim
   夏天 很多 人 去 海边 游泳。
   Xiàtiān hěnduō rén qù hǎibian yóuyǒng.
   Many people go to the seaside to swim in summer.

3. 游戏 **yóuxì** game
   孩子们 喜欢 玩 游戏。
   Háizimen xǐhuan wán yóuxì.
   Children love to play games.

4. 游人 **yóurén** tourist, traveler
   游人 止步。
   Yóurén zhǐbù
   No entrance. (literally, travelers stop)

5. 游览 **yóulǎn** go sight-seeing
   明天 我们 去 游览 故宫。
   Míngtiān wǒmen qù yóulǎn Gùgōng.
   Tomorrow we are touring the Imperial Palace.

The last stroke of 氵 goes up. 12 strokes

丶	丶	氵	氵	汒	汸	汸	汸	游	游	游	游	

228

泳　**yǒng**　swim

The character combines *water* 氵 and the phonetic 永 to give the idea of a style of swimming. It means *swim*.

Radical: 氵 '3 drops of water'　　　**Index # 32**

Character components: 氵 + 永　　　**Character configuration:**

Compounds, sentences and meanings

1. 泳　**yǒng**　swim
   夏天　很多　人　去　海边　游泳。
   Xiàtiān hěnduō rén qù hǎibian yóuyǒng.
   Many people go to the seaside to swim in summer.

2. 游泳　**yóuyǒng**　swim
   夏天　很多　人　去　海边　游泳。
   Xiàtiān hěnduō rén qù hǎibian yóuyǒng.
   Many people go to the seaside to swim in summer.

3. 蛙泳　**wāyǒng**　breast stroke
   中国　赢过　蛙泳　金牌。
   Zhōngguó yíngguo wāyǒng jīnpái.
   China had won a gold medal for breast stroke.

4. 自由泳　**zìyóuyǒng**　free style
   我的　自由泳　游得　不　好。
   Wǒde zìyóuyǒng yóude bù hǎo.
   My freestyle is not very good.

5. 泳道　**yǒngdào**　lane (in swimming)
   他　游　的　是　第三　泳道。
   Tā yóu de shì dìsān yǒngdào.
   He swam in the third lane.

The last stroke tapers off to the right.　　　**8 strokes**

丶	丶	氵	氵	汀	氻	泳	泳				

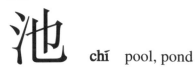

池　chí　pool, pond

The character combines *water* 氵 and the phonetic 也 to suggest a *pool* or *pond*.

Radical: 氵 '3 drops of water'　　　　**Index # 32**

Character components: 氵 + 也

Character configuration:

Compounds, sentences and meanings

1. 池　**chí**　pond
   我 家 后院 里 有 一个 养鱼池。
   Wǒ jiā hòuyuàn li yǒu yí ge yǎngyúchí.
   We have a fishpond in our backyard.

2. 游泳池　**yóuyǒngchí**　swimming pool
   宾馆 里 有 游泳池。
   Bīnguǎn li yǒu yóuyǒngchí.
   There's a swimming pool in the hotel.

3. 水池　**shuǐchí**　sink
   我 在 水池 洗菜。
   Wǒ zài shuǐchí xǐ cài.
   I washed the vegetables in the sink.

4. 浴池　**yùchí**　public bathhouse
   他 喜欢 去 浴池 洗澡。
   Tā xǐhuan qù yùchí xǐzǎo
   He likes to go to the bathhouse to bathe.

5. 池塘　**chítáng**　pond
   池塘 里 种了 荷花儿。
   Chítáng li zhòngle héhuār.
   There are water lilies in the pond.

The last stroke ends with a hook.　　　　**6 strokes**

丶　冫　氵　汜　池　池

fāng direction

The character came from the sketch of a plough showing a handle on both sides of the shaft. Thus, it suggests the idea of extension to both sides or *direction*.

Radical: 方 'direction'　　　　　**Index # 74**

Character component: 方

Character configuration: ☐

Compounds, sentences and meanings

1. 方 **fāng** method
   他 母亲 教导 有 方。
   Tā mǔqin jiàodǎo yǒu fāng.
   His mother taught him the right way to do it.

2. 方便 **fāngbiàn** convenient
   什么 时候 方便, 什么 时候 来。
   Shénme shíhou fāngbiàn, shénme shíhou lái.
   Drop in whenever it's convenient.

3. 方向 **fāngxiàng** direction
   他 往 学校 的 方向 走了。
   Tā wǎng xuéxiào de fāngxiàng zǒu le.
   He went in the direction of the school.

4. 方法 **fāngfǎ** method
   这 个 学习 方法 很 好。
   Zhè ge xuéxí fāngfǎ hěn hǎo.
   This is a good study method.

5. 方面 **fāngmiàn** aspect
   应该 考虑 各 方面 的 意见。
   Yīnggāi kǎolǜ gè fāngmiàn de yìjiàn.
   One should consider opinions from different quarters.

The last stroke bends and ends with a hook.　　　　　4 strokes

丶	一	亠	方								

Quiz 23 (221–230)

A. Look at the 16-character grid and CIRCLE words or phrases. They can be written horizontally or vertically. Look at the circled characters in the Key if unsure. COPY the word or phrase next to the grid and write the pinyin and meaning.

		Word or phrase			**Pinyin**	**Meaning**
游 多 下 雨	(i)	游	泳	池	yóuyǒngchí	swimming pool
泳 比 较 过	(ii)					
池 热 地 万	(iii)					
夏 常 方 海	(iv)					

B. Refer to the characters in the 16-character grid above and CONVERT the pinyin phrases into characters and check their English meaning in the Key.

(i)	Shànghǎi xiàtiān rè bu rè?								
(ii)	Bǐjiào rè, búguò cháng xiàyǔ.								
(iii)	Shànghǎi yóuyǒngchí duō bu duō?								
(iv)	Bùshǎo, hěnduō dìfang dōu yǒu.								

C. Match the Chinese words with their English meaning.

(i)

海边	direction
海外	seaside
夏 lǐng 时	aspect
热 qíng	comparatively
比较	overseas
方 xiàng	summer time
方 fǎ	enthusiastic
方面	method

(ii)

常见	rainy season
常常	common
下雨	swim
雨 jì	game
zhèn 雨	tour
游泳	often
游 xì	rain
游 lǎn	showers

231

周

zhōu   week

週

The character is used both as a full character (examples 4 and 5), and the simplified form for 週. The full form combines *field* 周 and *movement* 辶 to suggest the idea of making a circuit. It came to mean *cycle of time,* and then *week*.

Radical: 冂 'border'   **Index # 16**

Character components: 冂 + 土 + 口   **Character configuration:** ⬚

Compounds, sentences and meanings

1. 周 **zhōu** week
   上周 我 有 事儿, 没 去 跳舞。
   Shàngzhōu wǒ yǒu shìr, méi qù tiàowǔ.
   Last week I was busy, so I didn't go dancing.

2. 周日 **zhōurì** Sunday
   周日 晚上 我 都 没 空儿。
   Zhōurì wǎnshang wǒ dōu méi kòngr.
   I'm always busy on Sundays.

3. 周年 **zhōunián** anniversary
   今天 是 我 结婚 二十五 周年 纪念。
   Jīntiān shì wǒ jiéhūn èrshíwǔ zhōunián jìniàn.
   Today is my 25th wedding anniversary.

4. 周身 **zhōushēn** all over the body
   今天 我 觉得 周身 疼痛。
   Jīntiān wǒ juéde zhōushēn téngtòng.
   Today, my whole body aches.

5. 周围 **zhōuwéi** around
   这里 周围 环境 都 很 美。
   Zhèlǐ zhōuwéi huánjìng dōu hěn měi.
   The surroundings here are beautiful.

The second stroke ends with a hook.											8 strokes
丿	冂	月	冃	用	用	周	周				

232

 mò end

The character is a phonetic used as a character. It means *end*. It is important to write the second horizontal stroke shorter to avoid confusion with wèi 未 *'not yet'* .

Radical: 木 'tree'   **Index # 81**

Character components: 一 + 木   **Character configuration:** ☐

Compounds, sentences and meanings

1. **末** mò end
   今天 是 学期 最 末 一天。
   Jīntiān shì xuéqī zuì mò yì tiān.
   Today is the last day of the semester.

2. **周末** zhōumò weekend
   周末 我 一般 都 出去 玩儿。
   Zhōumò wǒ yìbān dōu chūqu wánr.
   I generally go out during the weekends.

3. **末期** mòqī last phase
   我 是 第二次 世界 大战 末期 出生 的。
   Wǒ shì dì'èr cì shìjiè dàzhàn mòqī chūshēng de.
   I was born during the last stage of the Second World War.

4. **末班车** mòbānchē last train/bus
   末班车 午夜 十二点 一刻 开。
   Mòbānchē wǔyè shí'èrdiǎn yíkè kāi.
   The last bus leaves at 12:15 a.m.

5. **末日** mòrì doomsday
   核子 战争 将 导致 世界 末日。
   Hézi zhànzhēng jiāng dǎozhì shìjiè mòrì.
   Nuclear wars will result in the end of the world.

The second stroke is shorter.   **5 strokes**

一	二	丰	才	末								

233

活　huó　live

The character combines *water* 氵 and *tongue* 舌 to symbolize *life*. It came to mean *active* or *vigorous*.

Radical: 氵 '3 drops of water'　　　　**Index # 32**

Character components: 氵 + 舌　　　　**Character configuration:**

Compounds, sentences and meanings

1. 活　**huó**　live
   我 爸爸 活到 八十五岁。
   Wǒ bàba huódào bāshíwǔ suì.
   My father lived to be eighty-five.

2. 活动　**huódòng**　activity
   这个 周末 你 有 什么 活动?
   Zhè ge zhōumò nǐ yǒu shénme huódòng?
   What activities have you planned for this weekend?

3. 活力　**huólì**　energy
   这个 小伙子 充满 活力。
   Zhè ge xiǎohuǒzi chōngmǎn huólì.
   This young man is full of energy.

4. 活泼　**huópò**　lively
   这 个 孩子 真 活泼。
   Zhè ge háizi zhēn huópò.
   This child is really lively.

5. 生活　**shēnghuó**　life
   在 中国 生活 要 用 汉语。
   Zài Zhōngguó shēnghuó yào yòng Hànyǔ.
   You have to use Chinese if you live in China.

The fourth stroke sweeps down from right to left.　　　　**9 strokes**

丶	冫	氵	汇	汇	汗	汗	活	活			

234

动　dòng　move

Full form

動

The full form combines *strength* 力 and *heavy* 重 to express the idea of *to budge something heavy* or *to move*.

Radical: 力 'strength'

Index # 31

Character components: 云 + 力

Character configuration:

Compounds, sentences and meanings

1. **动** dòng　move
   这　东西　一个　人　拿不动。
   Zhè dōngxi yí ge rén nábudòng.
   This thing can't be moved by one person.

2. **动身** dòngshēn　set out on a journey
   我们　明天　一早　就　动身。
   Wǒmen míngtiān yì zǎo jiù dòngshēn.
   We'll leave early tomorrow.

3. **动人** dòngrén　moving, touching
   这　个　电影　故事　很　动人。
   Zhè ge diànyǐng gùshi hěn dòngrén.
   The plot of this movie is very touching.

4. **动听** dòngtīng　pleasant to listen to
   她　唱歌　很　动听。
   Tā chànggē hěn dòngtīng.
   She sings beautifully.

5. **动物园** dòngwùyuán　zoo
   北京　动物园　有　大熊猫。
   Běijīng Dòngwùyuán yǒu dàxióngmāo.
   There are pandas in Beijing Zoo.

The last stroke tapers off.

6 strokes

一	二	云	云	动	动						

ài love

Full form

愛

The full form combines *hand* ⍩, *cover* ⌒ , *heart* 心 and *stop* 夂 to express the idea of someone standing still while cherishing *love* in his heart. The simplified form uses the idea of *companionship* 友 to express *love*.

Radical: ⍩ 'claw'

Index # 102

Character components: ⍩ + ⌒ + 友

Character configuration:

Compounds, sentences and meanings

1. 爱 **ài** love
   他 爱上 她了。
   Tā àishang tā le.
   He has fallen in love with her.

2. 爱情 **àiqíng** love
   他们 之间 已经 有了 很 深 dc 爱情 了。
   Tāmen zhījiān yǐjīng yǒule hěn shēn dc àiqíng le.
   They are deeply in love.

3. 爱护 **àihù** take good care of
   请 爱护 公物。
   Qǐng àihù gōngwù.
   Please take care of public property.

4. 爱惜 **àixī** value highly and use prudently
   他 不 知道 爱惜 东西。
   Tā bù zhīdao àixī dōngxi.
   He doesn't know how to look after things.

5. 爱好 **àihào** hobby
   你 有 什么 爱好?
   Nǐ yǒu shénme àihào?
   What hobbies do you have?

The last stroke firms and tapers off.

10 strokes

'	'	⺈	⍩	⍩	爫	𤔦	尹	爱	爱			

shuì sleep

The character combines *eyes* 目 and the phonetic 垂 which means *hang down* to suggest the idea that when the eyelids droop, you go to *sleep*.

Radical: 目 **'eye'**　　　　　　　　**Index # 118**

Character components: 目 + 垂　　　**Character configuration:**

Compounds, sentences and meanings

1. **睡　shuì** sleep
   昨晚 我 睡了 八 小时。
   Zuówǎn wǒ shuìle bā xiǎoshí.
   I slept for eight hours last night.

2. **睡觉　shuìjiào** sleep
   该 睡觉 了。
   Gāi shuìjiào le.
   It's time to go to sleep.

3. **午睡　wǔshuì** afternoon nap
   中国人 有 午睡 的 习惯。
   Zhōngguórén yǒu wǔshuì de xíguàn.
   Chinese have the habit of taking an afternoon nap.

4. **睡眠　shuìmián** sleep
   医生 说 我 睡眠 不足。
   Yīshēng shuō wǒ shuìmián bùzú.
   The doctor said that I don't have enough sleep.

5. **睡衣　shuìyī** pyjamas
   我 忘了 带 睡衣。
   Wǒ wàngle dài shuìyī.
   I forgot to bring my pyjamas.

The last horizontal stroke is shorter.　　　　　**13 strokes**

丨	冂	冂	月	目	目	目	睡	睡	睡	睡	睡	睡

jiāo/jué sleep; feel

The full form combines *feelings* 與 and *see* or *perceive* 見 to mean *feel*. It is pronounced as *jué*. Its other meaning is *sleep,* pronounced as *jiào.*

Radical: 见 'see'

Index # 93

Character components: ⺌ + 见

Character configuration:

Compounds, sentences and meanings

1. 觉 **jiāo** sleep
   一 觉 醒 来 已经 十点半 了。
   Yī jiāo xǐng lái yǐjīng shídiǎnbàn le.
   When I woke up it was already 10:30.

2. 睡懒觉 **shuì lǎnjiào** sleep in
   周末 我 喜欢 睡 懒觉。
   Zhōumò wǒ xǐhuan shuì lǎnjiào.
   At the weekend, I like to sleep in.

3. 睡午觉 **shuì wǔjiào** afternoon nap
   中国人 有 睡 午觉 的 习惯。
   Zhōngguórén yǒu shuì wǔjiào de xíguàn.
   Chinese have the habit of taking an afternoon nap.

4. 觉得 **juéde** feel
   我 觉得 我的 中文 进步了。
   Wǒ juéde wǒde Zhōngwén jìnbù le.
   I feel that my Chinese has improved.

5. 感觉 **gǎnjué** perception
   这 只是 我 个人 的 感觉。
   Zhè zhǐ shì wǒ gèrén de gǎnjué.
   This is only my personal feeling.

The last stroke is a vertical-bend hook.   9 strokes

丶	丷	⺌	⺌	兴	兴	兴	觉	觉			

238

呢

ne [particle]

The character combines *mouth* 口 and *the phonetic* 尼 to give the idea of a *question particle*.

Radical: 口 'mouth'

Index # 50

Character components: 口 + 尼

Character configuration:

Compounds, sentences and meanings

1. **呢** ne particle (rhetorical question)
   我 怎么 能 不记得呢?
   Wǒ zěnme néng bú jìde ne?
   How could I forget this?

2. **呢** ne particle (declarative sentence)
   远 得 很 呢。
   Yuǎn de hěn ne.
   It's a long way.

3. **呢** ne particle (to mark continuous action)
   他 还 在 睡觉 呢。
   Tā hái zài shuìjiào ne.
   He's still asleep.

4. **呢** ne particle (to ask a return question)
   我 叫 大伟, 你呢?
   Wǒ jiào Dàwěi, nǐ ne?
   My name is David, what's yours?

5. **呢** ne particle (to mark a pause)
   不 下雨 呢, 就去; 下雨呢, 就 不 去。
   Bú xiàyǔ ne, jiù qù; xiàyǔ ne, jiù bú qù.
   If it doesn't rain, we'll go; if it rains, we won't go.

The last stroke sweeps from right to left.							8 strokes
丶	冂	口	叮	叮	吓	呎	呢

运 yùn transport

Full form

運

The full form combines *war chariot* 軍 and *movement* 辶 to mean *carry people in a vehicle* or *transport*. The simplified form uses the simpler phonetic 云 .

Radical: 辶 'movement'

Index # 38

Character components: 云 + 辶

Character configuration: ⌞

Compounds, sentences and meanings

1. 运 **yùn** luck
   祝 你 好运!
   Zhù nǐ hǎo yùn!
   Good luck!

2. 运气 **yùnqi** luck
   我 最近 运气 不太 好。
   Wǒ zuìjìn yùnqi bú tài hǎo.
   I've had some bad luck recently.

3. 幸运 **xìngyùn** fortunate
   我 觉得 我 很 幸运。
   Wǒ juéde wǒ hěn xìngyùn.
   I think that I'm very fortunate.

4. 运动 **yùndòng** sport
   游泳 是 我 喜爱的 运动。
   Yóuyǒng shì wǒ xǐ'ài de yùndòng.
   Swimming is my favorite sport.

5. 运用 **yùnyòng** utilize
   她 把 学过 的 东西 运用 在
   Tā bǎ xuéguo de dōngxi yùnyòng zài
   生活 里。
   shēnghuó li.
   She applies what she learnt to everyday situations.

End the last stroke of 云 firmly.

7 strokes

丶	一	云	云	运	运						

dé/de/děi   obtain; [particle]; must

The character is pronounced *dé* when it means *obtain*; in the neutral tone *de* when it functions as *verbal particle*; and *děi* when it means *must*.

Radical: 彳 **'double person'**   **Index # 54**

Character components: 彳 + 日 + 寸   **Character configuration:**

Compounds, sentences and meanings

1. **得** **dé** obtain
   他 考试 得了第一 名。
   Tā kǎoshì déle dīyī míng.
   He came first in the exam.

2. verb + **得** verb + de verbal particle
   她 乒乓球 打得 不错。
   Tā pīngpāngqiú dǎde búcuò.
   She plays table tennis quite well.

3. **得意** **déyì** proud of oneself
   我 对自己的 成绩 感到 得意。
   Wǒ duì zìjǐ de chéngjī gǎndào déyì.
   I was proud of my results.

4. **得罪** **dézuì** offend
   我的 话 把 他 给 得罪了。
   Wǒde huà bǎ tā gěi dézuìle.
   My words offended him.

5. **得** **děi** certainly will
   要不 快 走, 我们 就 得 迟到 了。
   Yàobù kuài zǒu, wǒmen jiù děi chídào le.
   We'll be late if we don't hurry.

The second horizontal stroke is longer.   **11 strokes**

| 丿 | 彳 | 彳 | 彳 | 彳 | 彳 | 彳 | 得 | 得 | 得 | | |

Quiz 24 (231–240)

A. Look at the 16-character grid and CIRCLE words or phrases. They can be written horizontally or vertically. Look at the circled characters in the Key if unsure. COPY the word or phrase next to the grid and write the pinyin and meaning.

欢	活	喜	呢
运	动	周	末
步	睡	觉	跑
和	泳	游	爱

	Word or phrase			Pinyin	Meaning
(i)	活	动		huódòng	activity/activities
(ii)					
(iii)					
(iv)					

B. Refer to the characters in the 16-character grid above and CONVERT the pinyin phrases into characters and check their English meaning in the Key.

(i)	Zhōumò nǐ yǒu shénme huódòng?									
(ii)	Zhōumò wǒ ài shuì lǎnjiào.									
(iii)	Nǐ xǐhuan shénme yùndòng?									
(iv)	Wǒ xǐhuan yóuyǒng hé pǎobù.									

C. Match the Chinese words with their English meaning.

(i)

周年	zoo
周日	pleasant to listen to
生活	touching
动人	anniversary
动 tīng	spouse
动 wù 园	hobby
爱人	living
爱好 (pron. hào)	Sunday

(ii)

睡午觉	offend
睡 lǎn 觉	sports
睡衣	luck
觉得	sleep in
gǎn 觉	afternoon nap
运动	perception
运 qi	pyjamas
得 zuì	feel

可

kě   can, may

The character combines *mouth* 口 and the non-character 丁 which is sign of bending. The character may mean *to be acknowledged by hook or by crook.*

Radical: 一 'horizontal stroke'   **Index # 2**

or   口 'mouth'   **Index # 50**

Character components: 口 + 丁   **Character configuration:**

Compounds, sentences and meanings

1. 可 **kě** (used for emphasis)
   可 别 忘 了。
   Kě bié wàng le.
   Mind you don't forget it.

2. 可是 **kěshì** but
   我的 房间 比较 小, 可是 很 舒适。
   Wǒde fángjiān bǐjiào xiǎo, kěshì hěn shūshì.
   My room is a bit small, but it's very comfortable.

3. 可爱 **kě'ài** lovable, lovely
   多么 可爱的 孩子!
   Duōme kě'ài de háizi!
   What a cute child!

4. 可以 **kěyǐ** can, may
   这 间 屋子可以 住 两 个人。
   Zhè jiān wūzi kěyǐ zhù liǎng ge rén.
   This room can accommodate two people.

5. 可能 **kěnéng** possible
   很 可能 他 已经 到 家 了。
   Hěn kěnéng tā yǐjīng dào jiā le.
   He's most likely to be home by now.

The second stroke ends with a hook.   **5 strokes**

一	丁	叮	可	可							

242

以 yǐ with

The character combines *gather* レ and *people* 人 to represent the idea of *gathering people and their employment*. Later it came to mean *use* or *according to*.

Radical: 人 'person'

Index # 18

Character components: レ + 人

Character configuration:

Compounds, sentences and meanings

1. **以** **yǐ** with, by means of
   我们 不 应该 以 貌 取人。
   Wǒmen bù yīnggāi yǐ mào qǔ rén.
   We should not judge people solely by their appearance.

2. **以便** **yǐbiàn** in order to
   作好 准备, 以便 明天 一 早
   Zuòhǎo zhǔnbèi, yǐbiàn míngtiān yī zǎo
   动身。
   dòngshēn.
   Get ready so that we can start early tomorrow.

3. **以后** **yǐhòu** afterwards
   以后 你 会 有 机会 去 的。
   Yǐhòu nǐ huì yǒu jīhuì qù de.
   You will have a chance to go later.

4. **以前** **yǐqián** prior to, former
   她 是 我 以前 的 同事。
   Tā shì wǒ yǐqián de tóngshì.
   She's a former colleague of mine.

5. **以为** **yǐwéi** consider
   他 以为 那样 做 比较 好。
   Tā yǐwéi nàyàng zuò bǐjiào hǎo.
   He thinks it's better to do it that way.

Both dots finish firmly.

4 strokes

レ	レ	レノ	以							

共

gòng together

The character represents the idea of two hands lifting an object. Thus, it came to mean *together*.

Radical: 八 'eight'

Index # 17

Character components: 廿 + 八

Character configuration:

Compounds, sentences and meanings

1. **共 gòng** public
   今天 很 高兴 能 有 机会 跟 老
   Jīntiān hěn gāoxìng néng yǒu jīhuì gēn lǎo
   朋友 共 聚一堂。
   péngyou gòng jù yī táng.
   I'm very happy to have the opportunity to meet with old friends.

2. **共同 gòngtóng** common
   他们 之间 没有 共同 的 语言。
   Tāmen zhījiān méiyǒu gòngtóng de yǔyán.
   They don't have a common language.

3. **一共 yígòng** altogether
   你们 一共 多少 人?
   Nǐmen yígòng duōshao rén?
   How many people are there altogether in your group?

4. **公共 gōnggòng** public
   请 不要 在 公共 场所 吸烟。
   Qǐng búyào zài gōnggòng chǎngsuǒ xīyān.
   Please don't smoke in public places.

5. **共和国 gònghéguó** republic
   中华 人民 共和国。
   Zhōnghuá Rénmín Gònghéguó.
   The People's Republic of China.

The last stroke ends firmly.   **6 strokes**

一	十	廿	共	共	共						

244

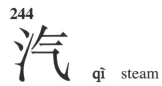

qì   steam

The character combines *water* 氵 and *gas* 气 to suggest the idea of *watery air* or *vapor*.

Radical: 氵 '3 drops of water'   **Index # 32**

Character components: 氵 + 气   **Character configuration:**

Compounds, sentences and meanings

1. 汽 **qì** vapor
   汽船 用 蒸汽 开动。
   Qìchuán yòng zhēngqì kāidòng.
   Steamships are driven by steam.

2. 汽油 **qìyóu** petrol
   最近 汽油 涨价 了。
   Zuìjìn qìyóu zhǎngjià le.
   Recently the price of gasoline has risen.

3. 汽水 **qìshuǐ** soft drinks
   这 是 什么 汽水？
   Zhè shì shénme qìshuǐ?
   What is this soft drink?

4. 汽车 **qìchē** automobile
   路上 有 很多 汽车。
   Lùshang yǒu hěnduō qìchē.
   There are lots of cars on the road.

5. 汽船 **qìchuán** steamship
   现在 很少 有 汽船 了。
   Xiànzài hěnshǎo yǒu qìchuán le.
   Nowadays steamships are rare.

The last stroke slants to the right.   **7 strokes**

丶	冫	氵	汙	汇	汽	汽					

huò or; perhaps

The character combines *spear* 戈, *border* 口 and *approximation* 一 to suggest the idea that the border is an approximation. Thus, it came to mean *perhaps*.

Radical: 戈 'spear'

Index # 85

Character components: 戈 + 口 + 一

Character configuration:

Compounds, sentences and meanings

1. 或 **huò** or
   无论 唱歌 或 跳舞，她 都 行。
   Wúlùn chànggē huò tiàowǔ, tā dōu xíng.
   She is good at both singing and dancing.

2. 或是 **huòshì** or
   无论 唱歌 或是 跳舞，她 都 行。
   Wúlùn chànggē huòshì tiàowǔ, tā dōu xíng.
   She is good at both singing and dancing.

3. 或者 **huòzhě** either ... or
   你 早上 或者 下午 来 都可以。
   Nǐ zǎoshang huòzhě xiàwǔ lái dōu kěyǐ.
   You may come either in the morning or in the afternoon.

4. 或许 **huòxǔ** perhaps, maybe
   他 或许 没有 赶上 火车。
   Tā huòxǔ méiyǒu gǎnshàng huǒchē.
   Perhaps he has missed the train.

The bottom horizontal stroke goes up slightly. **8 strokes**

一 厂 厂 口 豆 或 或 或

zhě -er, -ist

This character functions as a particle. It is often used after a verb, adjective or noun to indicate a class of persons or things. In 或者, it means *perhaps*.

Radical: 曰 'speech'

Index # 91

Character components: 耂 + 日

Character configuration:

Compounds, sentences and meanings

1. **者** **zhě** one of those who; the thing or things which
    独身主义者。
    Dúshēnzhǔyìzhě.
    One who prefers to be single.

2. **作者** **zuòzhě** author
    他 是 这 本 书 的 作者。
    Tā shì zhè běn shū de zuòzhě.
    He's the author of this book.

3. **读者** **dúzhě** reader
    这 本 书 的 读者 很 广。
    Zhè běn shū de dúzhě hěn guǎng.
    This book has a wide readership.

4. **记者** **jìzhě** reporter
    他 是 当 记者的。
    Tā shì dāng jìzhě de.
    He is a reporter.

5. **旁观者** **pángguānzhě** onlooker
    旁观者 清。
    Pángguānzhě qīng.
    The spectator sees most clearly.

The top horizontal stroke is shorter.   8 strokes

一	十	土	耂	耂	者	者	者					

huǒ fire

The character is a pictograph of a blazing flame.

Radical: 火 'fire'　　　　　　　　　**Index # 75**

Character component: 火　　　　　**Character configuration:** ☐

Compounds, sentences and meanings

1. **火　huǒ**　fire
   不要 让 小孩子 玩火。
   Bǔyào ràng xiǎoháizi wánhuǒ.
   Don't let children play with fire.

2. **火车　huǒchē**　train
   她 明天 坐 火车 去 西安。
   Tā míngtiān zuò huǒchē qù Xī'ān.
   She will be taking a train to Xian tomorrow.

3. **火柴　huǒchái**　matches
   请问， 有 没有 火柴?
   Qǐngwèn, yǒu méiyǒu huǒchái?
   Excuse me, do you have a match?

4. **火候　huǒhou**　duration and degree of heating
   炒菜 的 时候， 掌握 火候 很
   Chǎocài de shíhou, zhǎngwǒ huǒhou hěn
   重要。
   zhòngyào.
   Heat control is very important in stir-frying.

5. **火气　huǒqì**　temper
   他的 火气 很大。
   Tāde huǒqì hěn dà.
   He has a bad temper.

The last stroke tapers off.　　　　　　　　　　　**4 strokes**

丶	丷	少	火								

站

zhàn stand

The character combines *stand* 立 and *occupy* 占 to express the meaning of *stand* or *station*.

Radical: 立 'stand'

Index # 111

Character components: 立 + 占

Character configuration:

Compounds, sentences and meanings

1. 站 **zhàn** train/bus stop
   我 下 个 站 下车。
   Wǒ xià ge zhàn xiàchē.
   I get off at the next stop.

2. 火车站 **huǒchēzhàn** train station
   我 家 离 火车站 不 远。
   Wǒ jiā lí huǒchēzhàn bù yuǎn.
   My house is not far from the railway station.

3. 站立 **zhànlì** be on one's feet
   他 腿 疼, 不能 站立。
   Tā tuǐ téng, bùnéng zhànlì.
   His leg was so sore that he couldn't stand up.

4. 站稳 **zhànwěn** come to a stop
   等 车 站稳了 再下。
   Děng chē zhànwěnle zài xià.
   Wait till the bus/train stops completely before getting out.

5. 站住 **zhànzhù** stop, halt
   风 刮得 人 都 站不住 了。
   Fēng guāde rén dōu zhànbuzhù le.
   The wind was so strong that you could hardly stand.

The fifth stroke lifts slightly. | **10 strokes**

丶	二	产	立	立	立丨	立卜	立占	站	站			

249

知
    zhī   know

The character combines *arrow* 矢 and *mouth* 口 to suggest words flying like arrows from the mouth. To speak fast means the speaker *knows* the subject well.

Radical: 矢 'arrow'   **Index # 123**

or   口 'mouth'   **Index # 50**

Character components: 矢 + 口   **Character configuration:**

Compounds, sentences and meanings

1. 知 **zhī** be aware of, know
   这 话 不 知 是 谁 说 的。
   Zhè huà bù zhī shì shéi/shuí shuō de.
   I don't know who said this.

2. 知道 **zhīdao** know
   你 知道 邮局 在 哪儿 吗?
   Nǐ zhīdao yóujú zài nǎr ma?
   Do you know where the post office is?

3. 知己 **zhījǐ** bosom friend
   人生 难得 有 个 知己。
   Rénshēng nándé yǒu ge zhījǐ.
   It is difficult to find a true friend.

4. 知音 **zhīyīn** an understanding friend
   难得 有 个 知音。
   Nándé yǒu ge zhīyīn.
   It is difficult to find someone who really understands you.

5. 知识 **zhīshi** knowledge
   王 老师 的 知识 渊博。
   Wáng lǎoshī de zhīshi yuānbó.
   Teacher Wang is very knowledgeable.

The fifth stroke ends firmly.   **8 strokes**

ノ	㇏	㇒	乍	矢	知	知	知					

250

道 dào road

The character combines *movement* 辶 and *main* 首 to suggest going along a main path. It means *road*.

Radical: 辶 'movement'

Index # 38

Character components: 首 + 辶

Character configuration:

Compounds, sentences and meanings

1. **道 dào** way, method
   他 对 养生 之 道 很 有 研究。
   Tā duì yǎngshēng zhī dào hěn yǒu yánjiū.
   He's very knowledgeable about staying healthy.

2. **道路 dàolù** road
   走 前人 没有 走过 的 道路。
   Zǒu qiánrén méiyǒu zǒuguo de dàolù.
   Explore paths none have taken before.

3. **道理 dàoli** reason
   你的 话 很 有 道理。
   Nǐde huà hěn yǒu dàoli.
   What you said is quite reasonable.

4. **道歉 dàoqiàn** apologize
   我 得 向 你 道歉。
   Wǒ děi xiàng nǐ dàoqiàn.
   I owe you an apology.

5. **道义 dàoyì** morality and justice
   我们 应该 给 他 道义 上 的 支持。
   Wǒmen yīnggāi gěi tā dàoyì shang de zhīchí.
   We should give him moral support.

The top horizontal stroke is longer.   12 strokes

丶	丷	丷	䒑	产	芐	首	首	首	首	道	道

A. Look at the 16-character grid and CIRCLE words or phrases. They can be written horizontally or vertically. Look at the circled characters in the Key if unsure. COPY the word or phrase next to the grid and write the pinyin and meaning.

在	儿	哪	火
共	公	汽	车
知	道	或	站
可	以	者	也

	Word or phrase			Pinyin	Meaning
(i)	火	车	站	huǒchēzhàn	train station
(ii)					
(iii)					
(iv)					

B. Refer to the characters in the 16-character grid above and CONVERT the pinyin phrases into characters and check their English meaning in the Key.

(i)	Dào Zhōngguó Fàndiàn zěnme zǒu?								
(ii)	Kěyǐ zuò gōnggòngqìchē qù.								
(iii)	Huòzhě zuò huǒchē yě kěyǐ.								
(iv)	Wǒ zhīdao chēzhàn zài nǎr.								

C. Match the Chinese words with their English meaning.

(i)

可爱	altogether
可能	know
以前	reason
公共	cute
一共	apologize
知道	possible
道 li	before
道 qiàn	public

(ii)

汽车	gasoline
汽 yóu	railway station
汽 shuǐ	automobile
或 xǔ	temper
作者	soft drinks
火 chái	matches
火 qì	perhaps, maybe
火车站	author, writer

CHARACTER BUILDING 5 (201–250)

A. Memorize each of the following radicals and their English names. As a review exercise, write the pinyin and meaning of each example.

1. ［一］ 'horizontal stroke'

　　来（＿＿＿＿）＿＿＿＿＿＿；万（＿＿＿＿）＿＿＿＿＿＿．

　　面（＿＿＿＿）＿＿＿＿＿＿．

2. ［丨］ 'vertical stroke'

　　北（＿＿＿＿）＿＿＿＿＿＿；

3. ［丿］ 'downward-left stroke'

　　久（＿＿＿＿）＿＿＿＿＿＿；长（＿＿＿＿）＿＿＿＿＿＿；

4. ［亠］ 'top of 六'

　　京（＿＿＿＿）＿＿＿＿＿＿；就（＿＿＿＿）＿＿＿＿＿＿．

5. ［十］ 'ten'

　　南（＿＿＿＿）＿＿＿＿＿＿；直（＿＿＿＿）＿＿＿＿＿＿；

6. ［八］ 'eight'

　　共（＿＿＿＿）＿＿＿＿＿＿；典（＿＿＿＿）＿＿＿＿＿＿；

　　前（＿＿＿＿）＿＿＿＿＿＿；公（＿＿＿＿）＿＿＿＿＿＿．

7. ［人］ 'person'

　　从（＿＿＿＿）＿＿＿＿＿＿；以（＿＿＿＿）＿＿＿＿＿＿；

8. ［亻］ 'upright person'

　　住（＿＿＿＿）＿＿＿＿＿＿；作（＿＿＿＿）＿＿＿＿＿＿；

9. ［又］ 'again'

　　欢（＿＿＿＿）＿＿＿＿＿＿；对（＿＿＿＿）＿＿＿＿＿＿；

10. ［力］ 'strength'

　　动（＿＿＿＿）＿＿＿＿＿＿；助（＿＿＿＿）＿＿＿＿＿＿；

11. ［氵］ '3 drops of water'

　　游（＿＿＿＿）＿＿＿＿＿＿；泳（＿＿＿＿）＿＿＿＿＿＿；

　　池（＿＿＿＿）＿＿＿＿＿＿；海（＿＿＿＿）＿＿＿＿＿＿；

　　活（＿＿＿＿）＿＿＿＿＿＿；汽（＿＿＿＿）＿＿＿＿＿＿；

12. ［门］ 'door'

　　间（＿＿＿＿）＿＿＿＿＿＿；问（＿＿＿＿）＿＿＿＿＿＿；

13. ［辶］ 'movement'

　　运（＿＿＿＿）＿＿＿＿＿＿；道（＿＿＿＿）＿＿＿＿＿＿；

14. ［土］ 'earth'

　　坐（＿＿＿＿）＿＿＿＿＿＿；地（＿＿＿＿）＿＿＿＿＿＿；

15. ［口］ 'mouth'
　　呢（＿＿＿＿＿）＿＿＿＿＿＿＿；和（＿＿＿＿＿）＿＿＿＿＿＿＿；
　　可（＿＿＿＿＿）＿＿＿＿＿＿＿.

16. ［巾］ 'napkin'
　　常（＿＿＿＿＿）＿＿＿＿＿＿＿；帮（＿＿＿＿＿）＿＿＿＿＿＿＿.

17. ［夂］ 'top of 冬'
　　冬（＿＿＿＿＿）＿＿＿＿＿＿＿；夏（＿＿＿＿＿）＿＿＿＿＿＿＿.

18. ［纟］ 'silk'
　　经（＿＿＿＿＿）＿＿＿＿＿＿＿；练（＿＿＿＿＿）＿＿＿＿＿＿＿；

19. ［灬］ '4 dots of fire'
　　热（＿＿＿＿＿）＿＿＿＿＿＿＿；点（＿＿＿＿＿）＿＿＿＿＿＿＿.

20. ［方］ 'direction'
　　方（＿＿＿＿＿）＿＿＿＿＿＿＿；旁（＿＿＿＿＿）＿＿＿＿＿＿＿.

21. ［木］ 'wood'
　　末（＿＿＿＿＿）＿＿＿＿＿＿＿；本（＿＿＿＿＿）＿＿＿＿＿＿＿；

22. ［车］ 'vehicle'
　　车（＿＿＿＿＿）＿＿＿＿＿＿＿；较（＿＿＿＿＿）＿＿＿＿＿＿＿.

23. ［戈］ 'spear'
　　或（＿＿＿＿＿）＿＿＿＿＿＿＿；我（＿＿＿＿＿）＿＿＿＿＿＿＿.

24. ［见］ 'see'
　　觉（＿＿＿＿＿）＿＿＿＿＿＿＿；见（＿＿＿＿＿）＿＿＿＿＿＿＿.

B. Write the pinyin and meaning against the characters classified under the following radicals.

1. ［冫］ 'ice'　　　　　　　　　　　　　　　冷　（＿＿＿＿＿）＿＿＿＿＿＿＿
2. ［冂］ 'three-sided frame, closed top'　周　（＿＿＿＿＿）＿＿＿＿＿＿＿
3. ［刂］ 'upright knife '　　　　　　　　　到　（＿＿＿＿＿）＿＿＿＿＿＿＿
4. ［土］ 'scholar'　　　　　　　　　　　　喜　（＿＿＿＿＿）＿＿＿＿＿＿＿
5. ［己］ 'self'　　　　　　　　　　　　　　已　（＿＿＿＿＿）＿＿＿＿＿＿＿
6. ［火］ 'fire'　　　　　　　　　　　　　　火　（＿＿＿＿＿）＿＿＿＿＿＿＿
7. ［曰］ 'speech'　　　　　　　　　　　　者　（＿＿＿＿＿）＿＿＿＿＿＿＿
8. ［爪］ 'claw'　　　　　　　　　　　　　爱　（＿＿＿＿＿）＿＿＿＿＿＿＿
9. ［立］ 'stand'　　　　　　　　　　　　　站　（＿＿＿＿＿）＿＿＿＿＿＿＿
10. ［目］ 'eye'　　　　　　　　　　　　　　睡　（＿＿＿＿＿）＿＿＿＿＿＿＿
11. ［矢］ 'arrow'　　　　　　　　　　　　知　（＿＿＿＿＿）＿＿＿＿＿＿＿
12. ［雨］ 'rain'　　　　　　　　　　　　　雨　（＿＿＿＿＿）＿＿＿＿＿＿＿

C. Write the pinyin and meaning against the characters which share the following components. (Note that these components are not necessarily used as radicals.)

1.　［也］　池（＿＿＿＿）＿＿＿＿＿＿；　地（＿＿＿＿）＿＿＿＿＿＿．

2.　［匕］　老（＿＿＿＿）＿＿＿＿＿＿；　北（＿＿＿＿）＿＿＿＿＿＿．

3.　［日］　间（＿＿＿＿）＿＿＿＿＿＿；　晚（＿＿＿＿）＿＿＿＿＿＿．

4.　［友］　友（＿＿＿＿）＿＿＿＿＿＿；　爱（＿＿＿＿）＿＿＿＿＿＿；

REVIEW 5 (201–250)

The following are words and phrases classified under parts of speech. Write the pinyin and meaning.

Nouns	地方	（＿＿＿＿）＿＿＿＿＿；	地下	（＿＿＿＿）＿＿＿＿＿；
	地铁	（＿＿＿＿）＿＿＿＿＿；	铁路	（＿＿＿＿）＿＿＿＿＿；
	车	（＿＿＿＿）＿＿＿＿＿；	汽车	（＿＿＿＿）＿＿＿＿＿；
	火车	（＿＿＿＿）＿＿＿＿＿；	火车站	（＿＿＿＿）＿＿＿＿＿；
	北方	（＿＿＿＿）＿＿＿＿＿；	南方	（＿＿＿＿）＿＿＿＿＿；
	时间	（＿＿＿＿）＿＿＿＿＿；	冬天	（＿＿＿＿）＿＿＿＿＿；
	海边	（＿＿＿＿）＿＿＿＿＿；	海外	（＿＿＿＿）＿＿＿＿＿；
	夏天	（＿＿＿＿）＿＿＿＿＿；	泳道	（＿＿＿＿）＿＿＿＿＿；
	游泳池	（＿＿＿＿）＿＿＿＿＿；	方面	（＿＿＿＿）＿＿＿＿＿；
	周	（＿＿＿＿）＿＿＿＿＿；	周口	（＿＿＿＿）＿＿＿＿＿；
	周末	（＿＿＿＿）＿＿＿＿＿；	周年	（＿＿＿＿）＿＿＿＿＿；
	末期	（＿＿＿＿）＿＿＿＿＿；	活动	（＿＿＿＿）＿＿＿＿＿；
	生活	（＿＿＿＿）＿＿＿＿＿；	爱好	（＿＿＿＿）＿＿＿＿＿；
	爱人	（＿＿＿＿）＿＿＿＿＿；	午睡	（＿＿＿＿）＿＿＿＿＿；
	运动	（＿＿＿＿）＿＿＿＿＿；	汽油	（＿＿＿＿）＿＿＿＿＿；
	作者	（＿＿＿＿）＿＿＿＿＿；	读者	（＿＿＿＿）＿＿＿＿＿；
	站	（＿＿＿＿）＿＿＿＿＿；	道路	（＿＿＿＿）＿＿＿＿＿；
	知识	（＿＿＿＿）＿＿＿＿＿．		

Proper nouns	北京	（＿＿＿＿）＿＿＿＿＿；	南京	（＿＿＿＿）＿＿＿＿＿；
	东京	（＿＿＿＿）＿＿＿＿＿；	上海	（＿＿＿＿）＿＿＿＿＿；

Verbs	住	（＿＿＿＿）＿＿＿＿＿；	到	（＿＿＿＿）＿＿＿＿＿；
	到期	（＿＿＿＿）＿＿＿＿＿；	坐	（＿＿＿＿）＿＿＿＿＿；
	来	（＿＿＿＿）＿＿＿＿＿；	经过	（＿＿＿＿）＿＿＿＿＿；
	长大	（＿＿＿＿）＿＿＿＿＿；	喜爱	（＿＿＿＿）＿＿＿＿＿；

喜欢 (_____) _____ ; 下雨 (_____) _____ ;
游泳 (_____) _____ ; 活 (_____) _____ ;
爱 (_____) _____ ; 睡觉 (_____) _____ ;
觉得 (_____) _____ ; 知道 (_____) _____ .

Auxiliary verbs
可以 (_____) _____ .

Adjectives
喜欢 (_____) _____ ; 热 (_____) _____ ;
常见 (_____) _____ ; 动人 (_____) _____ ;
可爱 (_____) _____ ; 到家 (_____) _____ ;
公共 (_____) _____ ; 公用 (_____) _____ .

Location words
南边 (_____) _____ ; 中间 (_____) _____ ;
前面 (_____) _____ ; 后面 (_____) _____ ;

Time words (Adverbs)
久 (_____) _____ ; 不久 (_____) _____ ;
以前 (_____) _____ ; 以后 (_____) _____ ;

Adverbs
从前 (_____) _____ ; 从来 (_____) _____ ;
已经 (_____) _____ ; 经常 (_____) _____ ;
常常 (_____) _____ ; 比较 (_____) _____ ;

Conjunction
和 (_____) _____ ; 以便 (_____) _____ ;
或 (_____) _____ ; 或者 (_____) _____ ;

Prepositions
从 (_____) _____ ; 从...到 (_____) _____ .

Particles
呢 (_____) _____ .

WORD/SENTENCE PUZZLE 5

Find and CIRCLE words, phrases or sentences hidden in the puzzle. They can be found horizontally from left to right or vertically. The lines across and down are indicated by numbers. Write down the meaning next to the pinyin. The first one is done for you.

ACROSS (left to right)

2. Wǒ juéde wǒde Zhōngwén jìnbù le. *I think my Chinese has improved.*
6. Huǒchē zài tiělù shàng zǒu. _____
7. qìchēzhàn. _____
8. dúzhě. _____
9. (i) Zhōumò huódòng tài duō le. _____
9. (ii) xiàyǔ

298

11. cónglái _____

13. Zhè zhī māo hěn kě'ài. _____

DOWN

1. yì zhōunián. _____

2. Wǒ cháng qù yóuyǒng. _____

3. (i) shuìjiào _____

3. (ii) huódào yībǎi-líng-yī _____

4. huǒchē _____

5. Wǒ jiā lí huǒchēzhàn bú tài yuǎn. _____

7. (i) zhōngjiān _____

7. (ii) dìtiě _____

9. Nǐ zǎoshang huòzhě xiàwǔ lái dōu kěyǐ. _____

	1	2	3	4	5	6	7	8	9	10	11
1	买	西	睡	旁	早	看	见	做	起	母	明
2	每	我	觉	得	我	的	中	文	进	步	了
3	东	常	亲	它	家	旁	间	知	工	共	公
4	头	去	城	边	离	吃	面	条	你	期	进
5	起	游	呢	和	火	北	地	京	早	到	道
6	走	泳	南	火	车	在	铁	路	上	走	面
7	床	亲	汽	车	站	典	明	毛	或	在	现
8	一	者	方	比	不	睡	爱	读	者	经	长
9	周	末	活	动	太	多	了	晚	下	雨	饭
10	年	觉	到	岁	远	到	坐	早	午	就	久
11	卖	亲	一	池	住	冷	冬	从	来	已	做
12	往	能	百	离	太	狗	钱	路	都	店	面
13	千	用	零	远	这	只	猫	很	可	爱	现
14	时	街	一	较	夏	还	大	欢	以	喜	往

Alphabetical Index

chéng	城	137.1		dàodǐ	到底	202.3
chéngshì	城市	137.3		dàojiā	到家	202.4
chéngxiāng	城乡	137		dàoqī	到期	134.5/202.5
chī	吃	108.1		dào	道	250.1
chībuxià	吃不下	108.4		dàoli	道理	250.3
chīdexià	吃得下	108.3		dàolù	道路	250.2
chīfàn	吃饭	108.2		dàoqiàn	道歉	250.4
chīkǔ	吃苦	108.5		dàoyì	道义	250.5
chí	池	229.1		de	的	34.1
chítáng	池塘	229.5		dé (verb)	得	240.1
chuáng	床	118.1		de (verbal particle)	得	240.2
chuángshang	床上	118.2		déyì	得意	240.3
chuángdān	床单	118.3		dézuì	得罪	240.4
cí	词	165.1		děi	得	240.5
cídiǎn	词典	165.2/166.4		Déguó	德国	26.3
cíhuìbiǎo	词汇表	165.5		dì	地	205.1
cóng	从	203.1		dìdao	地道	205.5
cóng nàr qǐ	从那儿起	81.5		dìfang	地方	205.2
cóng ... dào	从 ... 到	203.2		dìtiě	地铁	206.4
cónglái	从来	203.3/211.5		dìtú	地图	205.3
cóngqián	从前	203.4		dìxià	地下	205.4
cóngxiǎo	从小	203.5		dì	弟	57.1
				dìdi	弟弟	57.2
				dìxí	弟媳	57.4
D				dìxiōng	弟兄	57.3
dà	大	91.1		dìyī	第一	1.5
dà xiōngdì	大兄弟	61.4		diǎn	点	103.1
dàgài	大概	94.5		diǎncài	点菜	103.4
dàgē	大哥	55.3		diǎntóu	点头	103.5
dàjiā	大家	91.3		diǎnzhōng	点钟	104.2
dàjiē	大街	188.3		diǎn	典	166.1
dàshēng	大声	91.2		diǎnlǐ	典礼	166.2
dàxiǎo	大小	91.4		diǎnxíng	典型	166.3
dàxiě	大写	42.4		diàn	电	129.1
dàxuéshēng	大学生	99.4		diànhuà	电话	129.5
dàxióngmāo	大熊猫	89.4		diànnǎo	电脑	129.4/151.4
dāncí	单词	165.4		diànshì	电视	129.3
dānrénchuáng	单人床	118.4		diànyǐng	电影	129.2
dào	到	202.1		diànyǐngyuàn	电影院	177.5
dàochù	到处	202.5				

J

K

L

lǐbian	里边	82.4
lǐtou	里头	82.5
liàn	练	162.1
liànwǔ	练武	162.5
liànxí	练习	162.2
liànxíběn	练习本	162.3
liànxítí	练习题	162.4
liǎng	两	60.1
liǎng cì	两次	60.3
liǎng ge	两个	60.2/45.2
liǎng suì	两岁	60.4
liǎngbànr	两半儿	60.5
liǎngpáng	两旁	174.3
líng	零	160.1
língjiàn	零件	145.3
língqián	零钱	146.4/160.4
língsuì	零碎	160.3
língxià	零下	160.2
língyòngqián	零用钱	160.5
liù	六	6.1
Liùyī	六一	6.4
Liùyuè	六月	6.2
lù	路	194.1
lùbiāo	路标	194.2
lùkǒu	路口	194.4
lùshang	路上	194.3
lùxiàn	路线	194.5
luànqībāzāo	乱七八糟	8.5
lǜshī	律师	70.5

M

mā	妈	66.1
māma	妈妈	66.2
mǎ	马	193.1
mǎhu	马虎	193.3
Mǎlāsōng	马拉松	193.5
mǎlù	马路	193.2
mǎshàng	马上	193.4
ma	吗	30.1

mǎi	买	138.1
mǎibudào	买不到	138.5
mǎibuqǐ	买不起	138.3
mǎideqǐ	买得起	138.2
mǎimài	买卖	138.4/153.5
mài	卖	153.1
màilì	卖力	153.2
màinòng	卖弄	153.4
màizuò	卖座	153.3
máng	忙	100.1
mánglù	忙碌	100.3
mángzhe	忙着	100.2
máng ma?	忙吗?	30.3
mángrén	忙人	100.4
māo	猫	89.1
māotóuyīng	猫头鹰	89.5
máo	毛	143.1
máobǐ	毛笔	143.3
máobìng	毛病	143.4
máoyī	毛衣	143.2/144.2
me	么	13.1
méi	没	53.1
méiyǒu	没有	53.2
méi guānxi	没关系	53.3
méi yìsi	没意思	53.4
méiwán-méiliǎo	没完没了	53.5
měi	美	29.1
Měiguó	美国	29.5
měihǎo	美好	29.3
měihuà	美化	29.4
měilì	美丽	29.2
Měiyuán	美元	156.2
měi	每	135.1
měi ge xīngqī	每个星期	135.4
měiměi	每每	135.5
měinián	每年	135.3
měitiān	每天	135.2
mèi	妹	58.1
mèifu	妹夫	58.4

xiè	谢	77.1
xiètiān-xièdì	谢天谢地	77.5
xièxie	谢谢	77.2
xīng	星	133.1
xīngqī	星期	133.2
Xīngqīliù	星期六	6.3
Xīngqīsān	星期三	3.4
xìngyùn	幸运	239.3
xìng	姓	23.1
xìngmíng	姓名	23.2
xìngshì	姓氏	23.3
xiōng	兄	61.1
xiōngdì	兄弟	61.2
xué	学	37.1
xuéfèi	学费	37.5
xuéqī	学期	134.4
xuésheng	学生	37.2
xuéshí	学识	48.5
xuéwèn	学问	20.5
xuéxí	学习	37.3
xuéxiào	学校	37.4/178.3

Y

yāsuìqián	压岁钱	146.5
yàng	样	73.1
yàngzi	样子	73.3
yàome	要么	13.5
.. yěba, ... yěba	也罢…也罢	68.5
yě	也	68.1
yě ... yě	也…也	68.2
yěhǎo	也好	68.5
yěxǔ	也许	68.3
yèjiān	夜间	216.5
yī	一	1.1
yī qiānwàn	一千万	155.3
yí cì	一次	1.4
yí ge	一个	1.2
yí kèzhōng	一刻钟	104.3
yíbàn	一半	107.2
yígòng	一共	243.3

yíhuìr	一会儿	41.3
yí kuài qián	一块钱	148.3
yíkuàir	一块儿	148.4
yíyàng	一样	73.4
yì běn (shū)	一本（书）	1.3
yì máo (qián)	一毛（钱）	143.5
yìqǐ	一起	117.5
yìzhí	一直	183.2
yī	衣	144.1
yīfu	衣服	144.3
yījià	衣架	144.5
yīliào	衣料	144.4
yī	医	98.1
yīkē	医科	98.5
yīshēng	医生	98.2
yīwùsuǒ	医务所	98.3
yīyuàn	医院	98.4/177.3
yí	宜	150.1
yírén	宜人	150.3
yímā	姨妈	66.4
yǐ	已	213.1
yǐjīng	已经	213.2
yǐwǎng	已往	213.3
yǐ	以	242.1
yǐbiàn	以便	242.2
yǐhòu	以后	172.5/242.3
yǐqián	以前	242.4
yǐwéi	以为	242.5
yīng	英	39.1
Yīngguó	英国	39.3
yīngjùn	英俊	39.2
yīnglǐ	英里	39.5
Yīngwén	英文	40.2
Yīngyǔ	英语	39.4
yǐng	影	130.1
yǐngmí	影迷	130.2
yǐngxiǎng	影响	130.4
yǐngyìn	影印	130.3
yǒng	泳	228.1
yǒngdào	泳道	228.5

Radical Index

1 stroke

[一] #2

一	yī	1
七	qī	7
三	sān	3
下	xià	114
上	shàng	113
万	wàn	155
天	tiān	122
不	bù	38
五	wǔ	5
可	kě	241
东	dōng	139
再	zài	189
百	bǎi	147
来	lái	211
两	liǎng	60
面	miàn	173
哥	gē	55

[丨] #3

中	zhōng	28
北	běi	208
电	diàn	129
师	shī	70

[丿] #4

九	jiǔ	9
千	qiān	154
么	me	13
久	jiǔ	212
午	wǔ	115
长	cháng/zhǎng	215
生	shēng	99
乐	lè/yuè	278
年	nián	126
后	hòu	172

[乙] (乛 丁 乚) #5

了	le	106
习	xí	163
也	yě	68
书	shū	164
电	diàn	129
买	mǎi	138

2 strokes

[亠] #6

六	liù	6
京	jīng	209
离	lí	181
商	shāng	140
就	jiù	158

[冫] #7

冷	lěng	219

[冖] #8

写	xiě	42

[讠] #9

认	rèn	47
识	shí	48
词	cí	165
说	shuō	49
语	yǔ	50
请	qǐng	19
谁	shéi/shuí	33
谢	xiè	77

[二] #10

二	èr	2
五	wǔ	5
元	yuán	156

[十] #11

十	shí	10
半	bàn	17
直	zhí	183
卖	mài	153
南	nán	210

[匚] #13

医	yī	98

[卜] #14

外	wài	192

[刂] #15

到	dào	202

[冂] #16

周	zhōu	231

[八] #17

八	bā	8
公	gōng	179
分	fēn	106
半	bàn	107
只	zhī/zhǐ	90/200
共	gòng	243
弟	dì	57
前	qián	171
首	shǒu	271

[人] #18

人	rén	27
个	ge	45
今	jīn	121
从	cóng	203
以	yǐ	242
会	huì	18

只	zhī/zhǐ	90/200
兄	xiōng	61
台	tái	152
叫	jiào	11
吃	chī	108
后	hòu	172
名	míng	14
吗	ma	30
吧	ba	159
知	zhī	249
和	hé	54
呢	ne	238
哪	nǎ	25
哥	gē	55
喜	xǐ	217

[口] #51

四	sì	4
因	yīn	297
园	yuán	180
国	guó	26

[巾] #52

常	cháng	225
师	shī	70
帮	bāng	169

[山] #53

岁	suì	93

[彳] #54

很	hěn	71
往	wǎng	73
得	dē/de/děi	240
街	jiē	188

[彡] #55

影	yǐng	130

[夕] #56

名	míng	14
岁	suì	93
多	duō	43

[夂] #57

冬	dōng	220
条	tiáo	187
夏	xià	222

[犭] #58

狗	gǒu	88
猫	māo	89

[饣] #59

饭	fàn	110

[己] #62

已	yǐ	213

[女] #65

女	nǚ	85
她	tā	32
好	hǎo	17
妈	mā	66
妹	mèi	58
姐	jiě	56
姓	xìng	23

[子] #67

子	zǐ	84
学	xué	37
孩	hái	87

[纟] #68

练	liàn	162
经	jīng	214

[马] #69

马	mǎ	193

4 strokes

[灬] #71

点	diǎn	104
热	rè	223

[文] #73

文	wén	40

[方] #74

方	fāng	230
旁	páng	174

[火] #75

火	huǒ	247

[心] #76

怎	zěn	72
您	nín	21

[王] #79

现	xiàn	101

[木] #81

本	běn	167
末	mò	232
床	chuáng	118
条	tiáo	187
校	xiào	178
样	yàng	73

[车] #84

车	chē	207
较	jiào	224

[戈] #85

我	wǒ	18
或	huò	245

[比] #86

比	bǐ	94

KEY

Quiz 1 (1–10)

A.

B. (i)

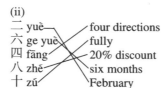

(ii)
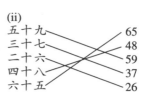

C. (i)

dì 一 ╳ third
dì 三 ╱ first
dì 一 cì ╲ third time
dì 三 cì ╳ first time
dì 五 cì — fifth time

(ii)

二 yuè ╲ four directions
六 ge yuè ╲ fully
四 fāng ╳ 20% discount
八 zhé ╳ six months
十 zú — February

D. (i)

1. dì 七
2. 四 jǐ
3. 七 chéng
4. 十 zú
5. 二 děng

(ii)

6. xīngqī 四
7. 九 zhě
8. 九九 biǎo
9. 五 yán 六 sè
10. 三 xīn 二 yì

Quiz 2 (11–20)

A.
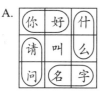

	Word or phrase	Pinyin	English meaning
(i)	你好	Nǐ hǎo	Hello!
(ii)	请问	Qǐngwèn . . .	May I ask . . .
(iii)	什么	shénme	what
(iv)	名字	míngzi	name

B.

	Pinyin	Characters	Translation
(i)	Wǒ wèn nǐ.	我问你。	I ask you.
(ii)	Nǐ wèn wǒ shénme?	你问我什么?	What did you ask me?
(iii)	Wǒ jiào shénme míngzi?	我叫什么名字?	What's my name?

C. (i)

好 kàn ╲ Come in
好 chī ╲ characters
Hàn 字 ╳ dictionary
yǒu 名 ╳ delicious
字 diǎn ╳ alphabet
请 jìnlai ╳ business card
字 mǔ ╳ pretty
名 piàn ╱ famous

(ii)

xué 问 ╲ question
问 tí ╲ etc.
叫 hǎn ╳ say hello to
问 hǎo ╳ what
请 jiào ╳ shout
什么 ╳ seek advice
什么 de ╳ how
zěn 么 ╱ learning

Quiz 3 (21–30)

A.

	Word or phrase	Pinyin	Translation
(i)	贵姓	Guìxìng	What's your name?
(ii)	哪国人	nǎguórén	which nationality
(iii)	中国	Zhōngguó	China

B.

	Pinyin	Characters	Translation
(i)	Qǐngwèn, nín guìxìng?	请问,您贵姓?	Excuse me, may I ask your name?
(ii)	Qǐngwèn, guìguó shì nǎguó?	请问,贵国是哪国?	Excuse me, which country do you come from?
(iii)	Qǐngwèn, nǐ shì nǎguórén?	请问,你是哪国人?	Excuse me, what nationality are you?

320

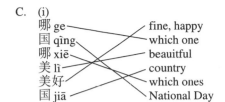
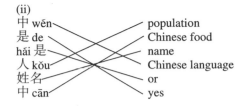

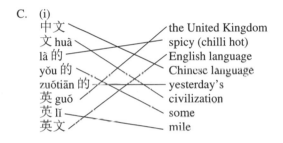

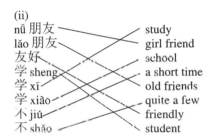
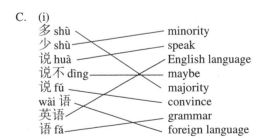
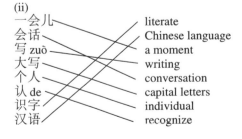

C. (i)

哪 ge	fine, happy
国 qīng	which one
哪 xiē	beauitful
美 lǐ	country
美好	which ones
国 jiā	National Day

(ii)

中 wén	population
是 de	Chinese food
hái 是	name
人 kǒu	Chinese language
姓名	or
中 cān	yes

Quiz 4 (31–40)

A.

她	朋	友
学	英	文
不	谁	的

Word or phrase	Pinyin	English meaning
(i) 朋友	péngyou	friend/s
(ii) 学英文	xué Yīngwén	learn English
(iii) 谁的	shuǐ/shéi'de	whose

B.

Pinyin	Characters	Translation
(i) Shuǐ/shéi de péngyou?	谁的朋友？	Whose friend is this?
(ii) Tā xué bù xué Zhōngwén?	她／他学不学中文？	Does she/he study Chinese?
(iii) Bù, tā xué Yīngwén.	不，她／他学英文。	No, she/he studies English.

C. (i)

中文	the United Kingdom
文 huà	spicy (chilli hot)
là 的	English language
yǒu 的	Chinese language
zuótiān 的	yesterday's
英 guó	civilization
英 lǐ	some
英文	mile

(ii)

nǚ 朋友	study
lǎo 朋友	girl friend
友好	school
学 sheng	a short time
学 xí	old friends
学 xiào	quite a few
不 jiǔ	friendly
不 shǎo	student

Quiz 5 (41–50)

A.

多	少	说
写	会	汉
认	识	语

Word or phrase	Pinyin	English meaning
(i) 多少	duōshao	how many/much
(ii) 说汉语	shuō Hànyǔ	speak Chinese
(iii) 认识	rènshi	recognize

B.

Pinyin	Characters	Translation
(i) Nǐ huì shuō Hànyǔ ma?	你会说汉语吗？	Can you speak Chinese?
(ii) Nǐ huì búhuì xiě Hànzì?	你会不会写汉字？	Can you write Chinese characters?
(iii) Nǐ huì xiě duōshao Hànzì?	你会写多少汉字？	How many Chinese characters can you write?
(iv) Tā búhuì xiě Hànzì.	他／她不会写汉字。	He/she can't write Chinese characters.

C. (i)

多 shù	minority
少 shù	speak
说 huà	English language
说不 dìng	maybe
说 fú	majority
wài 语	convince
英语	grammar
语 fǎ	foreign language

(ii)

一会儿	literate
会话	Chinese language
写 zuò	a moment
大写	writing
个人	conversation
认 de	capital letters
识字	individual
汉语	recognize

Character Building 1 (1–50)

A. 1. [一] 一 *yī*, one; 三 *sān*, three; 五 *wǔ*, five;
七 *qī*, seven; 不 *bù*, not.

2. [丿] 九 *jiǔ*, nine; 么 *me*, particle.

3. [讠] 请 *qǐng*, please; 谁 *shéi/shuí*, who; 认
rèn, recognize; 识 *shí*, know; 语 *yǔ*,
language; 说 *shuō*, speak.

4. [人] 人 *rén*, person, people; 个 *ge*, classifier;
会 *huì*, be able to.

5. [亻] 你 *nǐ*, you (singular); 他 *tā*, he, him; 什
shén, head word for *shénme*, what.

6. [口] 叫 *jiào*, be called; 哪 *nǎ*, which; 名
míng, given name; 吗 *ma*, question
particle.

7. [囗] 四 *sì*, four; 国 *guó*, country.

8. [女] 好 *hǎo*, good, well; 她 *tā*, she, her; 姓
xìng, be surnamed.

B. 1. [丨] 中 *zhōng*, middle
2. [八] 八 *bā*, eight
3. [宀] 写 *xiě*, write
4. [二] 二 *èr*, two
5. [亠] 六 *liù*, six
6. [十] 十 *shí*, ten
7. [又] 友 *yǒu*, friend
8. [氵] 汉 *Hàn*, ethnic Han race
9. [艹] 英 *yīng*, hero

10. [小] 少 *shǎo*, few
11. [夕] 多 *duō*, many/much
12. [文] 文 *wén*, script
13. [心] 您 *nín*, you (polite)
14. [戈] 我 *wǒ*, I, me
15. [日] 是 *shì*, to be
16. [贝] 贵 *guì*, expensive
17. [白] 白 *bái*, white
18. [羊] 美 *měi*, beautiful

C. 1. [夕] 名 *míng*, given name;
多 *duō*, many, much

2. [口] 名 *míng*, given name;
问 *wèn*, ask

3. [中] 中 *zhōng*, middle
贵 *guì*, honorific, expensive

4. [子] 好 *hǎo*, good, well;
学 *xué*, learn, study;
字 *zì*, character

5. [又] 汉 *Hàn*, ethnic Chinese;
友 *yǒu*, friend

6. [也] 他 *tā*, he, him;
她 *tā*, she, her

7. [人] 人 *rén*, people, person;
认 *rèn*, recognize

8. [小] 你 *nǐ*, you (singular);
少 *shǎo*, few, less

Review 1 (1–50)

A.

Pronouns
我 *wǒ*, I, me; 我的 *wǒde*, my, mine;
你 *nǐ*, you (singular); 你的 *nǐde*, your (singular);
他 *tā*, he, him; 他的 *tāde*, his;
她 *tā*, she, her; 她的 *tāde*, her, hers

Interrogative pronouns
什么 *shénme*, what; 哪 *nǎ*, which;
谁 *shéi/shuí*, who; 多少 *duōshao*, how many/much

Nouns
人 *rén*, person, people;
朋友 *péngyou*, friend;
中文 *Zhōngwén*, Chinese language;
英文 *Yīngwén*, English language;
汉语 *Hànyǔ*, Chinese language;
英语 *Yīngyǔ*, English language;
汉字 *Hànzì*, Chinese character;
中国 *Zhōngguó*, China;
英国 *Yīngguó*, the United Kingdom;
美国 *Měiguó*, the United States

Verbs
叫 *jiào*, be called; 姓 *xìng*, be surnamed;
是 *shì*, to be; 问 *wèn*, ask; 学 *xué*, learn, study;
写 *xiě*, write; 会 *huì*, be able to, can;
认识 *rènshi*, recognize

Numbers
一 *yī*, one; 二 *èr*, two; 三 *sān*, three; 四 *sì*, four; 五 *wǔ*, five; 六 *liù*, six; 七 *qī*, seven; 八 *bā*, eight; 九 *jiǔ*, nine; 十 *shí*,
ten

Classifiers
个 *ge*, classifier

Noun phrases
中文名字 *Zhōngwén míngzi*, Chinese name;
英文名字 *Yīngwén míngzi*, English name;
中国朋友 *Zhōngguó péngyou*, Chinese friend;
英国朋友 *Yīngguó péngyou*, English friend;
美国朋友 *Měiguó péngyou*, American friend;
谁的朋友 *shéi/shuí de péngyou*, whose friend;
哪国人 *nǎguórén*, which nationality

Word/Sentence Puzzle 1

ACROSS (left to right)

2. (i) Chinese friend/s
   (ii) can write
3. do/does not say
4. How many characters do you know?
8. Which is your country (polite)?

DOWN

1. What nationality are you?
2. United Kingdom
3. (i) become literate
   (ii) What's your surname (polite)?
5. (i) quite a lot
   (ii) yes
6. Can you speak Chinese?
7. American

	1	2	3	4	5	6	7
1		英				你	
2	中	国	朋	友		会	写
3				不	说		
4	你	认	识	多	少	汉	字
5	是	字				语	
6	哪					吗	
7	国	您					美
8	人		贵	国	是	哪	国
9		姓		的			人

Quiz 6 (51–60)

A.

姐	个	妹	弟
美	她	们	和
国	还	是	两
人	没	有	哥

	Word or phrase	Pinyin	English meaning
(i)	美国人	Měiguórén	American/s
(ii)	她们	tāmen	they (females)
(iii)	还是	háishi	or
(iv)	没有	méiyǒu	not have, none

B.

	Pinyin	Characters	Translation
(i)	Wǒ yǒu liǎng ge mèimei.	我有两个妹妹。	I have two younger sisters.
(ii)	Nǐ yǒu méiyǒu jiějie?	你有没有姐姐？	Do you have an older sister (or older sisters)?
(iii)	Tāmen shì Měiguórén.	她们是美国人。	They are Americans. (females)
(iii)	Ta yǒu gēge hé dìdi.	他有哥哥和弟弟。	He has an older brother (or older brothers) and a younger brother (or younger brothers).

C. (i)

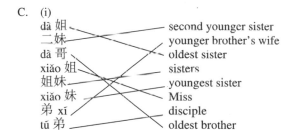

(ii)

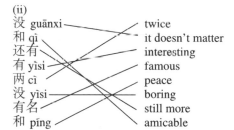

Quiz 7 (61–70)

A.

家	口	姐	人
和	兄	妹	还
老	弟	爸	有
师	几	妈	哥

	Word or phrase	Pinyin	English meaning
(i)	老师	lǎoshī	teacher
(ii)	兄弟	xiōngdì	brothers
(iii)	姐妹	jiěmèi	sisters
(iv)	还有	hái yǒu	still more

B.   **Pinyin**   **Characters**   **Translation**
  (i) Wǒ jiā yǒu sì kǒu rén.   我家有四口人。   There are four of us in our family.
  (ii) Bàba, māma, jiějie hé wǒ.   爸爸、妈妈、姐姐和我。 My father, mother, older sister and myself.
  (iii) Wǒ māma shì lǎoshī.   我妈妈是老师。   My mother is a teacher.
  (iv) Nǐ yǒu jǐ ge xiōngdì jiěmèi?   你有几个兄弟姐妹？   How many brothers and sisters do you have?

C. (i)

家 tíng — wife
老大 — master
hòu 妈 — oldest sibling
师 fu — stepfather
兄弟 — family
gū 妈 — stepmother
老 po — father's married sister
hòu 爸 — brother

(ii)

这 xiē — honest
家 wùshì — perhaps
这 yàng — these
人口 — in this way
老 shi — housework
也 xǔ — population
这 èr — accent
口 yīn — here

Quiz 8 (71–80)

A.

	Word or phrase	**Pinyin**	**English meaning**
(i)	怎样	zěnyàng	how
(ii)	父母	fùmǔ	parents
(iii)	母亲	mǔqin	mother
(iv)	身体	shēntǐ	health

B.   **Pinyin**   **Characters**   **Translation**
  (i) Nǐ fùmǔ shēntǐ hǎo ma?   你父母身体好吗？   How are your parents (in terms of their health)?
  (ii) Tāmen dōu hěn hǎo, xièxie.   他们都很好，谢谢。   They are fine, thank you.
  (iii) Nǐde Hànyǔ zěnmeyàng?   你的汉语怎么样？   How is your Chinese?
  (iii) Hái hǎo, xièxie.   还好，谢谢。   (I'm managing) all right, thank you.

C. (i)
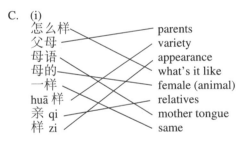

(ii)
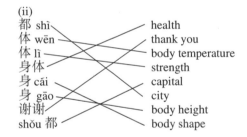

Quiz 9 (81–90)

A.

	Word or phrase	**Pinyin**	**English meaning**
(i)	男孩	nánhái	boy
(ii)	女孩	nǚhái	girl
(iii)	那儿	nàr	there
(iv)	儿子	érzi	son

B.   **Pinyin**   **Characters**   **Translation**
  (i) Nǐ gēge yǒu méiyǒu háizi?   你哥哥有没有孩子？   Does your older brother have any children?
  (ii) Wǒ gēge yǒu liǎng ge nǚ'ér.   我哥哥有两个女儿。   My older brother has two daughters.
  (iii) Nǐ jiā yǒu méiyǒu gǒu?   你家有没有狗？   Do you have a dog in your household?
  (iii) Méiyǒu, wǒ jiā yǒu yì zhī māo. 没有，我家有一只猫。 No, we don't. We have a cat.

C. (i)

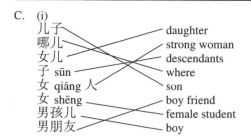

儿子 ——— daughter
哪儿 ——— strong woman
女儿 ——— descendants
子 sūn ——— where
女 qiǎng 人 ——— son
女 shēng ——— boy friend
男孩儿 ——— female student
男朋友 ——— boy

(ii)

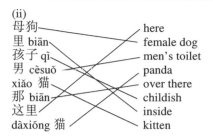

母狗 ——— here
里 biān ——— female dog
孩子 qì ——— men's toilet
男 cèsuǒ ——— panda
xiǎo 猫 ——— over there
那 biān ——— childish
这里 ——— inside
dàxióng 猫 ——— kitten

Quiz 10 (91–100)

A.

狗	比	医	猫
大	小	生	学
工	岁	很	忙
作	女	里	男

	Word or phrase	Pinyin	English meaning
(i)	大小	dàxiǎo	size
(ii)	工作	gōngzuò	work
(iii)	医生	yīshēng	doctor
(iv)	很忙	hěn máng	very busy

B.

Pinyin	Characters	Translation
(i) Nǐ jiějie zuò shénme gōngzuò?	你姐姐做什么工作?	What work does your older sister do?
(ii) Tāde gōngzuò máng bu máng?	她的工作忙不忙?	Is her work very busy?
(iii) Nǐ gēge bǐ nǐ dà jǐ suì?	你哥哥比你大几岁?	What's the age difference between you and your older brother?
(iii) Nǐ mèimei bǐ nǐ xiǎo jǐ suì?	你妹妹比你小几岁?	What's the age difference between you and your younger sister?

C. (i)

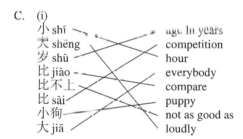

小 shí ——— age in years
大 shēng ——— competition
岁 shù ——— hour
比 jiào ——— everybody
比不上 ——— compare
比 sài ——— puppy
小狗 ——— not as good as
大 jiā ——— loudly

(ii)

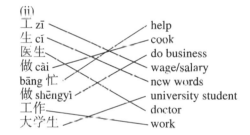

工 zī ——— help
生 cí ——— cook
医生 ——— do business
做 cài ——— wage/salary
bāng 忙 ——— new words
做 shēngyì ——— university student
工作 ——— doctor
大学生 ——— work

Character Building 2 (51–100)

A. 1. [一] 哥 gē, older brother; 两 liǎng, two (of something).

2. [丿] 生 shēng, birth, life; 九 jiǔ, nine; 么 me, particle .

3. [讠] 谢 xiè, thank; 谁 shéi/shuí, who; 语 yǔ, language; 说 shuō, speak; 认 rèn, recognize; 识 shí, know.

4. [八] 八 bā, eight; 弟 dì, younger brother.

5. [亻] 们 -men, plural suffix; 作 zuò, do; 体 tǐ, body; 做 zuò, make.

6. [阝] 那 nà, that; 都 dōu, all.

7. [氵] 没 méi, not have; 汉 Hàn, ethnic Chinese.

8. [宀] 家 jiā, home; 字 zì, character, script.

9. [辶] 这 zhè, this; 还 hái, still.

10. [小] 小 xiǎo, small; 少 shǎo, few.

11. [口] 口 kǒu, mouth; 只 zhī, classifier; 兄 xiōng, older brother (formal); 名 míng, given name.

12. [犭] 狗 gǒu, dog; 猫 māo, cat.

13. [女] 女 nǚ, female; 妈 mā, mother; 她 tā, she/her; 姐 jiě, older sister; 妹 mèi, younger sister.

14. [子] 子 zǐ, son/child; 学 xué, study learn; 孩 hái, child.

15. [心] 怎 zěn, how; 您 nín, you (polite).

16. [父] 父 fù, father (formal); 爸 bà, father.

17. [月] 有 yǒu, to have, to exist; 朋 péng, friend.

B. 1. [㇇] 也 *yě*, also
   2. [匚] 医 *yī*, treat, cure
   3. [儿] 儿 *ér*, son
   4. [几] 几 *jǐ*, how many
   5. [力] 男 *nán*, male
   6. [忄] 忙 *máng*, busy
   7. [工] 工 *gōng*, work
   8. [巾] 师 *shī*, teacher
   9. [山] 岁 *suì*, age in years

   10. [彳] 很 *hěn*, very
   11. [木] 样 *yàng*, appearance
   12. [匕] 比 *bǐ*, compare to
   13. [立] 亲 *qin*, kin
   14. [母] 母 *mǔ*, mother (formal)
   15. [老] 老 *lǎo*, old
   16. [身] 身 *shēn*, body
   17. [里] 里 *lǐ*, inside

C. 1. [子] 子 *zǐ*, child; 学 *xué*, study; 字 *zì*,
        character; 孩 *hái*, child; 好 *hǎo*, good.
   2. [儿] 儿 *ér*, son; 兄 *xiōng*, older brother
        (formal).
   3. [也] 也 *yě*, also; 她 *tā*, she/her; 他 *tā*, he/him.

Review 2 (51–100)

A.

Pronouns
我们 *wǒmen*, we/us; 我们的 *wǒmende*, our/ours;
你们 *nǐmen*, you/your (plural); 你们的 *nǐmende*, your/yours;
他们 *tāmen*, they (including females);
他们的 *tāmende*, their/theirs (including female);
她们 *tāmen*, they (female); 她们的 *tāmende*, their/theirs
(females).

Demostrative pronouns
这 *zhè*, this; 这些 *zhèxiē*, these; 这儿 *zhèr*, here; 这里 *zhèlǐ*, here; 那 *nà*, that; 那些 *nàxiē*, those; 那儿 *nàr*, there;
那里 *nàli*, there.

Interrogative pronouns
谁的 *shéi/shuí'de*, whose; 哪儿 *nǎr*, where; 哪里 *nǎli*, where; 怎么 *zěnme*, how; 怎样 *zěnyàng*, how, what;
怎么样 *zěnmeyàng*, what's it like; 几 *jǐ*, how many; 几个 *jǐ ge*, how many of (something).

Nouns
父亲 *fùqin*, father (formal); 母亲 *mǔqin*, mother (formal); 父母 *fùmǔ*, parents (formal); 哥哥 *gēge*, older brother;
姐姐 *jiějie*, older sister; 弟弟 *dìdi*, younger brother; 妹妹 *mèimei*, younger sister; 兄弟 *xiōngdì*, brothers;
姐妹 *jiěmèi*, sisters; 家 *jiā*, family, home; 国家 *guójiā*, nation; 大家 *dàjiā*, everybody; 人家 *rénjia*, other people;
孩子 *háizi*, child; 儿子 *érzi*, son; 女儿 *nǔ ér*, daughter; 身体 *shēntǐ*, health; 老师 *lǎoshī*, teacher; 医生 *yīshēng*, doctor;
学生 *xuésheng*, student; 狗 *gǒu*, dog; 猫 *māo*, cat; 岁 *suì*, age in years; 工作 *gōngzuò*, work.

Verbs
有 *yǒu*, have; 没有 *méiyǒu*, not have; 谢 *xiè*, thank;
做 *zuò*, do, make.

Adjectives
男 *nán*, male; 女 *nǔ*, female; 大 *dà*, big;
小 *xiǎo*, small; 忙 *máng*, busy.

Adverbs
很 *hěn*, very; 比 *bǐ*, compare.

Conjunctions
还 *hái*, still; 也 *yě*, also; 都 *dōu*, all

Numbers
两 *liǎng*, a couple

Classifiers
口 *kǒu* (for family members);
只 *zhī* (for animals, birds etc.).

Noun phrases
中国人口 *Zhōngguó rénkǒu*, population of China; 美国人口 *Měiguó rénkǒu*, population of the United States;
英国人口 *Yīngguó rénkǒu*, population of the United Kingdom; 小学生 *xiǎoxuéshēng*, primary school pupil;
中学生 *zhōngxuéshēng*, secondary school pupil; 大学生 *dàxuéshēng*, university student;
好学生 *hǎo xuéshēng*, good student; 好朋友 *hǎo péngyou*, good friend; 老朋友 *lǎo péngyou*, old friend;
男朋友 *nánpéngyou*, boy friend; 女朋友 *nǔpéngyou*, girl friend.

Word/Sentence Puzzle 2

ACROSS (left to right)

2. How many brothers and sisters do you have?
5. He speaks Chinese better than me.
7. (i) no
7. (ii) two jobs
9. boy
10. many primary school pupils and secondary school students
12. This dog is big.
13. kitten

DOWN

1. His parents are in good health.
3. Can you speak Chinese
4. female student
6. I have two cats and a dog.
8. second youngest brother
9. (i) male student;
   (ii) size
10. youngest sister

	1	2	3	4	5	6	7	8	9	10
1								二		小
2		你	有	几	个	兄	弟	姐	妹	
3		会								
4		说								
5	他	说	汉	语	比	我	说	的	好	
6	父		语			有				
7	母		不	是		两	个	工	作	
8	身		会			只				
9	体			女		猫			男	孩
10	很	多	小	学	生	和	中	学	生	
11	好		生		一					
12					这	只	狗	很	大	
13						狗			小	猫

Quiz 11 (101–110)

A.

工	忙	作	吃
少	多	了	早
现	在	分	饭
几	点	钟	半

Word or phrase	Pinyin	English meaning
(i) 现在	xiànzài	now
(ii) 几点钟	Jǐ diǎnzhōng	What time is it?
(iii) 分钟	fēnzhōng	minute
(iv) 吃早饭	chī zǎofàn	eat breakfast

B.

Pinyin	Characters	Translation
(i) Xiànzài jǐ diǎnzhōng le?	现在几点钟了?	What's the time now?
(ii) Xiànzài liùdiǎnbàn le.	现在六点半了。	It's now 6:30.
(iii) Nǐmen jǐ diǎn chī zǎofàn?	你们几点吃早饭?	When do you eat (your) breakfast?
(iii) Wǒmen qīdiǎnbàn chī zǎofàn.	我们七点半吃早饭。	We eat breakfast at 7:30.

C.

(i)
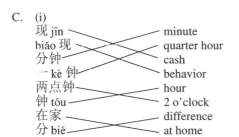

现 jīn ——— minute
biǎo 现 ——— quarter hour
分钟 ——— cash
一 kè 钟 ——— behavior
两点钟 ——— hour
钟 tóu ——— 2 o'clock
在家 ——— difference
分 bié ——— at home

(ii)
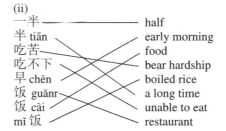

一半 ——— half
半 tiān ——— early morning
吃苦 ——— food
吃不下 ——— bear hardship
早 chén ——— boiled rice
饭 guǎnr ——— a long time
饭 cài ——— unable to eat
mǐ 饭 ——— restaurant

Quiz 12 (111–120)

A.

起	时	跑	步
床	晚	上	早
工	现	午	下
在	候	里	分

Word or phrase	Pinyin	English meaning
(i) 起床	qǐchuǎng	get out of bed
(ii) 跑步	pǎobù	jog
(iii) 晚上	wǎnshang	evening
(iv) 上午	shàngwǔ	a.m.

B. **Pinyin**

(i) Nǐ shénme shíhou qǐchuáng?

(ii) Wǒ qīdiǎnzhōng qǐchuáng.

(iii) Nǐ pǎo bu pǎobù?

(iv) Pǎo, yǒu shíhou pǎo.

Characters

你什么时候起床？

我七点钟起床。

你跑不跑步？

跑，有时候跑。

Translation

What time do you get up?

I get up at 7 o'clock.

Do you jog?

Yes, I do. Sometimes I jog.

C. (i)

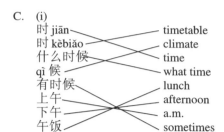

时 jiān — timetable

时 kèbiǎo — climate

什么时候 — time

qì 候 — what time

有时候 — lunch

上午 — afternoon

下午 — a.m.

午饭 — sometimes

(ii)

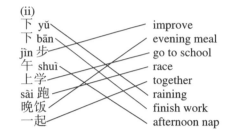

下 yǔ — improve

下 bān — evening meal

jìn 步 — go to school

午 shuì — race

上学 — together

sài 跑 — raining

晚饭 — finish work

一起 — afternoon nap

Quiz 13 (121–130)

A.

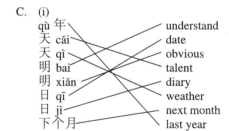

	Word or phrase	**Pinyin**	**English meaning**
(i)	今晚	jīnwǎn	tonight
(ii)	明天	míngtiān	tomorrow
(iii)	有空儿	yǒu kòngr	have free time
(iv)	看电影	kàn diànyǐng	see a movie

B. **Pinyin**

(i) Jīntiān shì Jiǔyuè-shíwǔrì.

(ii) Míngtiān shì wǒde shēngrì.

(iii) Jīnwǎn nǐ yǒu kòngr ma?

(iii) Wǒmen kàn diànyǐng zěnmeyàng?

Characters

今天是九月十五日。

明天是我的生日。

今晚你有空儿吗？

我们看电影怎么样？

Translation

Today is September 15th.

Tomorrow is my birthday.

Do you have free time tonight?

What if we see a movie?

C. (i)

qù 年 — understand

天 cái — date

天 qì — obvious

明 bái — talent

明 xiǎn — diary

日 qī — weather

日 jì — next month

下个月 — last year

(ii)

年 qīng — read

空 qì — television

空 tiáo — computer

看 shū — young

看 jiàn — air

电 nǎo — photocopy

电 shì — air-conditioning

影 yìn — see

Quiz 14 (131–140)

A.

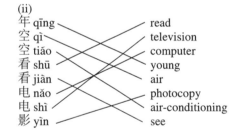

	Word or phrase	**Pinyin**	**English meaning**
(i)	星期	xīngqī	week
(ii)	昨晚	zuówǎn	last night
(iii)	买东西	mǎi dōngxi	do shopping
(iv)	进城	jìnchéng	go to the city

B. **Pinyin**

(i) Zuótiān wǒ jìnchéng le.

(ii) Nǐ jìnchéng zuò shénme le?

(iii) Wǒ qù mǎi dōngxi le.

(iii) Měi Xīngqīliù wǒ dōu jìnchéng.

Characters

昨天我进城了。

你进城做什么了？

我去买东西了。

每星期六我都进城。

Translation

Yesterday I went to the city.

What did you do in the city?

I did some shopping.

Every Saturday I go to the city.

C. (i)

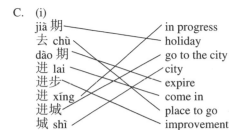

(ii)

买不起		thing
买卖		Western meal
东 nányà		can't afford
东 bian		business
东西		Western-style
西 fāng		east side
西 cān		South-East Asia
西 shì		the West

Quiz 15 (141–150)

A.

一	百	城	进
钱	商	便	宜
件	店	块	毛
西	东	生	衣

Word or phrase	Pinyin	English meaning
(i) 一百	yībǎi	one hundred
(ii) 商店	shāngdiàn	shop
(iii) 便宜	piányi	inexpensive
(iv) 毛衣	máoyī	woolen sweater

B.

Pinyin	Characters	Translation
(i) Chéngli shāngdiàn dōngxi guì ma?	城里商店东西贵吗？	Are the shops in the city expensive?
(ii) Zhè jiàn máoyī hěn piányi.	这件毛衣很便宜。	This woolen sweater is inexpensive.
(iii) Liǎngbǎi kuài qián yī jiàn, guì ma?	两百块钱一件贵吗？	Is it expensive to pay $200 (for a garment)?
(iii) Wǒ mǎi liǎng jiàn, piányi diǎnr?	我买两件便宜点儿？	Would it be cheaper if I bought two?

C. (i)

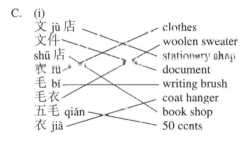

(ii)

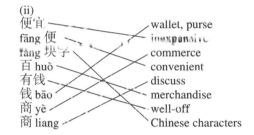

Character Building 3 (101–150)

A. 1. [一] 上 shàng, above; 下 xià, below; 东 dōng, east; 百 bǎi, hundred.

2. [丿] 午 wǔ, noon; 年 nián, year.

3. [乛] 了 le, particle; 买 mǎi, buy.

4. [乚] 电 diàn, electricity; 也 yě, also.

5. [亠] 商 shāng, merchant; 六 liù, six.

6. [八] 半 bàn, half; 分 fēn, minute.

7. [人] 人 rén, people; 今 jīn, present, now; 会 huì, be able to, would; 个 ge, classifier.

8. [亻] 候 hòu, wait; 件 jiàn, classifier; 便 biàn, convenient; 们 -men, plural suffix.

9. [口] 吃 chī, eat; 哪 nǎ, which; 名 míng, name; 吗 ma, question particle.

10. [宀] 宜 yí, appropriate; 字 zì, character, script.

11. [广] 床 chuáng, bed; 店 diàn, shop.

12. [辶] 进 jìn, enter; 还 hái/huán, still/return; 这 zhè, this.

13. [土] 在 zài, at; 城 chéng, city; 块 kuài, classifier.

14. [日] 日 rì, day; 早 zǎo, early; 明 míng, bright; 晚 wǎn, evening; 昨 zuó, yesterday; 星 xīng, star; 时 shí, time.

15. [月] 月 yuè, month; 期 qī, period.

16. [钅] 钟 zhōng, clock; 钱 qián, money.

17. [母] 每 měi, every; 母 mǔ, mother (formal).

B. 1. [厶] 去 qù, go
2. [饣] 饭 fàn, meal
3. [大] 天 tiān, day
4. [彡] 影 yǐng, shadow
5. [止] 步 bù, step
6. [毛] 毛 máo, hair
7. [穴] 空 kōng, empty
8. [衣] 衣 yī, clothing
9. [西] 西 xī, west
10. [目] 看 kàn, see
11. [足] 跑 pǎo, run
12. [走] 起 qǐ, rise

C. 1. [工]   工 *gōng*, work; 空 *kōng/kòng*, empty/
             leisure time.
    2. [土]   去 *qù*, go; 在 *zài*, at.
    3. [木]   床 *chuáng*, bed; 样 *yàng*, appearance.

    4. [日]   早 *zǎo*, early; 影 *yǐng*, shadow;
             星 *xīng*, star.
    5. [月]   期 *qī*, period; 明 *míng*, bright.
    6. [且]   宜 *yí*, appropriate; 姐 *jiě*, older sister.
    7. [乍]   昨 *zuó*, yesterday; 怎 *zěn*, how.

Review 3 (101–150)

Interrogative pronouns
什么时候 *shénme shíhou*, what time.

Nouns
天 *tiān*, day; 日 *rì*, day; 星期 *xīngqī*, week; 月 *yuè*,
month; 年 *nián*, year; 钱 *qián*, money; 床 *chuáng*, bed;
城 *chéng*, city; 学期 *xuéqī*, semester; 日期 *rìqī*, date;
商店 *shāngdiàn*, shop; 东西 *dōngxi*, thing;
文件 *wénjiàn*, document; 毛衣 *máoyī*, woolen sweater;
电影 *diànyǐng*, movie; 空儿 *kòngr*, free time;
小时 *xiǎoshí*, hour; 分钟 *fēnzhōng*, minute.

Verbs
吃 *chī*, eat; 买 *mǎi*, buy; 看 *kàn*, see; 去 *qù*, go; 跑步 *pǎobù*, jog; 起床 *qǐchuáng*, get out of bed.

Numbers
半 *bàn*, half; 百 *bǎi*, hundred.

Classifiers
块 *kuài*, piece; 毛 *máo*, ten cents unit; 件 *jiàn*, item.

Adjectives
早 *zǎo*, early; 晚 *wǎn*, late; 好吃 *hǎochī*, delicious; 有钱 *yǒuqián*, rich; 便宜 *piányi*, inexpensive; 空 *kōng*, empty.

Time words (Adverbs)
现在 *xiànzài*, now; 昨天 *zuótiān*, yesterday;
今天 *jīntiān*, today; 明天 *míngtiān*, tomorrow;
上午 *shàngwǔ*, a.m.; 下午 *xiàwǔ*, afternoon;
早上 *zǎoshang*, morning; 晚上 *wǎnshang*, evening;
每天 *měitiān*, every day; 今年 *jīnnián*, this year;
去年 *qùnián*, last year; 明年 *míngnián*, next year;
有时候 *yǒu shíhou*, sometimes;
上 (个) 星期 *shàng (ge) xīngqī*, last week;
这 (个) 星期 *zhè (ge) xīngqī*, this week;
下 (个) 星期 *xià (ge) xīngqī*, next week.

Adverbs
一起 *yìqǐ*, together; 一块儿 *yíkuàir*, together.

Prepositions
在 *zài*, at.

Particles
了 *le*, particle.

Word/Sentence Puzzle 3

ACROSS (left to right)

1. Today is September 25th.
3. What do you do in the evening?
5. We go to the city every Sunday.
8. What time do you get up every day?
10. I'm doing some shopping tomorrow.

DOWN

1. I'm free this evening.
2. Do you go jogging every day?
4. Did you see a movie yesterday?
5. week
6. Things are very cheap.
8. (i) $500   (ii) Where is the shop?
10. How much are woolen sweaters in the city?

	1	2	3	4	5	6	7	8	9	10
1	今	天	是	九	月	二	十	五	日	
2	天							百		
3	晚	上	你	做	什	么		块		
4	上									
5	我	们	每	个	星	期	天	都	进	城
6	有			期						里
7	空			昨						的
8		你	每	天	几	点	起	床		毛
9		每		你						衣
10	明	天	我	去	买	东	西			多
11		都		看		西		商		少
12		去		电		很		店		钱
13		跑		影		便		在		
14		步		了		宜		哪		
15		吗		吗				儿		

Quiz 16 (151–160)

A.

	Word or phrase	Pinyin	English meaning
(i)	太贵了	Tài guì le!	It's too expensive!
(ii)	电脑	diànnǎo	computer
(iii)	怎么样	zěnmeyàng	How is it?
(iv)	买东西	mǎi dōngxi	shopping

B.

	Pinyin	Characters	Translation
(i)	Zhè tái diànnǎo mài duōshao qián?	这台电脑卖多少钱？	How much is this computer?
(ii)	Yīwàn-èrqiān yuán	一万二千元。	It's ¥12,000 (Chinese dollars).
(iii)	Tài guì le, jiù yīwàn kuài ba.	太贵了，就一万块吧。	That's too expensive, what about ¥10,000?
(iii)	Yīwàn-líng-bābǎi, zěnmeyàng?	一万零八百怎么样？	What about ¥10,800?

C.   (i)

电脑 —— Taiwan
台 jiē —— 10 million
台 wān —— just in case
卖 zuò —— computer
卖 lì —— exert one's strength
一千万 —— stairs
百万 —— draw large audiences
万一 —— million

(ii)

美元 —— A.D.
元 dàn —— too expensive
gōng 元 —— American dollars
太 jíquán —— New Year's Day
太贵了 —— small change
太 yáng —— Taichi
zǒu 吧 —— sun
零钱 —— let's go

Quiz 17 (161–170)

A.
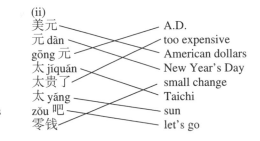

	Word or phrase	Pinyin	English meaning
(i)	帮助	bāngzhù	help
(ii)	词典	cídiǎn	dictionary
(iii)	练习	liànxí	practice
(iv)	读书	dúshū	study

B.

	Pinyin	Characters	Translation
(i)	Zhè shì yì běn shénme shū?	这是一本什么书？	What type of book is this?
(ii)	Zhè búshì shū, yě búshì cídiǎn.	这不是书，也不是词典。	This is neither a book nor a dictionary.
(iii)	Zhè shì Hànzì dú-xiě liànxíběn.	这是汉字读写练习本。	This is a character workbook.
(iii)	Tā bāngzhù wǒ xué Hànzì.	它帮助我学汉字。	It helps me to learn characters.

C.   (i)

习 sú —— calligraphy
练习本 —— dictionary
书店 —— custom
yuè 读 —— bookshelves
书 jià —— workbook
书 fǎ —— reading
生词 —— new words
词典 —— book store

(ii)

本 dī —— skills
本 lǐng —— assistant
本 lái —— typical
帮助 —— local
助手 —— help
典 xíng —— reading text
读书 —— study
读本 —— originally

Quiz 18 (171–180)

A.
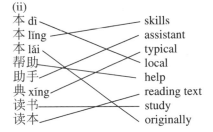

	Word or phrase	Pinyin	English meaning
(i)	前边	qiánbian	in front of, ahead
(ii)	旁边	pángbiān	next to, adjacent
(iii)	母校	mǔxiào	Alma Mater
(iv)	校园	xiàoyuán	campus

B.

Pinyin	Characters	Translation
(i) Qiánmian shì yīyuàn.	前面是医院。	There's a hospital ahead.
(ii) Xuéxiào hòumian shì gōngyuán.	学校后面是公园。	At the back of the school is a park.
(iii) Diànyǐngyuàn zài nǎr?	电影院在哪儿?	Where's the cinema?
(iii) Diànyǐngyuàn zài xuéxiào duìmiàn.	电影院在学校对面。	The cinema is opposite the school.

C. (i)

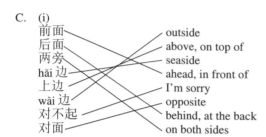

前面 — outside
后面 — above, on top of
两旁 — seaside
hǎi 边 — ahead, in front of
上边 — I'm sorry
wài 边 — opposite
对不起 — behind, at the back
对面 — on both sides

(ii)

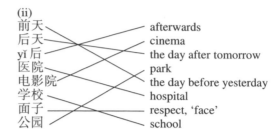

前天 — afterwards
后天 — cinema
yǐ 后 — the day after tomorrow
医院 — park
电影院 — the day before yesterday
学校 — hospital
面子 — respect, 'face'
公园 — school

Quiz 19 (181–190)

A.

	Word or phrase	Pinyin	English meaning
(i)	两条街	liǎng tiáo jiē	two streets
(ii)	一直走	yìzhí zǒu	go straight ahead
(iii)	再见	zàijiàn	goodbye
(iv)	往前走	wǎng qián zǒu	go straight ahead

B.

Pinyin	Characters	Translation
(i) Qǐngwèn, qù yīyuàn zěnme zǒu?	请问,去医院怎么走?	Excuse me, how do you get to the hospital?
(ii) Yìzhí wǎng qián zǒu.	一直往前走。	Go straight from here.
(iii) Lí zhèr yuǎn ma?	离这儿远吗?	Is it far from here?
(iv) Bù yuǎn, guò liǎng tiáo jiē jiù shì.	不远,过两条街就是。	It's not far, cross two streets and you are there.

C. (i)

离 kāi — long term
远 jìn — until
cháng 远 — distance
直 dào — depart
往往 — often
走 lù — out of fashion
走 yùn — lucky
过时 — on foot

(ii)

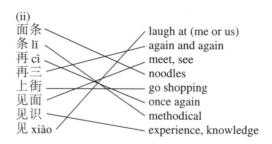

面条 — laugh at (me or us)
条 lǐ — again and again
再 cì — meet, see
再三 — noodles
上街 — go shopping
见面 — once again
见识 — methodical
见 xiào — experience, knowledge

Quiz 20 (191–200)

A.

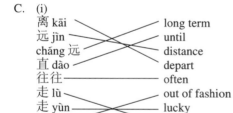

	Word or phrase	Pinyin	English meaning
(i)	右手	yòushǒu	right hand
(ii)	左手	zuǒshǒu	left hand
(iii)	马路	mǎlù	road
(iv)	外面	wàimian	outside

B.

Pinyin	Characters	Translation
(i) Xuéxiào lí zhèr yuǎn bu yuǎn?	学校离这儿远不远?	Is the school far from here?
(ii) Hěn jìn, guòle mǎlù jiù shì.	很近,过了马路就是。	It's very near, after you cross the road, you're there.
(iii) Nǐ néng yòng zuǒshǒu xiězì ma?	你能用左手写字吗?	Can you write with your left hand?
(iv) Bù néng, wǒ zhǐ néng yòng yòushǒu.	不能,我只能用右手。	No, I can't. I can only write with my right hand.

C. (i)

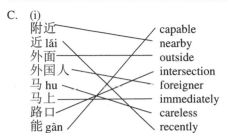

附近   capable
近 lái   nearby
外面   outside
外国人   intersection
马 hu   foreigner
马上   immediately
路口   careless
能 gàn   recently

(ii)

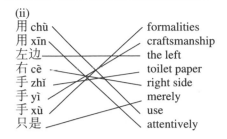

用 chù   formalities
用 xīn   craftsmanship
左边   the left
右 cè   toilet paper
手 zhǐ   right side
手 yì   merely
手 xù   use
只是   attentively

Character Building 4 (151–200)

A.   1. [一] 再 *zài*, again; 万 *wàn*, ten thousand; 面 *miàn*, surface.

    2. [丿] 千 *qiān*, thousand; 后 *hòu*, behind.

    3. [乛] 习 *xí*, practice; 书 *shū*, book.

    4. [亠] 离 *lí*, distance from; 就 *jiù*, then.

    5. [讠] 读 *dú*, read; 词 *cí*, word.

    6. [二] 二 *èr*, two; 元 *yuán*, dollar.

    7. [十] 直 *zhí*, straight; 卖 *mài*, sell.

    8. [八] 典 *diǎn*, standard; 前 *qián*, in front of; 公 *gōng*, public.

    9. [厶] 能 *néng*, can; 去 *qù*, go.

   10. [又] 对 *duì*, correct; 友 *yǒu*, friend.

   11. [力] 助 *zhù*, assistance; 男 *nán*, male.

   12. [宀] 它 *ta*, it; 字 *zì*, character, script.

   13. [辶] 远 *yuǎn*, far; 过 *guò*, pass; 边 *biān*, side; 近 *jìn*, near.

   14. [工] 工 *gōng*, work; 左 *zuǒ*, the left.

   15. [大] 太 *tài*, extreme; 天 *tiān*, day.

   16. [口] 台 *tái*, platform; 右 *yòu*, the right.

   17. [口] 园 *yuán*, garden; 国 *guó*, country.

   18. [巾] 帮 *bāng*, help; 师 *shī*, teacher.

   19. [彳] 往 *wǎng*, toward; 街 *jiē*, street.

   20. [木] 本 *běn*, root; 校 *xiào*, school.

   21. [月] 脑 *nǎo*, brain; 期 *qī*, period.

   22. [走] 走 *zǒu*, walk; 起 *qǐ*, rise.

   23. [足] 路 *lù*, road; 跑 *pǎo*, run.

B.   1. [卜] 外 *wài*, outside
    2. [阝] 院 *yuàn*, courtyard
    3. [夂] 条 *tiáo*, classifier
    4. [纟] 练 *liàn*, practice
    5. [马] 马 *mǎ*, horse

    6. [方] 旁 *páng*, next to
    7. [手] 手 *shǒu*, hand
    8. [用] 用 *yòng*, use
    9. [雨] 雨 *yǔ*, rain

C.   1. [卖] 卖 *mài*, sell; 读 *dú*, read
    2. [寸] 对 *duì*, correct; 过 *guò*, pass
    3. [力] 边 *biān*, side; 助 *zhù*, assist

    4. [月] 脑 *nǎo*, brain; 明 *míng*, bright
    5. [巴] 吧 *ba*, suggestion particle; 爸 *bà*, father
    6. [口] 右 *yòu*, the right; 名 *míng*, name

REVIEW 4 (151–200)

Pronouns
它 *tā*, it; 它们 *tāmen*, they.

Nouns
脑 *nǎo*, brain; 电脑 *diànnǎo*, computer;
零钱 *língqián*, small change; 读本 *dúběn*, reading text;
练习本 *liànxíběn*, workbook; 书 *shū*, book;
书店 *shūdiàn*, book store; 词 *cí*, word;
生词 *shēngcí*, new words; 词典 *cídiǎn*, dictionary;
帮手 *bāngshǒu*, assistant; 助手 *zhùshǒu*, assistant;
面子 *miànzi*, face (respect); 医院 *yīyuàn*, hospital;
电影院 *diànyǐngyuàn*, cinema; 学校 *xuéxiào*, school;

校园 *xiàoyuán*, campus; 母校 *mǔxiào*, Alma Mater;
公里 *gōnglǐ*, kilometer; 公园 *gōngyuán*, park;
远近 *yuǎnjìn*, distance; 面条 *miàntiáo*, noodles;
街 *jiē*, street; 见识 *jiànshi*, experience, knowledge;
外国人 *wàiguórén*, foreigner; 外人 *wàirén*, stranger;
路 *lù*, road; 马路 *mǎlù*, sealed road;
路口 *lùkǒu*, turning, intersection; 手 *shǒu*, hand.

Verbs
卖 *mài*, sell; 读 *dú*, read; 读书 *dúshū*, study;
练 *liàn*, practice; 练习 *liànxí*, practice; 学习 *xuéxí*, study;
帮 *bāng*, help; 帮助 *bāngzhù*, help; 帮忙 *bāngmáng*,

help; 住院 *zhùyuàn*, be hospitalized; 走 *zǒu*, walk; 过 *guò*, pass; 上街 *shàngjiē*, go shopping; 见 *jiàn*, see; 见面 *jiànmiàn*, see; 用 *yòng*, use.

Auxiliary verbs
能 *néng*, possible.

Numbers
零 *líng*, zero; 千 *qiān*, thousand; 万 *wàn*, ten thousand;
百万 *bǎiwàn*, million; 一千万 *yìqiānwàn*, ten million.

Classifiers
台 *tái*, (for equipment); 元 *yuán* (for dollar unit);
件 *jiàn* (for clothing); 条 *tiáo* (for long and slender objects).

Adjectives
远 *yuǎn*, far; 直 *zhí*, straight; 近 *jìn*, near;
对 *duì*, correct; 过时 *guòshí*, be out of fashion.

Location words
前 *qián*, in front of; 后 *hòu*, behind;
前面 *qiánmian*, in front of; 后面 *hòumian*, behind;
前边 *qiánbian*, in front of; 两旁 *liǎngpáng*, on both sides;
旁边 *pángbiān*, next to; 上边 *shàngbian*, above;
外边 *wàibian*, outside; 对面 *duìmiàn*, opposite;
外面 *wàimian*, outside; 路上 *lùshang*, on the road or
journey; 左 *zuǒ*, the left; 左边 *zuǒbian*, left hand side;
右 *yòu*, the right; 右边 *yòubian*, right hand side.

Time words (Adverbs)
前天 *qiántiān*, the day before yesterday; 后天 *hòutiān*, the day after tomorrow; 以后 *yǐhòu*, afterwards.

Adverbs
千万 *qiānwàn*, be sure to; 就 *jiù*, then; 一直 *yìzhí*, straight; 直到 *zhídào*, until; 往往 *wǎngwǎng*, often; 再 *zài*, again;
再三 *zàisān*, repeatedly; 马上 *mǎshàng*, immediately; 只 *zhǐ*, only; 只是 *zhǐshì*, merely.

Conjunction
不过 *búguò*, but, however.

Prepositions
离 *lí*, distance from.

Particles
吧 *ba*, (for suggestion).

Word/Sentence Puzzle 4

ACROSS (left to right)
1. She can't use a computer.
4. There's a big shop in front of my house.
7. (i) left hand side
7. (ii) Are you going to school today?
8. assistant
9. outside
10. dictionary
12. Is the cinema far from here?
14. eat noodles

DOWN
2. I can write with my left hand.
4. next to the hospital
5. I'm asking you for a favor.
6. She has a dog in her house
7. Where are we meeting tomorrow?
9. I'm sorry.
10. The shop is outside the school (campus).
11. bookshop

	1	2	3	4	5	6	7	8	9	10	11
1						她	不	会	用	电	脑
2						家					
3						里					书
4		我	家	前	面	有	一	个	大	商	店
5		能				狗			店		
6		用		请		明			在		
7		左	边	你	今	天	去	学	校	吗	
8	助	手		帮		我			园		
9		写		忙		们			外	面	
10		字	典			在			边		
11			医			哪		对			
12	电	影	院	离	这	儿	远	不	远		
13			旁			见		起			
14			边		吃	面	条				

Quiz 21 (201–210)

A.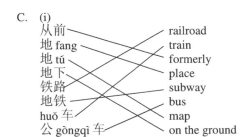

	Word or phrase	Pinyin	English meaning
(i)	怎么走	zěnme zǒu	How do you get to . . .?
(ii)	中国城	Zhōngguóchéng	Chinatown
(iii)	下车	xiàchē	get off from the bus/train
(iv)	坐地铁	zuò dìtiě	take the subway

B.

	Pinyin	Characters	Translation
(i)	Wǒ zhù zài chénglì.	我住在城里。	I live in the city.
(ii)	Dào nǐ jiā zěnme zǒu?	到你家怎么走?	How do I get to your house?
(iii)	Nǐ cóng zhèr zuò dìtiě.	你从这儿坐地铁。	You take the subway from here.
(iv)	Dào Zhōngguóchéng xiàchē jiù shì.	到中国城下车就是。	Get off at Chinatown (station) and you're there.

C. (i)

从前 — formerly
地 fang — place
地 tú — map
地下 — on the ground
铁路 — railroad
地铁 — subway
huǒ 车 — train
公 gòngqì 车 — bus

(ii)

北京 — Beijing
北 fāng — the north
到期 — expire
京 jù — Beijing opera
南 bù — southern part
住 zhái — residence
坐 wèi — seat
北 Měizhōu — North America

Quiz 22 (211–220)

A.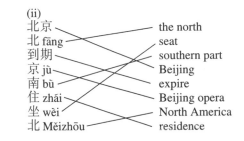

	Word or phrase	Pinyin	English meaning
(i)	多久	duō jiǔ	how long? (time)
(ii)	时间	shíjiān	time
(iii)	已经	yǐjīng	already
(iv)	喜欢	xǐhuan	be fond of

B.

	Pinyin	Characters	Translation
(i)	Nǐ lái Běijīng duō jiǔ le?	你来北京多久了?	How long have you been in Beijing?
(ii)	Yǐjīng hěn cháng shíjiān le.	已经很长时间了。	(I've) already been here for quite a long time.
(iii)	Nǐ xǐhuan Běijīng ma?	你喜欢北京吗?	Do you like Beijing?
(iv)	Hái hǎo, dōngtiān lěng yìdiǎnr.	还好,冬天冷一点儿。	It's okay, (but) it's a bit cold in winter.

C. (i)

从来 — all along
来回 — a return journey
不久 — not long
已经 — already
经常 — often
经过 — pass through
长大 — grow up
长 jiāng — the Yangtze River

(ii)

时间 — time
中间 — middle
fáng 间 — room
喜欢 — be fond of
欢喜 — happy
欢 yíng — welcome
冷 shuǐ — unboiled water
冬天 — winter

Quiz 23 (221–230)

A.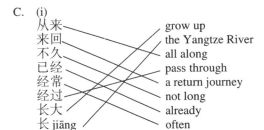

	Word or phrase	Pinyin	English meaning
(i)	游泳池	yóuyǒngchí	swimming pool
(ii)	下雨	xiàyǔ	It's raining.
(iii)	比较	bǐjiào	rather
(iv)	地方	dìfang	place

B.   **Pinyin**   **Characters**   **Translation**
(i)   Shànghǎi xiàtiān rè bu rè?   上海夏天热不热?   Is Shanghai hot in summer?
(ii) Bǐjiào rè, búguò cháng xiàyǔ.   比较热,不过常下雨。   (It's) rather hot, but it rains often.
(iii) Shànghǎi yǒuyǒngchí duō bu duō?   上海游泳池多不多?   Are there many swimming pools in Shanghai?
(iv) Bùshǎo, hěnduō dìfang dōu yǒu.   不少,很多地方都有。   Quite a few, many places have them.

C.   (i)   (ii)

海边 ——————— direction   常见 ——————— rainy season
海外 ——————— seaside   常常 ——————— common
夏 lìng 时 ——————— aspect   下雨 ——————— swim
热 qíng ——————— comparatively   雨 jì ——————— game
比较 ——————— overseas   zhèn 雨 ——————— tour
方 xiàng ——————— summer time   游泳 ——————— often
方 fǎ ——————— enthusiastic   游 xǐ ——————— rain
方面 ——————— method   游 lǎn ——————— showers

Quiz 24 (231–240)

A.   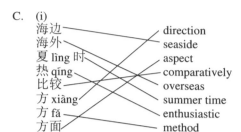   **Word or phrase**   **Pinyin**   **English meaning**
(i)   活动   huódòng   activity
(ii) 运动   yùndòng   sport
(iii) 周末   zhōumò   weekend
(iv) 睡觉   shuìjiào   sleep

B.   **Pinyin**   **Characters**   **Translation**
(i)   Zhōumò nǐ yǒu shénme huódòng?   周末你有什么活动?   What do you do on the weekend?
(ii) Zhōumò wǒ ài shuì lǎnjiào.   周末我爱睡懒觉。   During the weekend, I love to sleep in.
(iii) Nǐ xǐhuan shénme yùndòng?   你喜欢什么运动?   What sports do you like?
(iv) Wǒ xǐhuan yóuyǒng hé pǎobù.   我喜欢游泳和跑步。   I like swimming and jogging.

C.   (i)   (ii)

周年 ——————— zoo   睡午觉 ——————— offend
周日 ——————— pleasant to listen to   睡 lǎn 觉 ——————— sports
生活 ——————— touching   睡衣 ——————— luck
动人 ——————— anniversary   觉得 ——————— sleep in
动 tīng ——————— spouse   gǎn 觉 ——————— afternoon nap
动 wù 园 ——————— hobby   运动 ——————— perception
爱人 ——————— living   运 qi ——————— pyjamas
爱好 (pron. hào) ——————— Sundays   得 zuì ——————— feel

Quiz 25 (241–250)

A.   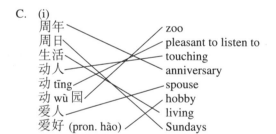   **Word or phrase**   **Pinyin**   **English meaning**
(i)   火车站   huǒchēzhàn   train station
(ii) 知道   zhīdao   be aware of something
(iii) 或者   huòzhě   or, perhaps
(iv) 可以   kěyǐ   can, possible

B.   **Pinyin**   **Characters**   **Translation**
(i)   Dào Zhōngguó Fàndiàn zěnme zǒu?   到中国饭店怎么走?   How to get to the China Hotel?
(ii) Kěyǐ zuò gōnggòngqìchē qù.   可以坐公共汽车去。   (You) can take the bus.
(iii) Huòzhě zuò huǒchē yě kěyǐ.   或者坐火车也可以。   Alternatively, you can take the train.
(iv) Wǒ zhīdao chēzhàn zài nǎr.   我知道车站在哪儿。   I know where the bus stop/train station is.

C. (i)

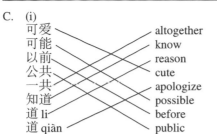

可爱		altogether
可能		know
以前		reason
公共		cute
一共		apologize
知道		possible
道 li		before
道 qiàn		public

(ii)

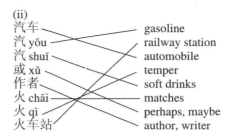

汽车		gasoline
汽 yóu		railway station
汽 shuǐ		automobile
或 xǔ		temper
作者		soft drinks
火 chái		matches
火 qì		perhaps, maybe
火车站		author, writer

Character Building 5 (201–250)

A. 1. [一] 来 lái, come; 万 wàn, ten thousand;
       面 miàn, face.

    2. [丨] 北 běi, north.

    3. [丿] 久 jiǔ, a long time;
       长 cháng/zhǎng, long/grow.

    4. [亠] 京 jīng, capital; 就 jiù, then.

    5. [十] 南 nán, south; 直 zhí, straight.

    6. [八] 共 gòng, together; 典 diǎn, standard;
       前 qián, in front of; 公 gōng, public.

    7. [人] 从 cóng, from; 以 yǐ, with.

    8. [亻] 住 zhù, live, stay; 作 zuò, work.

    9. [又] 欢 huān, happy; 对 duì, correct,
       opposite.

    10. [力] 动 dòng, move; 助 zhù, help.

    11. [氵] 游 yóu, swim; 泳 yǒng, style of
       swimming;
       池 chí, pool, pond; 海 hǎi, sea;
       活 huó, live, living; 汽 qì, air.

    12. [门] 间 jiān, space; 问 wèn, ask.

    13. [辶] 运 yùn, transport; 道 dào, road.

    14. [土] 坐 zuò, sit; 地 dì, earth.

    15. [口] 呢 ne, particle; 和 hé, and;
       可 kě, possible.

    16. [巾] 常 cháng, often; 帮 bāng, help.

    17. [冬] 冬 dōng, winter; 夏 xià, summer.

    18. [纟] 经 jīng, classic; 练 liàn, practice.

    19. [灬] 热 rè, hot; 点 diǎn, dot.

    20. [方] 方 fāng, direction; 旁 páng, next to.

    21. [木] 末 mò, end, 本 běn, base, classifier.

    22. [车] 车 chē, vehicle; 较 jiào, rather, compare.

    23. [戈] 或 huò, or, perhaps; 我 wǒ, I, me.

    24. [见] 觉 jué/jiào, feel/sleep; 见 jiàn, see.

B. 1. [冫] 冷 lěng, cold

    2. [冂] 周 zhōu, week

    3. [刂] 到 dào, arrive

    4. [士] 喜 xǐ, be fond of

    5. [己] 已 yǐ, already

    6. [火] 火 huǒ, fire

    7. [日] 者 zhě, -er, -ist

    8. [爪] 爱 ài, love

    9. [立] 站 zhàn, stand; station

    10. [目] 睡 shuì, sleep

    11. [矢] 知 zhī, know

    12. [雨] 雨 yǔ, rain

C. 1. [也] 池 chí, pool, pond; 地 dì, earth.

    2. [比] 老 lǎo, old; 北 běi, north.

    3. [日] 间 jiān, space; 晚 wǎn, night.

    4. [友] 友 yǒu, friend; 爱 ài, love.

Review 5 (201–250)

Nouns

地方 dìfang, place; 地下 dìxià, ground; 地铁 dìtiě, subway; 铁路 tiělù, railway; 车 chē, vehicle; 汽车 qìchē, vehicle; 火车 huǒchē, train; 火车站 huǒchēzhàn, train station; 北方 běifāng, north (of a country); 南方 nánfāng, south (of a country); 时间 shíjiān, time; 冬天 dōngtiān, winter; 海边 hǎibian, seaside; 海外 hǎiwài, overseas; 夏天 xiàtiān, summer; 泳道 yǒngdào, lane (in a swimming pool); 游泳池 yóuyǒngchí, swimming pool;

方面 fāngmiàn, aspect; 周 zhōu, week; 周日 zhōurì, Sunday; 周末 zhōumò, weekend; 周年 zhōunián, anniversary; 末期 mòqī, end of a period; 活动 huódòng, activity; 生活 shēnghuó, life; 爱好 àihào, hobby; 爱人 àiren, spouse (used in China only); 午睡 wǔshuì, afternoon nap; 运动 yùndòng, sport; 汽油 qìyóu, gasoline; 作者 zuòzhě, author, writer; 读者 dúzhě, reader; 站 zhàn, station; 道路 dàolù, road; 知识 zhīshi, knowledge.

Proper nouns
北京 *Běijīng*, Beijing; 南京 *Nánjīng*, Nanjing; 东京 *Dōngjīng*, Tokyo; 上海 *Shànghǎi*, Shanghai.

Verbs
住 *zhù*, live, stay; 到 *dào*, arrive; 到期 *dàoqī*, expire; 坐 *zuò*, sit, ride on (bus, train, ferry, plane); 来 *lái*, come; 经过 *jīngguò*, pass through; 长大 *zhǎngdà*, grow up; 喜爱 *xǐ'ài*, be fond of; 喜欢 *xǐhuan*, be fond of;

下雨 *xiàyǔ*, rain; 游泳 *yóuyǒng*, swim; 活 *huó*, live, alive; 爱 *ài*, love; 睡觉 *shuìjiào*, sleep; 觉得 *juéde*, feel; 知道 *zhīdao*, know.

Auxiliary verbs
可以 *kěyǐ*, can.

Adjectives
欢喜 *huānxǐ*, happy; 热 *rè*, hot; 常见 *chángjiàn*, common; 动人 *dòngrén*, touching; 可爱 *kě'ài* cute; 到家 *dàojiā*, excellent; 公共 *gōnggòng*, public; 公用 *gōngyòng*, public.

Location words
南边 *nánbian*, southern side; 中间 *zhōngjiān*, middle; 前面 *qiánmian*, ahead; 后面 *hòumian*, behind.

Time words
久 *jiǔ*, long time; 不久 *bùjiǔ*, not a very long time; 以前 *yǐqián*, formerly, before; 以后 *yǐhòu*, afterwards.

Adverbs
从前 *cóngqián*, formerly; 从来 *cónglái*, all along; 已经 *yǐjīng*, already; 经常 *jīngcháng*, often; 常常 *chángcháng*, often; 比较 *bǐjiào*, comparatively.

Conjunction
和 *hé*, and; 以便 *yǐbiàn*, so as to; 或 *huò*, or; 或者 *huòzhě*, or/maybe.

Prepositions
从 *cóng*, from; 从...到 *cóng ... dào*, from ... to.

Particles
呢 *ne*, particle.

Word/Sentence Puzzle 5

ACROSS (left to right)

2. I think my Chinese has improved.
6. The train is running on railway tracks.
7. bus stop.
8. reader (person)
9. (i) There are too many things to do on the weekend.
9. (ii) raining
11. all along
13. This cat is very cute

DOWN

1. first anniversary
2. I often go swimming.
3. (i) sleep
3. (ii) live up to 101
4. train
5. My house is not too far from the station
7. (i) the middle
7. (ii) subway
9. You can come either in the morning or in the afternoon.

	1	2	3	4	5	6	7	8	9	10	11
1			睡								
2		我	觉	得	我	的	中	文	进	步	了
3		常			家		间				
4		去			离				你		
5		游			火		地		早		
6		泳		火	车	在	铁	路	上	走	
7			汽	车	站				或		
8	一				不			读	者		
9	周	末	活	动	太	多	了		下	雨	
10	年		到	远					午		
11			一					从	来		
12			百						都		
13			零		这	只	猫	很	可	爱	
14			一						以		